BEING SAFE

BEING SAFE

Mel Mandell

Saturday Review Press

NEW YORK

This book is dedicated to the more than six million Americans who this year will be the victims of serious crimes, including two and a half million burglarized, more than a million whose cars will be stolen, more than three hundred thousand who will be held up at the point of a gun or knife, another three hundred thousand victims of aggravated assault, the hundreds of thousands of victims of purse-snatchers and pick-pockets, the fifty thousand females who will be raped, and finally the three thousand who can't be helped or protected any more by the police or by reading books because they will be murdered by criminals.

CONTENTS

BEING SAFE

Chapter I

CRIME CAN BE
CONTROLLED

All of us are the victims of crime. Even if we are not among the millions victimized directly each year, we pay dearly and daily for crime in the following ways:

• With the many billions of tax dollars expended on our antiquated, cumbersome and ofttimes self-defeating system of criminal justice.

• In escalating premiums for insurance against car theft and burglary, if we can, in fact, obtain coverage.

• In inflated prices on the goods and services we buy—to make up for shoplifting and the various forms of employee dishonesty, such as pilferage, executive embezzlement and collusion with professional criminals.

• In inflated prices or rentals on the residences we own or rent to make up for widespread employee pilferage of materials and tools, dishonest faking of contractor payrolls and bribery of municipal employees.

• In the many petty inconveniences forced on us by businesses victimized by crime: buses, taxis and gas stations that can't make change; neighborhood stores that close before dark and/or remain locked all day, opening only to recognized customers; guards who search packages before we can leave a supermarket or department store.

• In poorer schooling for our children resulting from widespread vandalism of schools compounded by illegal disruptions by activists (and we are then taxed more or charged higher fees to repair the estimated $200 million in annual damage).

• In the hundreds of millions spent by citizens for do-it-yourself security in the form of locks, alarms, guns, self-protection training courses and watchdogs (much of it not spent wisely, as I show in Chapter IX, "How to Buy Security Products and Services").

But most of all we pay in an ever-heavier burden of fear and anxiety, especially if we live in one of the crime-ridden cities.

Besides the anxiety and sometimes outright terror, crime lowers the quality of life in subtler ways. To deter crime calls for measures that make life in the city less attractive, less civil, less private and more constricted. For example, in Chapter VI on "Apartment House Security," I unhappily urge impolite behavior for women. For example, if a woman is opening the locked front door of an apartment building and a young male stranger comes up, the proper course now is not to hold the door open for him. Prudence calls for hopping inside and slamming the door in his face. Gross incivility? Of course, but the alternative to general bad manners is far worse: widespread terror stimulating wasteful excessive turnover of apartments, contributing strongly to the abandonment of sorely needed housing, and soon extending to entire neighborhoods. It's happening already in some of our great cities.

Crime helps destroy communities in other ways, such as intensified racial polarization in cities where whites see blacks and other minority groups as the source of criminality. The ghettos are indeed the breeding grounds of a disproportionate number of criminals, but people living in ghettos are also the most often victimized by criminals and limited police protection.

If you are one of the rare ones who has never suffered or witnessed an overt crime, your chances of continued freedom from that form of fear are limited. Just consider the growing, pervasive nature of crime in America as reported by the FBI in its annual *Uniform Crime Reports:* *

• Almost six million serious crimes reported in 1970, up 11 percent over 1969.

• Purse-snatchings up 332 percent from 1960 to 1970.

• In 1970, 921,400 cars were stolen, up 6 percent over 1969.

• There is no escape to the suburbs. Where the FBI breaks down a category of crime by "city," "rural" and "suburban," the last is invariably the area suffering the greatest increases. For example, in robberies, rural areas experienced a 14 percent increase from 1969 to 1970, large cities with over 250,000 people experienced an increase of 16 percent, while suburban areas surrounding those large cities experienced a 20 percent increase in the same year.

• Although the majority of crimes were committed at night, daytime burglaries of residences rose 337 percent from 1960 to 1970.

To make matters even worse, the level of criminality is going to rise before it ever drops. Why? Because of many

---

* There is strong evidence that the *Uniform Crime Reports* considerably understate the extent and seriousness of crime. Sample surveys of areas of Boston, Chicago and Washington, D.C., known for high crime rates indicate that the actual crime rate was *four* times that reported. Sociologist Albert J. Reiss, Jr., of the University of Michigan, estimates that the real crime rate is at least twice as high as that reported in the *Uniform Crime Reports,* but not increasing as fast as indicated by the reports.

factors. Let me just cite one obvious one: that portion of the population most prone to criminal acts—young men from fifteen to twenty-four years of age—is growing faster than other subpopulations.

When young men in this category, which includes many of the returning Vietnam veterans, can't find work, they get into trouble. And the unemployment rate among this group is higher than that of any other. (With a nod to the liberated women among my readers, you may take some grim satisfaction in learning that young women are taking advantage of their new status and turning in unprecedented numbers to the criminal life: crimes committed by women, starting, of course, from a much lower base, are rising much faster than among men.)

The outlook is made even more depressing because the threshold age for crime is dropping. Younger and younger children are engaging in more and more serious crimes. For example, in some housing projects in New York teenage boys have invented a new form of robbery in which the penis becomes a long-range weapon.

For years the Housing Authority has had to cope with clever, agile boys who circumvent all locks and barriers to take joyrides on tops of elevators. Some of the private housing complexes experience the same headache. It's dangerous. Each year many are injured and a few boys are killed, either by falling down the shafts or by being decapitated by the descending counterweights. Now the problem has taken on a new dimension. By law, each elevator cab must have a trapdoor in the roof to permit passengers to get out in case of breakdown. Lately, some boys who ride on top peek through the trapdoor, waiting for one or two women to enter the cab. Then they suddenly throw open the trapdoor, expose themselves and threaten to urinate on their prey unless the women hand up their money. The distraught women comply. Boys practicing this new form of terror are reportedly as young as nine years old.

The Housing Authority has called in experts, and hopefully they will soon come up with some electrical or electronic devices or circuitry that will stop this tragicomic delinquency.

I could go on citing page after page of fear-breeding statistics and situations except that I don't want to be boring or add to the generally high and sometimes unreasonable level of fear of crime and violence. Some sense of fear is purposeful because it motivates citizens to take sensible precautions against crime and to support intelligent community measures to deal with it; but too much fear either paralyzes or stimulates an unreasoned or even hysterical overreaction that could result in silly or inefficient measures, vigilantism, lynch-mob tactics or unjust repression. None of these will solve our pervasive crime problem. In fact, some of these overresponses are in themselves highly criminal.

What is abundantly clear is that crime can no longer be controlled by the professionals. No one needs to be reminded that our patchwork system of criminal justice (the police, courts and prisons) can't cope effectively with the problem. However, I would like to stress just one key fact. The police cannot do a complete job of deterring crime when by tradition they rarely patrol where most crimes are committed—indoors.

If the police and other government agencies can't control crime, then it is obvious that each citizen must take on some of the job himself or herself. Of course, citizens have always played a role in crime control: the police must rely on reports from victims and witnesses to lead them to the scene of crimes and obtain descriptions of the "perpetrators" (that ponderous official designation for unconvicted criminals). It is absolutely essential that citizens continue to participate in that reporting role. Beyond participating in the primarily passive role of reporter, what I offer the average citizen in this book is a regimen of sane, reasonable ways in which he can protect himself, his family, his guests and his and their property. And they work!

Many of the same techniques and devices apply in business. If you are an employer, you have an obligation to protect your employees and whatever property they keep or bring onto your premises. Conversely, if you are an employee, you have a moral obligation to protect the property of your employer and that of your fellow employees. Protecting your employer could also mean protecting your job: one of the primary causes of the failure of small businesses is their inability to recover from severe losses due to crime. In Chapter X, "Security on the Job," I summarize some of the primary approaches and equipment to protect businesses against criminal attack.

All of us also have a general communal role to play in controlling crime. By backing legislation and speaking up in public and private meetings, each of us can lend his weight to a complex of measures that would make our society respond in a late-twentieth-century manner to our late-twentieth-century crisis of crime. Here is what I, as a "law-and-order liberal," recommend in a multifaceted response:

1. Support legislation that helps inhibit and control crime, such as gun-control laws and reform of the system of criminal justice. For example, we need to move closer to the British system of setting very low bail for lesser crimes and *no* bail for serious crimes. In the United States, the first-time criminal, often a juvenile, who can't raise a $1,000 bail is held in detention and exposed to the malevolent influence of mature criminals. In contrast, the professional criminal quickly finds

a bondsman to post much higher bails, and then he goes out to commit more crimes to pay the bail bondsman.

2. Support—or do not oppose—authorization of more money to pay higher police salaries (astonishingly low in many cities, especially when compared to "safe" jobs in industry) and for additional services such as transportation and school guards, more judges, more probation officers, modern prisons with effective rehabilitation services, truly separate facilities for juvenile offenders and many other services that help nip criminal careers in the bud or turn long-time criminals to productive or at least benign activities.

3. Indirectly, by (a) helping provide equal opportunity for the minority groups and slum dwellers who unfortunately breed a disproportionate number of criminals; (b) helping to raise the often incredibly low standard of living of these minority groups; (c) supporting those who would ensure equal treatment in the courts and reasonable bail for minority groups.

4. If you are an employer, hire those with criminal records who have shown that they are sincerely trying to "go straight." (If all employers discriminated against those with criminal records, the nation would suffer a severe shortage of manpower: 40 percent of all male children now living in the United States will be arrested for a nontraffic offense during their lives.)

5. Support proposals to put the police back on the beat where they can deter really serious crimes such as robbery, assault, car theft and burglary. If these common crimes, which induce widespread terror or cause heavy losses, are to be contained, the police can't be burdened with suppression of socially unpopular or "immoral" behavior. By these I mean: social gambling; sabbath violations; homosexuality between

consenting adults; public alcoholism unaccompanied by disorderly or otherwise unlawful behavior; "breaches of the peace" (mostly between spouses); pornography; minor drug usage (as distinct from the serious crime of drug distribution); and unorganized prostitution, where the prostitutes are not engaged in violent crimes such as mugging.* In particular, assigning police to trap or harass streetwalkers is a demeaning task that may corrupt the former and certainly doesn't deter or rehabilitate the latter.

6. Support proposals to relieve the police of such minor or nonpolice duties as handing out parking tickets, secretarial tasks, ceremonial appearances and towing of illegally parked cars.

7. Set a good example to children and neighbors by not violating any laws or cutting corners, such as "fixing" or ignoring traffic tickets.

8. Work to eliminate prohibitions against the sale of alcoholic beverages in one county or state when they can be purchased openly in an adjoining area. The bootlegging that results reproduces on a lesser scale the breakdown of respect for law that this nation is still suffering from as a result of Prohibition.

9. Oppose all vigilantism and any group that takes the law into its own hands (Ku Klux Klan, Black Panthers, Jewish Defense League, Weathermen, etc.).

10. Support laws permitting legal organized gambling such as offtrack betting corporations, including betting on sporting events other than horse racing, lotteries, and supervised casinos. Since a large segment of the population will never give up gambling, let's at least channel these obsessions to some

---

* When I began working on this book in late 1969 I thought of prostitution as one of the "victimless" crimes. With the sharp rise in robbery associated with prostitution, especially in such cities as Los Angeles and New York, I have been forced to change my view of the benignity of prostitution.

useful purpose, and thereby simultaneously deny to organized crime one of its most lucrative sources of revenue.

11. Support setting up treatment centers for addicts, in particular those pathetic young men who became addicted while serving in Vietnam.

Some of you may be opposed to most of these general recommendations and most of you will no doubt disagree with at least a few. Realist that I am, I don't expect what is in essence a restructuring of society to come about. And even if strongly supported, such a restructuring would take decades. In the meanwhile, we still have to protect ourselves until the current generation of criminals dies out, reforms or is imprisoned. For this reason, I stress what is the thrust of this book: to eliminate, or at least not create, criminal opportunities.

Such actions, which I detail in the succeeding chapters, are no long-range or permanent cure for crime. But they do work to reduce crime in your community and protect what is most dear to you. In some as yet unquantified way, denying criminal opportunities does deter youngsters from entering a life of crime. For instance, criminologists believe that stealing cars is perhaps the most common way in which young men are launched on criminal careers. Merely by adhering to the prime rule of pocketing your ignition key every time you leave your car, you may prevent some youngster from taking your car for a joyride. Denial of that one opportunity may be all that stands in the way of a series of increasingly criminal thefts leading to a first commitment to prison. And once a young man enters our prisons, he will be schooled in the techniques of far more serious crimes.

Denying criminal opportunities calls for action on three levels:

1. Individual action—the way you discipline yourself and

those members of your family or employees under your influence or authority.

2. Community action—essential when the apartment house in which you live is your "community" (see Chapter VI).

3. Locality-wide action—supporting the police and other elements in the criminal justice system by joining either the auxiliary police or volunteer communication networks such as React and City-Wide React (see p. 160), or helping to organize antiburglary systems such as Operation Identification (see p. 23).*

Unlike the authors of some previous books on do-it-yourself security, I take a strong stand against arming oneself in any way. Handguns are what I object to most strongly, but I also caution against the use of such nonlethal weapons as hat pins, razors and repellent chemicals such as Mace. Handguns are illegal, especially if concealed, in many states; some other lesser weapons, such as Mace, are also illegal.

Why do I counsel a nonviolent response to crime? Because I think that no amount of property is worth the risk of injury, maiming or death to the owner. Let's take the crime of mugging, which is really robbery. Today, the term "mugging" is applied to any robbery of an individual in which force or the threat of force is used. (Decades ago it was called "yoking," in which one criminal came up behind the victim, caught him around the neck in the crook of an arm and lifted him off the ground. While he was held in this helpless position, an accomplice went through the victim's pockets.) The New York police have found that in over 99 percent of muggings, the victim (usually a woman) is not harmed as long as she does not resist.

* For information on forming a viable anticrime unit in your locality, write to the National Alliance for Safer Cities at 165 East Fifty-sixth Street, New York, N.Y. 10022 (telephone: 212–PL1–4000 ext. 257).

The same advice applies to many criminal situations. If you come home to find a burglary in progress, don't rush in to trap or catch the burglar. The best advice is to withdraw quietly to the nearest phone to call the police.

If a teenager snatches your purse, the smart response is to let it go. Otherwise, he may knock or pull you to the ground. Many older women have been severely injured resisting purse-snatchers, usually to protect but a few dollars.

Nevertheless, many have or will rashly arm themselves with guns or knives. What risks they run! In many localities gun owners are subject to arrest for carrying a concealed weapon. This justifiable regulation is gaining in application all over the country. In Dallas, concurrent with the recent inauguration of sale of drinks-by-the-glass, a new law states that anyone caught carrying a gun in a bar is subject to up to five years in jail.

The penalties are even higher if a gun owner attempts to board an airplane. With the refinement of metal-detecting instruments, there's a good chance that any weapons carried by passengers will be detected, subjecting them to arrest on very serious grounds. (Ever since weapon-detecting apparatus have been set up at most airports to prevent hijacking, hundreds of gun bearers have been arrested, and many discarded guns and knives have been found in departure lounges, usually in potted plants.)

Those who keep weapons in their homes or places of business run the greatest risk of all—accidental discharge. Each year, according to the National Safety Council, about thirteen hundred Americans are accidentally killed in their homes by firearms and another eleven hundred are killed outside of their homes (about half in hunting accidents). The National Safety Council does not compile any figures on those injured accidentally by firearms, but based on the known ratio of thirteen injuries to each two deaths caused accidentally by firearms, it is reasonable to assume that many thousands more are injured accidentally by firearms in the home.

Chance arming of criminals is another great risk. A captain in the New York Police Department told me that he is opposed to citizens keeping handguns at home because this is a leading source of weapons for the underworld. When burglars find a gun in a home or place of business, they keep it, either for their own use or for sale to other criminals.

The National Rifle Association and other groups that dote on guns are, of course, very much opposed to all efforts to limit the sale of guns and register them. One of the arguments against gun control offered by the NRA is based on the Constitution. Whenever a gun nut talks about gun control, he first goes through his little catechism about "constitutional rights." These worshippers of gunmetal are about as dedicated to the preservation of the Constitution and the constitutional rights of others as are criminals who cite the Fifth Amendment every time they clam up before a grand jury. If gun control in any way violates the Constitution, one might ask why New York State's tough Sullivan Act controlling handguns has not been declared unconstitutional in the decades since its enactment.

Another argument offered by the NRA is that armed citizens prevent crimes or catch criminals. Each month in *The National Rifleman*, the publication of the NRA, there is a report of a citizen's apprehension of a criminal in a column called "The Armed Citizen." Since the publication is a monthly, this provides opportunity to publish only twelve such incidents each year. Obviously, there are many more such incidents. I asked the NRA to estimate their number, but they couldn't even offer a guess.

Let's make the very liberal estimate of two thousand criminals caught or shot each year by armed citizens. Is the apprehension of that number of criminals each year worth the accidental deaths due to firearms of an equal or greater number of honest citizens, plus the injuring of tens of thousands more? Obviously not, especially if you consider that some goodly fraction of those comparatively few criminals caught by armed citizens would have been caught anyway by the police.

The "armed citizen" argument is not very strong, and I doubt that even the most militant of NRA members really believe it. Let's face it: the NRA membership opposes gun controls because they love to own, shoot and play with guns. The psychology of gun owning is complex, fed by all the Westerns, the nostalgia for the lost frontier and perhaps some unfulfilled need to assert one's manhood.

If you are a gun lover, nothing that I write here will dissuade you from owning guns. But consider the price this country is paying and could pay because it's so easy to obtain guns. First, the criminals get all the guns they need. Secondly, too many angry people are able legally to own long guns. Sometimes those long guns are used in civil disturbances bordering on guerilla warfare. We can ill afford the urban guerilla warfare that is so common in parts of Latin America.

Gun lovers ride around with that silly bumper sticker that proclaims "If guns are outlawed, only the outlaws will have guns." I am not suggesting that *all* guns be outlawed, just handguns, which are not suitable for hunting. I would also like to see all long guns banned from cities over fifty thousand in population. Hunters who live in cities larger than that should be required to check their rifles, shotguns and ammunition at government-operated gun depositories on the outskirts of cities when they return from hunting. Remember, the hunting season is only a few weeks or at most a few months long. Why keep the guns about all year?

In the meantime, I'd be delighted if all states merely adopted gun-registration laws. Sometimes the only offense for which a known or professional criminal can be arrested is the fact that he is carrying a concealed illegal weapon.

Enough about guns. The majority of Americans, particularly women living alone, don't keep handguns in their homes for protection—and are well advised not to. If they are to protect themselves against criminals, it will be through deterrence, not by playing policeman.

Because I've lived in New York City most of my life, and have talked about crime with New York City police officials, this book might appear to favor the residents of big cities, particularly New York. In a sense, this is a book for city dwellers. Until you realize that the crime problems of the central cities are now following escapees to the suburbs. Crime in the suburbs is rising at a faster rate than crime in the central cities. In particular, school vandalism is more of a suburban than urban problem. Drug addiction, with its associated crimes against property, is no stranger to the suburbs.

Because of the scarcity of land, high-rise apartment construction is now common in the suburbs, making Chapter VI, "Apartment House Security," just as pertinent to suburbanites as urbanites. Professional car thieves may not operate as much in the suburbs, but suburbs are plagued with juvenile joyriders. And every suburbanite who works in the central city should be aware of the dangers of victimization by the city's more concentrated population of criminals.

Fire protection, which I discuss in Chapter V, "Electronic Security Systems," is germane for several valid reasons: many of the security systems include provisions for fire and even smoke detection; arson is often associated with the crimes of vandalism and civil disorder; if you live in an apartment building, the community action required to create a secure building can be extended with little effort to include fire protection; and security provisions can sometimes be in conflict with municipal or building regulations to promote fire protection.

Of course, it is going to cost money to protect yourself. However, even though I discuss many different security devices and systems in this book, I am very much against excessive spending for security. Spending must be in proportion to the threat.

On the other hand, it is obvious that government has to spend a lot more to control crime. Crime is one of the truly great threats to our system of government and to the very existence of our society, and surely a greater threat than the radicalism so many of us fear. Nevertheless, even on the governmental level mere changes in procedure can do much at no cost—and even *save* money. For example, it is estimated that in New York City alone, the annual cost of holding persons who have not yet been convicted of a crime is $10 million. Much of this could be saved by a program of letting out without bail those arrested persons who have strong enough roots in a community to provide reasonable assurance that they will show up in court when their cases are tried.

Another no-cost measure that would reduce crime is permanent Daylight Saving Time. Why not extend daylight during the winter months so that those of us who work regular hours could come home during daylight instead of after the sun has set? As I write this, various bills have been introduced in both houses of Congress that would permit each state to legislate year-round daylight saving. Unfortunately, another bill (S. 664) to limit daylight saving to the period from May

30 to September 30 has been reported out of the Senate Commerce Committee. Fortunately, the House Commerce Committee is taking its sweet time with a similar bill to emasculate the Daylight Saving Time law.

What I am really calling for in this book is the expenditure of something other than money to control crime on all levels—individual, communal and governmental. I mean that scarce commodity, self-discipline. If you are not prepared to exercise self-discipline to protect yourself, then you'd better set this book aside.

Chapter II

COMMONSENSE
MEASURES

Many years ago when I was in the U.S. Navy, one of my fellow officers performed an interesting ritual just before he was to relieve another watch officer at sea; he read *The Rules of the Road,* the world-accepted guidelines for ship movements relative to other vessels. He wanted to be ready just in case he encountered one of the rare emergencies at sea.

I have prepared something similar to guide the individual in an increasingly hostile and criminal world. "Commonsense measures," are what I call them. I don't expect you to read them every day, but they are designed for quick and frequent scanning. In particular, when you are about to enter a situation to which one of these lists apply, I urge you to read it. For example, if you've lived in a private home all your life and you move into an apartment, read "Commonsense Measures for Apartment Dwellers." And induce the other members of your family to do the same.

The appendices at the end of this chapter are designed for

duplication, either laboriously by typewriter or quickly on a flatbed photocopier that can handle bound books. Post the list of phone numbers near each phone, and if you live in an apartment house, show the tenants committee my suggested "Security Manual" and urge them to adapt it to the building and distribute a copy to each tenant.

Commonsense Measures for Everyone, Everyday

• Keep your money in the bank. Although the Federal Deposit Insurance Corporation (FDIC), which insures all savings bank accounts up to $15,000 per account, has been in existence for over thirty-five years, there are still tens of thousands of Americans who fear leaving their money in the bank. Some are old enough to remember the Great Depression, during which so many banks closed their doors, wiping out their depositors. Others are recent immigrants to the United States. There was nothing like the FDIC in the old country and these uninformed people still haven't heard about it. Money in the bank not only earns interest, but it is safe from fire as well as robbery.

• Don't keep a lot of cash on your person or in your home. Pay by check, traveler's checks, money orders or credit card. If you don't have a checking account, get one. If you don't want to bother with a checking account because you will use it infrequently (while paying monthly charges), try to make payments by money order or ask a good friend or relative to write a check for you in return for the amount in cash. When withdrawing substantial sums from your savings account, ask the bank to prepare it for you in the form of a cashier's check or checks. You can then fill in the name of the company or person to receive the amounts. Sometimes there is a small charge for this service. It's worth it.

• Keep all stock certificates in a safe-deposit box or in the custody of your broker. Your home safe is not secure enough, particularly if you have a large number of certificates. Stock and bond certificates stolen from homes, or from business premises, are a negotiable item of trade in the underworld. They are mostly used as collateral for risky loans. During the fiscal year that ended June 30, 1971, the Department of the Treasury received requests from 64,344 Americans for the issuance of U.S. Savings Bonds that were lost, destroyed or stolen. An average of three bonds was involved in each instance. If you lose Savings Bonds, you must file an application for replacements at the Bureau of the Public Debt, Division of Loans and Currency Branch, 536 South Clark Street, Chicago, Ill. 60680. Application form PD 1048 can be obtained from that office or from any Federal Reserve bank. It takes about six months to obtain replacements.

• Avoid all dealings with "readers and advisors," fortune tellers, gypsies, spiritualists and other self-appointed or unlicensed counselors, particularly those who claim "great powers," such as curing by "laying on of hands." Somehow those "blessed hands" work their way into your purse or pockets, your bank account and your safe-deposit box. If you—or more likely your parents or an elderly friend or former employee— are approached by anyone, either in person or over the phone, with a scheme that somehow involves giving or temporarily leaving a large sum of money with that person or a supposedly "neutral" party, report the incident as quickly as possible to the police or the district attorney. Confidence games and the various forms of medical quackery are far too varied and complex to report in detail in this book. However, they are the work of true criminals. Con men never use force, but they often murder: the police report that those elderly persons victimized by flimflammers often die soon afterward because they are so crushed by the loss of all or a large part of their savings.

• Don't leave outgoing mail containing checks lying about

your home—or office. Mail them promptly. Conversely, don't delay depositing of incoming checks. Delivery boys, messengers and others have been known to take such checks and successfully cash them. Even though you are not liable, banks have been known to give innocent parties in such situations a hard time and to delay reimbursement for many weeks.

• If you foul up a deposit slip in the bank, don't just crumple it. Rip it into small pieces before dropping it into the wastebasket. Forgers have been known to retrieve a crumpled deposit slip, which tells them your name and account number. In the event of a forgery, you are not responsible. However, you may not notice the forgery yourself—until one of your own checks bounces because of "inadequate funds." At the least, straightening out your account is a great annoyance.

• To otherwise foil forgers, write the amount of a check with no blank spaces—so a "check raiser" can't change a 7 into 70, for instance. Remove each check before filling it out so that the impression of your signature can't be picked up from the next check if your checkbook is stolen or lost. When mailing a check, enfold it with the bill or a blank sheet of paper so that a forger or thief holding the envelope up to the light can't tell there's a check inside. If any of your blank checks turn up missing, notify your bank in writing immediately.

• Cut down on the number of incoming checks subject to theft. Arrange for all dividend and bond-interest checks to be sent directly to your bank for inclusion in either your savings or checking account. Bank officers have forms to arrange such transfers (the bank sends you a notice each time they receive such checks), which cost you nothing to execute. There's another payoff to such arrangements: the earlier such checks are deposited to your account, the sooner they begin earning dividends.

• If you receive Social Security checks, go to your bank and arrange for these checks to be sent directly to your bank for credit to your savings or checking account. All you have to do is fill out a power of attorney. Pending the readdressing of checks, or if you do not arrange such a readdressing, always go to the bank to deposit or cash your Social Security check with a friend, neighbor or young escort. The mailbox thieves and purse-snatchers know when Social Security checks arrive.

• If a criminal holds you up with a gun, knife or other weapon or threatens physical harm, calmly agree to his demands and turn over all valuables. But study him carefully for future identification.

• Report all crimes, no matter how petty, despite your justifiable doubts that the criminals will be apprehended. Even if the criminal is not apprehended, these reports are of value. They help the police to use their limited forces more effectively and provide a truer picture of the level of crime in your neighborhood and municipality.

• Make a list of the serial numbers of all valuables: cars, watches, TV sets and other portable appliances, bikes (serial number is on crank hanger or toe plate), golf clubs and other expensive sports gear, guns, typewriters, cameras, etc. If you have any valuable paintings or other art objects, have them appraised and obtain appraisal forms. Photograph all valuable or antique silver that is not appraised. Place these lists, appraisal forms and photos in your safe-deposit box. You may need them to establish an insurance or income-tax claim.

• If you live in one of the growing number of cities in which the police and/or some civic organization have established a computer identification program (CIS) or a property identification program (Operation Identification), use it. Under these programs, citizens mark their valuable portable property with their driver's license numbers. If a computer identification program has been set up, then citizens file their numbers, addresses and business and home phone numbers with the police. The police enter this information into their computer and issue decals to be pasted on front and rear doors. The decal says: "All valuable items on these premises have been registered with the police department's computer identification program." Where CIS is not yet available, participating citizens mount decals that state: "All valuables inside have been engraved so that law enforcement agencies can readily identify them." Burglars and thieves soon find that they can't dispose of property marked with the telltale numbers and that they can be arrested if it is found in their possession. In Monterey Park, California, the CIS program has cut burglaries in registered residences to a negligible level. The tool most commonly used to mark property is the electric engraver, also known as the electric engraving pen. It's a hand tool with a carbide tip that is driven up and down at thousands of strokes per minute by a small electric motor. These tools are most commonly stocked in hobby shops. I found only one store in all of New York City that carried this tool, and it was out of stock. If you can't buy one locally,* a leading manufacturer sells them by mail at the list price of $14.95. The address is Dremel Manufacturing Company, P.O. Box 518, Racine, Wisconsin 53401.

• If you have a valuable or beloved pet, protect it against loss with an identification tag. Stainless-steel tags are provided for only $1.50, including engraving, by Tag-A-Long,

---

* In many towns with CIS programs, electric engraving pens have been made available by local insurance agencies or some civic organizations. In addition, tenants or block associations, clubs and groups of neighbors have purchased the pens on a cooperative basis for the use of their members. A bill was introduced in the 1971–1972 session of Congress by Representatives Claude Pepper of Florida and Leslie Aspin of Wisconsin to authorize $2 million in federal funds to make the pens available in interested communities.

Inc., Box 212, Westbury, N.Y. 11590. To further protect a valuable dog, you should register it with a service such as the Canine Bureau of Identification, 17 Battery Place, New York, N.Y. 10004 (telephone: 212–269–1200). Here's how this and similar services operate. Accept the unique number assigned by the service or use your own Social Security number and arrange for this number to be tattooed on the right flank or thigh of your dog. (It's painless.) Complete the registration form (three copies), give one to the vet and forward the other two to the service. The service will validate one and return it to you with a tag to go on the dog's collar. The tag says: "Warning, registered dog. If found, telegraph collect tattoo no. on flank or ear to: Canine Bureau of Identification, N.Y.C. 10004." Keep the validated form in your safe-deposit box. The charges for this service are $5 for the life of the dog as long as it is owned by the person who registered it. If you sell or give the dog away, the cost of modifying the registration form is only $2. However, your vet may charge you as much as $25 to tattoo the dog. For the names, addresses and phone numbers of other animal registration services, look in your local classified phone book under that heading or contact the nearest branch of the American Kennel Club.

• Keep a record of the identification numbers of all your credit cards and charge plates in the event of theft. A friend of mine has devised a quick way to maintain a record of all his credit cards. He places them face down on a photocopier and makes "copies" of them en masse. He keeps one copy at home, gives one to his secretary and keeps the other one with him, separate from the wallet in which he holds his credit cards.

• Many issuers of credit cards give recipients two copies of their cards. Most card holders keep one at home. If you have no good reason to keep a second card or don't have a safe in which to keep the cards secure, destroy them. In the event of a burglary, you may be too distraught to notice that the cards are missing—until long after the thief, or the person to whom he sold the cards, has run up big bills. Although recent federal legislation limits your liability in the event your credit cards are stolen, you are still liable for the first $50 of unauthorized use *on each card.* (See Chapter XI, "Crime Insurance," for information on low-cost insurance to protect you against liability for that first $50.)

• If you have a car, keep the ignition key on a chain separate from the trunk key and your house keys. (The two-part key chains that separate easily are recommended.)

• Make a list of all emergency numbers and post copies next to each phone in your home. (Use the list in Appendix I to this chapter as a guide.)

• Place a small table right next to the entrance of your home or apartment. Thus, if you are burdened with packages, you can deposit them on the table and immediately close the door behind you. Otherwise, you are liable to leave the front door open while you go into the kitchen or some other room deep inside your residence to put down the packages. Intruders have been known to follow burdened ladies into their homes.

• Install a phone next to your bed and a slide bolt on the door of your bedroom. In the rare event that you detect an intruder in another room in your residence, lock the door from the inside with the slide bolt and phone the police. If you have children, other relatives, guests or employees sleeping in other rooms, you may be reluctant to lock yourself in your bedroom to call the police. Nevertheless, this is still the best procedure. The intruder is not likely to realize that you are calling (assuming he has not cut the phone line—see discussion in Chapter VII, Part A, on buried phone lines).

If he does realize you have called the police, he will exit quickly, and not harm anyone.

• If you keep any guns in your home, buy a lockable trigger guard for each one and use it. They can be purchased in gun shops for about $5. The chances of some member of your family injuring or killing another relative or friend with a gun are far higher than your chances of using a gun on a criminal.

• Practice fire drills at least twice a year. Figure out alternative exits in the event the front door or staircase is blocked. Show your children how to crawl away in case of heavy smoke. Also show them how to climb out of the windows in their bedrooms if fire or smoke traps them. Instruct them to feel the middle of closed doors first to find out if the fire is burning beyond them.

• Don't show off to strangers. Don't point out your valuables—jewelry, furniture, handwoven rugs, paintings, bric-a-brac, objets d'art, liquor cabinet, etc.—to strangers such as door-to-door sales personnel, meter readers, TV repairmen, painters, delivery boys and such. Sometimes they pass on information to criminal cohorts, either deliberately or innocently.

• Women living alone should list only their first initial in the phone directory—and on mailboxes and apartment-house listings.

• If any street lamps go out on your block, report the outage to the proper authorities as quickly as possible. Keep after them until the lamp is repaired.

Telephone Harassment and Confidence Games

• If you receive an obscene, hate or denunciatory phone call, hang up—don't argue or try to reason with the caller. If the calls persist, contact your phone company. In larger cities, the phone company has created an annoyance call bureau to which such complaints are directed. The phone company office number in many cities is 811.

• If a stranger calls claiming that he has a misdirected package and offers to deliver it personally, or urges you to come for it, ask him to return it to the post office or United Parcel Service for delivery.

• If you lose some jewelry, other valuables or a pet and offer a reward for their return via an advertisement in the newspapers, don't rush out to meet a stranger with the reward. Instead, ask the caller to bring your property to your home or place of business. First, ask him to describe the lost property in detail. If he can't, hang up.

• If anyone calls up claiming to be taking a poll or making a survey, refuse to answer all questions about your appearance, income, place of business, how much money you have in the bank, sexual habits or state of health. Sometimes the callers are employees of collection agencies attempting (illegally in most states) to find out where to garnishee your salary. However, the caller could be a confidence man setting you up for a killing. In rare instances, a burglar may be trying to find out when you're going on vacation. (Because many companies close down for company-wide vacations the same two weeks each year, merely finding out where you work could tell a burglar when you're on vacation.)

• If you receive a call from someone claiming to be a policeman, FBI agent, some kind of "peace officer" or a government official, ask the caller to visit in person if he poses any questions about you, your family, friends or neighbors that you consider sensitive, private, irritating—or none of his damn business. If the person seeking information is indeed who he claims to be, he will agree to come to your home and identify himself properly. (You are, nevertheless, *not* obligated to answer his questions.) In the meantime, call the local organization of which he is a part and ask if such a person does work there and if he is indeed seeking information legitimately; also ask his superior for a physical description of him. On occasion, the caller will claim to be out of town, thereby precluding a personal visit. In this event, ask for his official phone number and tell him you will call back *collect* in a few minutes. If he insists that his organization can't accept collect calls, tell him he must make an exception in this case. Before calling back, check the number of his organization by calling the information operator in that locality. You are still under no obligation to answer his questions.

• Instruct your children not to give out any information over the phone to strangers.

Commonsense Measures to Take When Away from Home

Your home is your castle. Once you leave it you are far more likely to be victimized—by muggers, pickpockets, purse-snatchers, car clouts and sneak thieves. Confidence men also operate in the streets but are just as likely to initiate their schemes while you are at home. The best way to protect yourself away from home is not to place yourself in a very lonely street or building with no others in sight. Here is a list of ways to lower vulnerability:

• If you live in a private home, always leave any outside lights burning when it is dark (or mount an automatic control in the base that is actuated by sunlight to turn the light off— see Chapter IV, Part B). This light makes the return home of members of your family and yourself much safer and is the helpful thing to do for your neighbors and any passersby.

• If you are returning home at night, take a cab if you can afford it—and ask the driver to wait until you are inside the door. If you take public transportation at night and your home is not within a short, well-lighted walk from the nearest stop, take a cab from the bus, subway or railroad station— and then ask the driver to wait.

• If you are taking a subway at night, stand near the change booth until the train arrives. Women traveling on the subway should not stand close to the edge of the platform. A new type of purse-snatcher reaches out from between cars or from windows of trains as they leave the station to grab the purses of women within arm's length.

• When walking in the street during darkness, stay close to the curb. If the street is very dark, walk in the middle of the street.

• Obey your instincts! If you're walking down the street and you sense danger ahead from some person standing in the shadows or you sense you are being tracked by someone on foot or in a car, don't put aside your fears. Criminals appear to give off little signals or clues to their intentions in the way they walk or look—and many potential victims get the message. If you sense an impending attack, run into the nearest building or cross the street to avoid encountering danger ahead.

• Don't let any strangers stop you in the street and engage you in conversation, particularly at night.

• Don't let any strangers stop you for a match or cigarette.

• In particular, women and elderly men should not give directions requested by young men in cars, particularly if the motor is running and the car is in a position to pull away quickly. (Purse-snatchers and muggers have been operating from older—usually stolen—cars, using the device of asking directions to draw in their victims on deserted streets, often in daylight.)

• Avoid cars occupied by young men parked at crosswalks with the motor running (see immediately above).

• Avoid crowds of adolescents leaving school. If you see such a crowd approaching, cross the street. If the youths follow you, start screaming.

• Avoid parking on deserted streets or in large, lonely parking lots after dark, and sometimes in daylight if the neighborhood has a reputation as dangerous.

• Drive your car with the doors locked from the inside. If someone tries to enter your car at a stoplight, step on the gas.

• Never leave your purse or wallet unattended or unguarded. This means keeping your wallet or purse with you at work, while visiting washrooms (men should not leave their wallets in their jackets if they hang their jackets outside the commode booth and women should hang their purses on the hook behind the door, if it cannot be reached from outside, not on the floor), while trying on new clothes at a shop and while engaged in sports (if you can't keep your valuables with you, such as in a tennis, golf or bowling bag), check them with the management.

• Men should never carry their wallets in their back pockets, even if the pocket is buttoned—particularly when not wearing a jacket. When wearing a jacket, keep your wallet in your inside jacket pocket and keep your jacket buttoned. When not wearing a jacket, keep your wallet in one of your deep side pockets. Even better, use a money clip to separate your cash from your credit cards and licenses.

• Women, if you have heeded my earlier recommendation not to keep too much money on your person, then you shouldn't be carrying much money—or other valuables— in your purse. Therefore, if a robber demands or grabs your purse, let him have it. Even if you do have some valuables in your purse, let him have it. If you resist a purse-snatcher, he will pull at the purse until the strap breaks or you are pulled to the ground. The mugger may strike, stab or even shoot you. There's nothing in your purse worth a stay in the hospital. Don't carry your valuables in big, open purses or in a small bag sitting on top of a large, open shopping bag. (Pickpockets will take your purse or wallet without detection.) Women have been counseled to select purses with long belts so that they can be secured across the chest Sam Browne fashion. I disagree. A purse worn in that manner is a signal to a purse-snatcher that valuables are present. The determined snatcher will simply pull at the purse with all his might, hoping to break the belt or catches.

• Women, when in the theatre, should *never* place their purses on an adjacent empty seat. Clever pickpockets sitting behind the empty seat can open the purse, lift the wallet or change purse, remove all cash and other valuables and return the wallet or change purse without the owner becoming aware of the theft. If you are occupying a balcony seat, you may be able to place your purse safely under your seat—it usually can't be reached from behind. But the safest course is to hold your purse in your lap.

• Carry house keys separately from any documents that reveal your address or which could be used to trace your address (through a telephone book listing for example).

• Don't check topcoat or overcoat with your keys in the pocket.

• In the event that your keys are taken by a thief, and the thief can determine your address, immediately arrange for a locksmith to change all affected cylinders or the pins in those cylinders.

• Have your keys in hand before you reach your front door, so that you don't have to spend a long time fumbling for the right keys. One type of robber waits for his victim to open the front door, then rushes up, shoves the victim inside and robs both victim and residence.

• If you are walking on a deserted or dark street, you may sense that you are being followed. If you walk at a faster pace and your shadow also moves faster, don't hesitate to drop your purse or wallet into the nearest mailbox. Then stand beside the box. The suspected mugger will most likely pass you by. However, if he does accost you, simply tell him that all your valuables have been deposited in the box. As soon as he leaves, call the superintendent of the nearest post office and inform him of your action. He will most likely send a postal inspector around to open the box and return your property. (This happens dozens of times a day in New York.)

• Automatic cash-dispensing machines actuated by bank credit cards will soon be servicing people all over the country, beginning with installations outside banks. Naturally, muggers will be attracted to any machine that hands out from $25 to $200 in crisp new bills. If you are operating one of these machines late one night and you sense that a mugger is lurking nearby waiting to take both cash and credit card from you, punch the wrong personal code into the machine (to operate these machines, you must insert your credit card and a four- to six-digit code that only you are supposed to know). If you do this three times in succession, the machine will not return your card, making you less attractive as a victim. If you are not accosted by muggers, you need only call the bank the next day to retrieve your card. If you are accosted or have strong suspicions that you would have been attacked, call the police immediately.

• If you are making a bank deposit at night via the night depository and the depository door is covered by a sign announcing the machine is out of order and you should place your deposit in a "temporary" depository sitting on the street nearby, don't do it. This clever fraud was actually pulled off successfully in Detroit.

• Professional burglars read the social and obituary columns. If there is a wedding or other celebration or a death in your family, ask a friend or neighbor to stay in your home or apartment while your family is away for many hours attending the celebration or the memorial services and interment.

• Automatic phone-answering machines are now used by many thousands of small businessmen, salesmen and others, such as doctors and actors, who don't have secretaries to answer their phones. If you now have or if you buy such a machine, don't record messages that indicate just when you are returning. If a burglar dials your number and hears a message that ends, "And I will return after 5 P.M.," he knows that he has several hours in which to burglarize your home or office. Instead, use vague phrases such as "I will return shortly."

• Note the location of all police emergency call boxes near your home and place of employment. Also, note the location of fire-alarm boxes.

• Every time you use a credit card, make sure that your own card has been returned to you (some part-time thieves employed in shops and restaurants will substitute a stolen card that has outlived its usefulness, to obtain a fresh card; this form of theft is more commonly perpetrated on tourists and out-of-towners).

Commonsense Measures for Home Owners

• Hire a master locksmith to check the condition of locks on all doors, the garage door and accessible windows—and the doors themselves. Follow his recommendations. If he suggests that you install a peephole in the front door, have him install one; then use it.

• Own at least one battery-operated transistor radio, plus

spare batteries, so that you can receive instructions from municipal, police and other authorities in the event of a power outage that cuts off all radio and TV broadcasting.

• If there is only one light at the front door, have a second light installed to insure illumination in case the first light goes out. Install bulbs that provide good illumination.

• Leave some lights on all night in front of your home, even if this is not required by municipal regulations, as a neighborly gesture. Then try to convince all your neighbors to do the same. Criminals avoid well-lighted streets.

• Cut down or trim back all hedges that obscure ground-level or basement windows.

• Cut down or trim back any sturdy tree branches that extend close to upper windows, porches or roof areas leading to upper windows.

• Remove any trellises that could be used to climb up to upper windows or porches or roof areas leading to upper windows.

• Install a burglar and fire-alarm system that matches your risk (see Chapter V). If your home has many valuables, install a communicating system that alerts a guard service or the local police, if the police permit an indicator in their head-quarters. Check the system at least once a month. If you install a system that depends on phone lines, have the phone company install a buried phone line that can't be cut by a burglar. The cost of burial runs about $250.

• If electric, gas and water meters are in your basement, arrange with the various utilities for yearly readings with all intervening meter readings supplied by you via postcard.

Commonsense Measures for Apartment Dwellers

Maintaining the security of an apartment house is a coop-erative venture. You can't do it all by yourself. But one individual can make a strong contribution to the building's security by mobilizing all the other tenants. The only way to do this is by forming a tenants committee, as I point out in Chapter VI, "Apartment House Security." Such a committee can organize tenant patrols, request security evaluations by local authorities and issue a security manual. A security manual is a check list of commonsense measures for the apartment-house dweller. To make it simple to prepare such a manual, I have provided a model in Appendix II to this chapter.

One more important point: the security of a building will be lowered sharply if many strangers enter and leave without hindrance. To cut down on the number of strangers, buildings should bar all solicitors for cosmetics, vacuum cleaners, encyclopedias and magazine subscriptions. You should inform any such solicitors who come to your door that they have no right to enter the building and if they don't leave, you will call the police. This may work a hardship on some hardworking individuals (don't worry about the Fuller Brush Company, Avon Products or the publishers of encyclopedias), but it makes a lot of sense.

Commonsense Measures on the Job

• Don't bring a lot of money with you to work. If paid in cash, deposit the money as soon as possible. If paid by check, deposit the check at a nearby bank, taking only enough cash for immediate needs.

• For men: don't leave your wallet in your jacket if you remove your jacket.

• For women: don't leave your purse at or in your desk while away from your desk. If you go to the powder room, don't leave your purse on the floor of the commode booth near the door (female sneak thieves have been known to snatch purses, particularly in public rest rooms).

- Don't leave cash or other valuables behind in your desk.
- Don't leave your address among your papers in your desk (burglars have been known to "hit" the homes of employees of burglarized commercial premises after finding out their home addresses from papers left behind in desks into which the burglars have broken).
- Don't resent security measures imposed by your employer: they will protect your property and person as much as the company's property.
- Cooperate with an employer who restricts free passage of visitors on his premises. Don't invite friends, family, insurance agents, Avon ladies or other visitors who have no business with the company. Enforce the company rule requiring delivery people to leave coffee, lunch, mail and packages at the reception desk. The fewer visitors on the premises, the easier it is to prevent the petty thievery that has demoralized some offices.
- In the unlikely event that armed robbers invade your place of business, don't play hero or attempt to subdue or flee from the robbers. Give them all that they ask for.
- If a workman approaches your desk to remove an office machine, or if you find a strange mechanic removing your typewriter, ask to inspect his authorization to remove the machine, or call the office manager to ask if he has authorized the removal of the machine. Those who steal office machines often masquerade as mechanics. Their favorite time for a "hit" is just before closing.
- If you work in a retail establishment handling a lot of cash, suggest that the owner install a drop depository safe (see p. 267) to which only the owner or an armored car service has the combination.
- Report all drug peddlers who operate on company premises. (Many large plants are "serviced" by drug distributors who are also employees.)

Commonsense Measures to Take When Traveling

How to protect yourself and your family when traveling begins with a series of precautions taken before leaving home. The object is to protect your residence in your absence so that you can have peace of mind on this score while traveling and will not be shocked by a burglary on your return.

There are certain obvious steps: suspend deliveries of milk, newspapers and magazines and arrange for a friend or neighbor to either pick up the mail left at your doorstep or empty your mailbox. The lighting controls discussed in Chapter IV that automatically turn on certain lights, the radio and at least the bedroom air conditioner also make sense. Do not suspend phone service; a "suspended service" indication in response to a burglar's call tells him he has plenty of time to burglarize your home. Obviously, phone service can't be suspended if your residence is equipped with the type of security system that communicates with a central monitoring station or the local police.

If you are a home owner, these simple measures plus arranging for continued trimming of the lawn are certainly useful. But they are far from foolproof. Apparently, professional burglars have organized networks of informers, probably among delivery men, to tell them when a family is away on vacation. The informants would most likely know if your home is equipped with a burglar alarm system. So the burglars will come equipped with tools to circumvent it: they have loads of time to figure out how to break in without setting off an alarm.

The best deterrent is the "house-sitter." House-sitters should be reliable, responsible people who enjoy living in a home (or penthouse—which also needs a house-sitter). Sometimes house-sitters are a family from another part of the country or even overseas who use your home as a local vacation base. Some of the airlines, notably Pan American, arrange for families overseas to swap homes with American families for lower-cost vacations.* Usually, however, house-sitters are more mature students or retirees for whom living in a home is a real treat. Depending on how much they need the quarters and how important it is for you to have your home occupied, the consideration ranges from no fee to some moderate fee, often related to the privileges that are available to the house-sitter: car, swimming pool, liquor, food, etc. Fees range from a low of $2 up to $15 per day if a dog must be walked or children minded. Obviously, one of the big advantages of engaging a house-sitter is that you don't have to kennel your dog or cut off deliveries.

Finding a suitable house-sitter takes time. The best sources are friends or relatives. Or you might invite a trusted employee to live in your house. Another sensible approach is to work through the housing office of a local college or university. You might be lucky enough to work out a deal with a member of the faculty. Other sources are local hospitals whose interns or residents would be delighted with a chance to live away from the hospital dorm. Finally, you might consider your local police department. Some unmarried policemen might jump at the chance to move in for a few weeks.

Your last choice should be to advertise. Naturally, the ads should list a box number, not your home address or phone number. If you are forced to seek a house-sitter through an ad, place it well in advance of your departure so that you have time to screen all applicants.

Once you've selected a house-sitter, plan to have him over several days before you leave so that you can take him through

---

* Contact your local airline office or your travel agent for information on how to swap a home with an overseas family.

the house or apartment and point out all features and deficiencies, especially how to work your alarm system. Supplement this tour with a check list of all that should be known
to the house-sitter. I am assuming that you have previously
prepared the list of emergency phone numbers suggested in
Appendix I to this chapter and that you will give a copy
to the house-sitter. And, of course, that you are covered by
liability insurance in case the house-sitter falls or injures
himself in some way. Finally, leave a copy of your itinerary
behind.

Now for some additional commonsense measures to take
before leaving and while on your way:

• Don't permit any announcements of your impending vacation to appear in local or company newspapers. Don't boast
about your upcoming trip to strangers or shop personnel.

• Take a minimal amount of cash with you. Use traveler's
checks, credit cards or personal checks. (If you are going outside the United States, personal checks are useless, and they
may be difficult to cash in the United States far from home.)

• If you are traveling abroad, you will most likely need
small amounts of the local currency for tips. To avoid the
nuisance of attempting to convert one of your traveler's
checks into local currency immediately on arrival, buy a few
dollars' worth of the currency of each nation you plan to
visit. Your local bank may sell packets of such currencies,
or can tell you where to buy them.

• Don't buy expensive luggage. It attracts thieves at airports and hotels. Even though I recommend that all luggage
be locked—it's a minor deterrent—the locks on even the most
costly of luggage present no challenge to determined thieves.
Besides, baggage handlers and baggage-handling systems
will soon scratch or gouge fancy luggage.

• If you are traveling by air, don't overpack luggage. In

some airports, luggage handlers with larceny on their minds have been known to drop luggage deliberately, which can pop it open. Overpacked luggage is most subject to this form of "breaking and entering."

• Home owners should inform neighbors on either side that they will be away and for how long. Also inform the local police. Arrange for a friend or relative to inspect your empty home at frequent intervals.

• Apartment dwellers should inform neighbors on the same floor and the super of the building how long they will be away. Arrange for a friend or relative to inspect your empty apartment at regular intervals.

• If home or apartment is equipped with a burglar alarm, call in the local service representative to check it prior to leaving.

• If garbage is not collected every day, don't put any out when you leave if the next collection is several days off; this is an invitation to burglars and vandals. Instead, arrange for a neighbor to put your garbage out on the next collection day.

• Place all stock and bond certificates and all jewelry not taken on the trip in your safe-deposit box. Take the minimum amount of jewelry with you; when not wearing it, always leave it in your hotel safe—never in the trunk of your car.

• Store all valuable furs with a furrier.

• If car is to be used on trip, have it thoroughly checked by your mechanic. If car is not to be used, home owners should put it in the garage for length of vacation. Apartment dwellers who do not have a year-round garage should either store the car in a garage or leave it with a responsible friend. Avoid leaving your car at an airport parking lot for extended periods.

• Don't tell any service personnel you deal with why you are suspending deliveries, checking car, storing furs, etc.

• Pay phone, gas, water and electric bills so that no utility personnel need call during your absence to check on status of bills.

• Take your Blue Cross, Blue Shield and other medical-insurance identification with you. Pay medical-insurance premiums to take you through trip.

• If going overseas, check expiration date of passport.

• Bring will up to date.

• Discuss trip with physician. Take names of physicians known to your physician in towns to be visited. If your physician cannot provide you with the names of overseas physicians, they can be obtained from a directory of English-speaking physicians in 174 overseas cities that is available at a cost of $5 from Intermedic, 777 Third Avenue, New York, N.Y. 10017 (telephone: 212-421-5378).

• Take a Travelock: The Travelock, originated by Yale but now made by others as well, has many uses for the traveler. At night it can be used to prevent entry by unauthorized key holders or those who can "loid" (force the latch back with a thin piece of metal or plastic) the often inadequate locks in hotels while you are asleep. During the day, when you are away from your room and you want the maid to clean it, you can use this lock to close off a closet in which are placed such valuables as furs and cameras and other items too bulky to place in the hotel safe or which you want to use every day. If the closet has a sliding door or other door that can't be locked with a Travelock, place your valuables in the bathroom and use the lock to secure it. Later, when you return, you can ask the maid to come in and tidy up the bathroom.

• During the summer, don't leave your car windows open to cool the car. Crack the windows just a fraction of an inch and don't leave anything on the seats or in the glove compartment.

• Check all bills carefully. Demand itemization, especially of hotel bills. In particular, check bills for rented cars with extra diligence. A friend of mine was disconcerted to find that the clerk at a leading Italian rental agency had added in the date when he totaled the bill. "1971" in lira is over $3 in U.S. currency.

• If you deal with a foreign travel agency while overseas, check your bills very carefully. Some are notorious for padding bills by inclusion of charges for side trips never taken, telegrams never sent and inflated amounts for air and rail travel tickets (which should be checked against published rates available in directory form in the agent's office).

• Way in advance of leaving, prepare a check list of what to take with you and what has to be done just before leaving. Without such a list, you're liable to rush away and neglect some vital security measure. Keep this check list and use it for even short trips.

• Don't pack your car with luggage and other valuable items the night before leaving to get an early start. You are merely providing opportunities for car clouts.

• Avoid visiting cities with high levels of crime, unless you are prepared to take special precautions. For example, Nairobi, the capital of Kenya, is experiencing a wave of street crimes. Even those in cars are not immune: the robbers deliberately cause a minor accident, then rob the occupants of the other car when they get out to examine the damage. Your travel agent should be able to counsel you on crime-ridden cities. If he can't, find another, more knowledgeable agent.

• If your car does break down, stick with it. Use your emergency flashers and wait for a police car or other help to discover you—even if it takes hours.

• Don't allow yourself to be flagged down by anyone other than a policeman.

• If you have to stop for directions at night other than at a gas station, avoid getting out of your car. Run your window down halfway and keep the doors locked.

• Leave copies of itinerary with house-sitter, lawyer, employer, secretary, neighbors, close friends and relatives.

• If going on a vacation with a camping trailer in tow, check regulations of all states (and Mexico and Canada as well if they are to be visited) pertaining to weight of trailer relative to weight of car. Check state regulations on use of "cars only" highways and tunnels. If going into Mexico and/or Canada, check that your car insurance applies in those nations.

• Lock all windows and back doors prior to leaving. Don't pull all shades down to the same level.

Commonsense Measures for Children

Older children have always bullied younger, smaller children. However, in some of our cities, particularly New York, oppression of younger by older kids has taken on criminal overtones. Smaller children or children by themselves or in groups of two or three are stopped by groups of older kids who demand money, watches, bus passes (during the school year) or bicycles, if the victims are riding. Sometimes the oppressors wait outside the city's private schools because they know that the children who attend usually have affluent parents.

Advising or directing a child on ways to avoid being "shaken down" or robbed by older children is very difficult. You don't want your child to be subjected to a frightening, even traumatic, experience, yet in seeking ways to protect your child, you may make him afraid to walk the streets by himself.

I would like to pass on the advice given to me by the administrator of the Ethical Culture School, where my son was formerly a student.

• When traveling to and from school, but especially when leaving school, children should organize little groups somewhat like the car pools that grown-ups organize to go back and forth to work.

• If waylaid by older children who outnumber them, advise your children to accede to their demands. However, if they are not outnumbered, advise your children to make a run for it.

• Remind your children to report all incidents to school authorities and their parents. (When oppressed by children in the same school, younger children are understandably reluctant to report any incidents for fear of reprisal.)

• If the incident occurs near your home, try to find the offending children—and then try to find out where they live and report their behavior to their parents.

• Report the incidents, no matter how small, to the local police precinct. If they receive enough reports, the police may assign a patrolman to cover the area about the school at dismissal time.

• If your child is consistently bullied or oppressed by juvenile criminals, send him to the Y or some reputable school to learn jujitsu or some other form of defense. I doubt that your child will become an expert, but the training will give him much more self-confidence and lower his fear of walking the streets.

• Schools should not permit anyone to pick up or remove a child from the school without the written permission of the parents or guardian. And the validity of the document should be checked by a phone call. Tell your children not to go off with any stranger who waits for them as they leave school, even if the stranger claims to have been sent by you.

Appendix I

To encourage your family and yourself to call those in authority and others when a crime occurs or when help is needed, you should compile a list of their phone numbers and mount a copy next to each phone in your home. I assume that most of you have the number of your physician near your phone. Here's a model list of numbers that you can adapt for your needs and those of your community:

Next-door
   neighbors_____
Family doctor_____
   Office No._____
   Home No._____
Pediatrician_____
   Office No._____
   Home No._____
Family dentist_____
Husband's place
   of business_____
Family lawyer_____
Grandparents
   (or other close relative)_____
Local hospital_____
Police emergency_____
Police precinct_____
Fire department_____
Volunteer ambulance
   service_____
Landlord or
   managing agent_____
Superintendent
   of building_____
Head of tenants association
   (or president of cooperative)_____

School office_____
Oil-burner
   repair service_____
Street lights
   not working_____
Health department_____
Medical society_____
District attorney_____
FBI_____
Building violations_____
Sanitation
   complaints_____
Bulk sanitation
   collection_____
Air-pollution
   complaints_____
Undertaker_____
Traveler's Aid_____
Automobile Club_____
Water supply
   complaints_____
Repair service for
   burglar alarm_____
Electrical or gas
   emergency_____
Western Union_____

Appendix II

Model "Security Manual" for Apartment Buildings

To be adapted by landlords, managing agents or tenants committees and distributed to all present tenants and to each new tenant who moves into the building. A copy should also be given to each employee of the building. At regular intervals the manual should be updated and reissued to all tenants and employees.

Dear neighbor:

The security of this building depends on the cooperation of everyone who lives and works here. If only one or two tenants do not follow the rules, then all of us are threatened. Even though no crimes [or "very few crimes"] have been reported in this building, it is important that the security of the building be kept at the highest level consistent with dignified living. If even a single intruder finds the building an "easy mark," he will spread the word to his "buddies," who can be depended upon to swarm down on us.

Please read this manual carefully, ask each member of your family old enough to read to go over it and even read it to those in your family who can't read. In particular, ask your children to follow those rules that apply to them.

If we all follow the suggestions listed here, we will enjoy living in this building. If we don't, some of us will flee—which would most likely be a hardship to those who leave and deprive the rest of us of desirable neighbors.

Landlord, Agent or Committee

• Get to know as many of your neighbors as possible. When new tenants move into the building or onto your floor, make a point of introducing yourselves to them.
• Don't leave your house keys with anyone whom you don't know very well or who might be careless with the keys. The law

does *not* require that you leave a duplicate set of your keys with the super or landlord. However, it does make sense to leave a duplicate set with a trusted friend in the building, and then inform the super of this fact: he might need to get into your apartment to shut off an overflow of water or check for fire. (If you do leave your keys with the super, place them in an envelope, seal the envelope and write your name across the seal.)

• Don't "hide" copies of your front-door keys near the door— such as under the mat, on top of the frame or in a potted plant. Burglars know to look in such places.

• Always double-lock the door, even for a short absence.

• Don't leave the keys to the front doors of the building and your apartment on your auto key ring when parking in an attended lot or when your car is serviced. It takes only a few minutes to duplicate a key, and any mechanic who does so will likely know your address too.

• [For buildings with doormen] Request all guests to ask the doorman to announce them.

• [For buildings with door-opener intercoms] Use the buzzer system properly by opening the main door only to identified callers; request your visitors not to hold the door open for others.

• [For buildings with intercoms] When you enter the building make sure you close the door behind you and make sure that you do not permit strangers to enter without being announced. Point to the sign on the door: "Key or buzzer must be used." If the closer on the front door is inoperative, please report this immediately to the super and/or agent.

• [For buildings with intercoms] Please tell your children not to let strangers into the building—even if they feel embarrassed at not holding the door open for an adult. Tell them to point to the sign if someone tries to follow them in without buzzing.

• [For buildings with a garage in the basement] After entering the garage, make sure that no one sneaks into the building before the automatic door closes. If someone does manage to slip in, inform the [doorman, guard, super, police] immediately.

Commonsense Measures

- Please don't leave small children alone in your apartment, even for a few minutes. Instruct your older children not to let anyone enter the apartment while you are away.
- Use the peephole in your apartment door to identify callers before opening the front door.
- Don't leave notes on the front door, buzzer panel or the front door of your apartment indicating that you are away and when you will return.
- Don't open the door to strangers or repairmen unless properly identified. Request all solicitors and door-to-door salesmen to leave the building, then call the [doorman, guard, super] and inform him that some unauthorized people are in the building. Use the phone or intercom to inform your neighbors of the presence of unauthorized canvassers.
- If someone who arouses your suspicions enters the elevator with you, don't hesitate to step out of the elevator. Always stand near the front door of the elevator. (If the elevator is of such construction that someone can conceal himself from those entering, always peek into it before entering.)
- Get into the habit of greeting the doorman or guard [if your building has such] each time you enter the building. In this way he will get to know who belongs in the building and who is a stranger.
- Report all incidents and crimes to the local police precinct and the [super, agent, landlord, security committee].
- If you have any reasonable ideas on how to raise the level of security of the building, please communicate them to the [security committee, landlord, agent].
- Don't allow baby-sitters to have their friends visit them while you are gone.
- Please report any lobby, stairwell or corridor lights that are inoperative.
- Please report any inoperative locks on the doors leading into the lobby or basement or out onto the roof.

Chapter III

PROTECTING DOORS
AND WINDOWS

"Only a small percentage of all break-ins are accomplished by picking of locks." This assertion by the president of a locksmithing firm with a dozen locksmiths out repairing, replacing and adding locks to apartment doors in Manhattan should be a touchstone to all those concerned about the rapidly rising rate of burglaries. The way to protect your home against burglars is not merely by going along with the latest fad in "pick-resistant" lock cylinders. Security of doors —and windows—takes much more, as detailed in this chapter. Nevertheless, I recommend the installation of certain pick-resistant lock cylinders, but not merely because they resist picking!

Door Security

To make your front and rear doors (and the door between garage and home) secure, you must begin with the door itself, not the lock. Too many home owners waste $30, $40, $75, sometimes $100 installing excellent lock sets on doors that do not deserve a $5 lock. If your front or rear doors have glass or wooden panels, the least skilled of burglars or any neighborhood vandal can knock out a panel, then reach in and turn the doorknob or release the deadbolt (the deadbolt is the heavy bolt, usually with a rectangular face, that is thrown into place by the extra turn of the key or by the inside turn knob).

Paneled doors are highly insecure. In 1971 I delivered to the *Ladies' Home Journal* an article entitled "Burglar-Proofing Your Home." In the article, I warned against paneled doors. The managing editor of the magazine read the article on acceptance and most likely several times over again prior to its publication in July, 1971. Yet he never replaced or reinforced the paneled door to his apartment in one of the many converted brownstones in New York. Guess what happened over one summer weekend? He returned to find a neat hole in one panel large enough for a hand to reach through—and a stripped apartment. No one observed the burglar, but I doubt that he took more than several minutes to quietly cut the hole with a rasp, which can be purchased at any hardware store.

Replace any paneled front or back doors with a hollow metal door. If you don't want a metal door for esthetic reasons, a good, solid-core one-and-three-quarter-inch-thick wooden door without panels will be satisfactory. If your landlord won't replace the door or permit you to replace it, have the door reinforced with either a sheet of heavy-gauge galvanized steel or three-quarter-inch-thick plywood.

Despite my warnings, some of you will not replace or reinforce paneled doors. Is there some other way to make them more secure? There is. A lock set with two cylinders can be installed. Double-cylinder lock sets can be locked from the

inside with a key and can't be opened without one. Nevertheless, a paneled door still represents insecurity. Faced with a
double-cylinder lock set, the determined burglar may simply
kick or cut out enough panels—and the supporting wooden
members in between—to climb through your front door!
(Later in this chapter I explain why double-cylinder lock
sets can actually lower security.)

If you reside in a home with a glass-paneled outer vestibule or back door backed by a more secure inner door, it
makes sense to mount a lockable door bolt on these outer
paneled doors; otherwise a burglar can enter the paneled door
to attack the inner door secure in the knowledge that he can't
be seen from the outside. Lockable door bolts, mounted on
the inner surface of door, can be opened only with a key.
They cost a mere $4 to $5 apiece and are made by a number
of suppliers including The Stanley Works, whose products
are available locally throughout the country. However, the
key for such a lock should be hung near the door, but out of
reach of a burglar who breaks through a panel, in case you
have to exit quickly during a fire.

It's the Frame That Counts

A good door requires a good frame, one in which it fits
quite snugly. Steel is best, but a sturdy wooden frame will
also do. Unfortunately, according to Edwin F. Toepfer, one
of America's top lock consultants, hasty and sloppy work-
manship make the wooden frames of entrance doors in most
homes of recent construction completely inadequate. To
avoid any time-consuming delay in fitting door frames, the
door buck, the opening into which the frame is mounted, is
made a bit oversize, says Toepfer. The frame is then secured
with the aid of small wedges of wood. In time, with repeated
slamming of the door, these wedges will slip out of place,

which allows for some play in the door frame. In addition, the normal settling that affects every new building will distort the frame.

Burglars take advantage of this loosening of the door frame to jimmy open doors with short crowbars or tire irons. The crowbar simply expands the opening between door and frame until the deadbolt pops out of the strike, the flat piece of metal mounted on the frame. Years ago, a clever burglar employed a very sophisticated tool in the guise of an elegant walking stick to spread weak door frames. The metal knob at the top of his stick was actually part of a long, heavy threaded bolt. At the tip end of the stick was a series of one-inch-long segments that screwed into each other. The burglar would casually walk up to an entrance door, hold his stick up horizontally to "measure" the width of the door frame, then move off to unscrew enough of the segments at the tip so that the stick would fit loosely into the frame. Later, at night or after working hours, he would attack the door with his stick, spreading the frame with only a few turns of the knob until the deadbolt was exposed. Today's burglars are not so elegant. To spread the steel frames on modern doors, they use an auto jack held horizontally.

Toepfer suggests a simple test to tell if a door frame is weak. He uses two pieces of 2-by-4 wood purchasable as scrap in a lumber yard. Holding one piece perpendicularly against the frame, the other is cut so that it just fits between the first piece and the other side of the frame. Pressing inward on the perpendicular piece tends to spread the frame. If there is much play in the frame, it should be reinforced or replaced. In performing this test, you don't have to push very much on the lever piece; if you do you will crack the plaster around the door frame.

If you have a weak door frame or a loose-fitting door, yet

are not permitted or are not in a position to replace them, there is an alternate security method that I can recommend. A "jimmy-guard" should be mounted on the frame opposite the lock and extending above and below it at least a foot. A jimmy-guard is an angle iron with an L-shaped cross section. It acts as a lip protecting the latch and deadbolt from attack, even if the door and frame are spread apart. Even if your door and frame are acceptable, a jimmy-guard is a recommended deterrent. If you install one yourself or have it installed by a locksmith (cost, $10 to $12), nonretractable or one-way screws must be used.

Check Hinges Too

There's one more aspect of doors and frames that must be checked—the hinges. If a door opens inward, its hinges are not exposed, and there is no problem. However, if the door opens outward, its hinges are exposed. Determined burglars have been known to drive or cut the hinge pins out, which permits them to push or pull the door away. Most entrance doors open inward, but if you have an entrance door that opens outward, you must protect the hinges. Various methods include flanging with a hammer or welding or insertion of a set screw or flat-headed self-tapping screw through a portion of the hinge that is not exposed when the door is closed.

Automatic Closing

The entrance door to your home or apartment should be equipped with an automatic closing feature. In the event that you or a member of your family enters so burdened with packages that you can't pull the door shut behind you, that door should nevertheless close with sufficient force to operate the latch. The closing action should be quick enough so that no intruder can slip in while the occupant who just entered is depositing the packages in some other room. (You will remember that under "Commonsense Measures" I recommend that every resident, to avoid the above risk, place a small table near the entrance door for the express purpose of depositing packages.)

There is a very simple low-cost way of closing doors. It is the spring hinge, and, as its name implies, it is a hinge with a built-in spring designed to force the door shut. A set of spring hinges for a door costs about $10. In time, the springs loosen or lose some of their strength. This means that they must be rewound, a simple operation that takes about three minutes. However, this calls for a special tool. The super or handyman in an apartment building should possess one of these tools, or a local locksmith called in to do other work could also tighten the springs in the hinge. If your front door is not equipped with spring hinges, and no spring hinges are available that fit it, an automatic closer should be installed. These cost as much as $50 installed.

Locks—Secure and Insecure

If you have a substantial door that fits snugly into a sturdy frame, you can now consider investing in locks that will make that door reasonably secure.

The first locks were invented about four thousand years ago. Since the first locks were made, new forms of locks have been created numbering into the hundreds. The locks that protect homes and apartments come in three categories: key-in-knob, mortise and rim.

Key-in-knob locks are very popular with builders because they require less effort to install in doors than the older mortise locks, yet make a very neat appearance. To install a key-in-knob lock in a door the carpenter or locksmith need only cut two round holes through the door using a template to accurately position them. What's more, these holes can be made in the field, while it is usually much more time-consuming to mortise a door in the field.

Because the lock cylinder is in the knob, it is vulnerable to attack. The cheaper locks of this variety can actually be hacked off with a sledgehammer or heavy stone, although few burglars would use such a noisy means of entry. Even the sturdiest of key-in-knob locks can be twisted off with an inexpensive pipe wrench, available in most hardware stores. that grips the knob in a short length of bicycle chain. Once the knob has been broken or twisted off, the burglar can draw the dead-locking latch back through the exposed hole in the lock.

Mortise locks, which fit into a square or rectangular cavity mortised in the outer edge of the door, suffer from another form of vulnerability. When used in wooden doors, they tend to weaken the door. The lock is usually covered by only a thin outer wooden lamination. I've seen wooden doors equipped with mortise locks that were shattered around the lock by some heavy blows or kicks.

Mortise and key-in-knob locks are primary locks. This means that every entrance door should be equipped with one or the other. Such primary locks have latches that lock the door automatically when the door swings into the frame. In addition to the latch, primary locks should also be equipped with some form of deadbolt that can't be loided. Key-in-knob locks don't have deadbolts, but an equivalent feature known as a dead-locking latch.

Unfortunately, many front doors in older apartment build-ings (and in older hotels as well) are equipped with primary locks *without* a deadbolt feature. (I suggest that you get up right now and check the lock in your front door for a dead-bolt.) If the lock does not have a deadbolt, it should be replaced as quickly as possible with a primary lock equipped with a deadbolt. Most of the primary locks without deadbolts are mortise locks. The replacement lock set should have a long deadbolt. An extension of three-quarters of an inch is recommended, but a one-inch deadbolt is even better. Don't settle for a deadbolt that extends only one-half inch out from the lock. If the gap between the door and frame is one-quarter of an inch, this would mean that you are depending on only one-quarter of an inch of metal to secure your door against jimmying or forcing.*

Rim Locks

Rim locks are "auxiliary" locks, which means their function is to supplement the primary lock with its latching action. A rim lock is the kind that fits on the inside surface of the door (of course, a hole—usually one and one-quarter inches in diameter—has to be cut through the door to accommodate the cylinder into which one inserts the key). There are two kinds of deadbolt constructions in the most popular of rim locks: one in which the deadbolt moves horizontally; and a second in which the deadbolt action is vertical, securely gripping the portion of the lock mounted on the frame. This drop-bolt type is familiar to many as the Segal lock. I recommend it because it prevents the frame from being spread. However, some of the first type come with long, heavy deadbolts that offer excellent security.

Even if your front door is equipped with a primary lock with a deadbolt that extends at least three-quarters of an inch into the strike, the lock should be supplemented with a

* In New York, the City Council passed a law, effective after March 31, 1971, requiring that all apartment entrance doors in new and "altered" multiple dwellings be equipped with "heavy-duty" primary locks with a "heavy-duty" deadbolt. This has been interpreted to mean a deadbolt that extends at least three-quarters of an inch into the strike.

rim lock. This lock will increase the security of your door in two special ways. First, this "private" lock means that you have strong assurance that no one can enter your apartment with a duplicate or master key. (I will amplify this aspect of master keying later in this chapter in the section on care of keys.) Secondly, a rim lock is a strong deterrent to a burglar.

I had a firsthand opportunity to confirm the deterrent effect of an auxiliary lock. While I was visiting a locksmith's shop to examine some new locks, the locksmith received a phone call from a very agitated young man who could not enter his apartment because a would-be burglar had so damaged his door that he couldn't operate the lock. The locksmith invited me to join him on the call. The man lived in an apartment building in Manhattan's Greenwich Village. Of the five apartments on the landing, his was the only one not equipped with a rim lock. The criminal was experienced enough not to bother with any of the doors with rim locks. However, he was not skillful enough—or didn't have enough time—to defeat the mortise lock. Nevertheless, he did so much damage with a crowbar that the locksmith was unable to force the deadbolt back; he had to cut it off with a short hacksaw. The door, strike and frame were all badly damaged. (While awaiting repairs on the door and frame, the occupant of the apartment was able to protect himself with a new rim lock.)

Special Auxiliary Locks

A snugly fitting hollow metal door bolstered with a rim lock provides excellent security. Unfortunately, many residents for one reason or another require even more security. Perhaps their landlords are unwilling to spend $100 to $200 to provide good doors—and the apartment dweller doesn't want to invest in a door that he must leave behind. Or the settling of the building would make replacement of the door and frame very expensive. There are some rim locks to meet such situations.

The brace lock * is widely used on wooden—and steel— doors that can be forced inward easily. It has a brace that fits from the lock into a hole in the floor. When the key is turned from the outside, the brace slips out of its grip in the portion of the lock mounted on the inner surface of the door. The Magic Eye Company makes a version of the brace lock in which the brace moves only enough to permit the door to open partially. At this point, the occupant has to reach in further to unlock the lock to permit the brace to move away enough to enter the apartment. This extra unlocking feature means that someone who drills a small hole in the door large enough to poke a wire or coat hanger through won't be able to pull the brace out of place. On the other hand, there is a risk in any locking arrangements that force the occupant to spend an inordinate amount of time unlocking his door, a consideration that I amplify later in this chapter. Brace locks cost from $30 to $40 to install.

One more point in relation to brace locks: keep the hole in the floor free of dirt and anything that prevents the brace from fitting snugly.

The crossbar or double-bolt is another lock that offers extra protection. The lock, which is mounted in the center of the door, controls two locking bars that fit horizontally across the door, sliding into heavy pockets mounted on the frame. Costing about $60 to $90 installed, this lock is for commercial establishments in buildings that are deserted at night or over weekends. It is very rarely installed in homes and apartments. However, if you are in a neighborhood

---

* Also known as the "police lock" after the name of the leading manufacturer, the Fox Police Lock Company, New York, N.Y.

where no one is likely to observe a burglar at work, particularly on a back door, you might consider locking bars.

Another form of special lock popular with apartment dwellers in New York is the chain lock. This is a $6 lock mounted on the inner surface of the door that permits the door to open three or four inches to the length of the chain. Some apartment dwellers use them as a supplement to peepholes. Louis Tohn, head of Buy-Rite Locksmiths, one of Manhattan's busiest, refers to these locks as "junk." He claims that a burglar can snap the chain by throwing his weight against the door. (Some locksmiths claim that the chain lock gives burglars the impression that someone is home, a dubious advantage.)

There's an additional objection to chains on doors. It is now standard operating procedure for burglars to first chain any entrance doors equipped with chain locks. Then if the occupant arrives while the burglar is at work, he or she won't be able to enter the apartment. And the noise of the chain snapping taut will warn the burglar to leave. Of course, you don't want to enter the apartment while the burglar is present. Few burglars are violent, but in a panic some might hurt you in their rush to get away. However, if you are chained out of your apartment, you have the problem of getting back in.

That's just what happened to a neighbor of mine whose apartment was entered through the fire-escape window by an obviously slight burglar who bent outward the members of an inadequate accordion gate. She called the police, one of whom proceeded to kick down and heavily damage the front door despite the poor woman's pleas. The proper way to enter the apartment would have been to use bolt cutters or a hacksaw to cut the chain, which was too short to permit anyone to reach in and unlatch it. However, street patrolmen are not equipped with such tools. For this reason, I removed the chain lock that was attached to my front door when I moved in. (That burglars who enter via fire escapes first check the front door is an argument in favor of double-cylinder lock sets.)

Pick-Resistant Cylinders

The portion of the lock that is getting inordinate attention these days is the cylinder. This is the part into which the key fits. It contains pins, tumblers or wafers that are shifted by the key. If you insert the right key, the pins line up, permitting the entire cylinder to turn, which action draws the bolt back.

Skillful locksmiths (and the rare burglar skilled as a "pickman") use special tools called picks to move the pins into place, enabling them to open the lock without a key. Some cylinders, particularly the less expensive ones, are relatively easy to pick. As a result, various pick-resistant * lock cylinders have been developed. Tohn says that "they are the greatest thing that ever happened to New York's locksmiths." Customer demand for installation of these cylinders is high despite the fact that few burglaries are based on picking. (Of course, if you live in one of the luxury high-rises that attract burglars, a pick-resistant cylinder is needed.)

Many cylinders are designated pick-resistant, including those made by Ace, Duo, Eagle, Gem and Sargent. Perhaps the most resistant to picking of all the new cylinders is the Medeco. Although the key to the Medeco lock appears quite conventional, it is different in a very significant way. The pins turn or twist as the key is inserted. As a result, it is very difficult to pick. At first, the manufacturers of the Medeco

---

* Some cylinders are also referred to as "pickproof." However, governmental agencies frown on this designation and the Underwriters' Laboratories does not accept it.

cylinder actually offered a large cash reward to anyone who could pick their device. Many master locksmiths failed. Edwin Toepfer claims that he picked a Medeco, but that it took him an inordinate length of time, in itself a significant deterrent. In addition, the Medeco that Toepfer picked was so damaged that it could not be used again. (So that it could stand as evidence of illegal entry if picked.)

The first man to pick a Medeco cylinder was former Detective-Sergeant Robert McDermott of the New York police (Now a vice-president of Holmes Protection, Inc.). McDermott told me that it took him seventy minutes to pick the lock, after much previous study developing his technique. He won a prize of $1,000 for the feat. In McDermott's opinion, the Medeco is the most pick-resistant of all cylinders.

I have received some reports from locksmiths of Medeco keys breaking off in the cylinders. The Medeco key fits its cylinder very snugly. It must be withdrawn straight. I suspect that some people, accustomed to loosely fitting keys, were careless in withdrawing their keys from the Medeco cylinder, and broke them.

Despite my lack of concern that a burglar skilled in picking would attack my own door lock, I had a Medeco cylinder installed in a Segal lock (Toepfer says that Segal makes a "poor" standard cylinder for an otherwise excellent lock set). My reason was simple: I wanted a key that could be duplicated only with great effort if I gave it to a painter, workman or repairman. The keys to Medeco lock cylinders can only be duplicated easily by a locksmith who knows the code to that key. Even if he has a key to work with, he can't duplicate it quickly. And very few locksmiths have invested the $1,750 required to buy the special machine that decodes and cuts Medeco keys. On the other hand, most of the keys in use today can be duplicated on machines that cost from $60 to $400.

This means that if you issue a Medeco lock to an employee and the employee returns the key at the end of his employment, that person, if disgruntled, is not likely to be able to enter the premises when you are away. Of course, you have to check immediately on return of the key to make sure that it is the one that fits the designated lock and not a substitute. Nevertheless, the cylinder should be changed.

I don't doubt that some burglars have bought key-cutting machines. However, there is no great need to buy these machines: so many locksmiths' trucks have been broken into that I am sure some of the portable versions of these key cutters are in the hands of professional burglars, along with all the other useful tools that locksmiths carry.

Another cylinder recommended as highly pick-resistant is the Sargent Keso, also known as the Maximum Security. It offers one important security advantage: the keys can only be duplicated easily at the factory on a special key cutter. However, while some experts praise the Keso, many locksmiths claim it is easily picked by a variety of methods. Since this cylinder is not available to the public (it is sold directly for installation in commercial buildings and for new apartment-house construction), the controversy over its merits is an academic question as far as the public is concerned.

Cylinders with tubular keys are recommended by more and more locksmiths. This is the type of cylinder that one sees in pay-phone boxes and vending machines. It is more pick-resistant than the garden variety of cylinders that take flat keys, but that is not its chief recommendation. According to Myril Zion, one of New York's leading locksmiths, many burglars gain entry in the following manner. They drive a heavy screwdriver into the keyway of a cylinder that takes a flat key, then twist the screwdriver with a Vise-Grip, an unconventional wrench sold in most hardware stores for $3 to $5, depending on size. In this manner, they can unlock many doors, of course destroying the cylinder in the process. Sometimes, when they pull the screwdriver out, the cylinder comes out too. As a result, many victims of this manner of break-in believe that the cylinder was removed to permit manipulation of the deadbolt. However, the removal of the cylinder is merely a by-product of the break-in. Cylinders with tubular keyways can't be attacked in this manner.

The Proof Lock

Are you much concerned about theft because you frequently leave duplicates of front-door keys with building employees, painters, acquaintances, employees or others in whom you don't have complete trust? The Medeco cylinder, despite the difficulty of duplication associated with it, may not offer enough security. Under these circumstances, you might consider the Proof Lock. The invention of a very clever young Chinese-American named Sam Hsu, the "pick-resistant" Proof Lock has the unique ability to "trap" duplicate keys at the option of the resident. In other words, under one setting of the cylinder, duplicate keys open the lock. When the setting is changed from the outside by means of a control key, only the master key opens the lock: all the other keys not only fail to open the lock but are trapped—until released by the control key. When originally introduced a few years ago, the Proof Lock was far too expensive for general distribution. I have been told that arrangements are being made to manufacture this unusual cylinder in the Orient for sale in the U.S. shortly at a more reasonable price, about $30. It will also be offered as part of a drop-bolt lock set of the Segal variety.

I have received private information that there will soon be available another lock cylinder that can be set to reject certain keys. Although this cylinder will not trap the keys, it will be reasonable in cost.

Protective Plates

To protect lock cylinders from direct attack, it makes sense to reinforce the door with steel plates. If the cylinder face is flush with the door, a flat plate will do. I bought a brass-plated Fox protective plate with four carriage bolts (the ones with no slot for screwdrivers) for $2.50 and installed it myself in about half an hour. (Because some of the old paint flaked off the inside of the door where the bolts came through, I had to touch up around the bolts and also cover the few scratches I made with the hacksaw that I used to cut the overlength bolts to size.)

For lock cylinders that project from the surface of the door, a protective plate with a sort of bubble in the middle is required. All of these plates have holes in the middle that are large enough to permit the key to enter, but smaller than the diameter of the cylinder.

Because installation of these plates is a bit tricky, it makes sense to have them put in by a locksmith at the time you have other work done. A locksmith will charge from $10 to $25 to install a plate, depending on how far he has to travel.

Front Doors for Apartment Buildings

The main doors leading into apartment buildings are a special problem. Usually they are not deadbolted; the locking action is based on a spring-operated latch. This calls for a sturdy door closer that quickly forces the door shut. But a proper door closer may make the door difficult to open for children and the elderly.

Many of these doors are fully or partially glass-paneled. Of course, this means that the determined intruder can break or cut a pane to enter. Often the intruder does not have to break the glass—the job has already been done for him by vandals or accidentally. To prevent entry, the glass portion of a door should be backed by some form of vandal-resistant metal guard through which a hand cannot fit. A series of rather lightweight door grills in various sizes is available from Ideal Security, 215 East Ninth Street, St. Paul, Minn. 55101. For greater protection, I recommend a grill made of expanded metal, which is heavy-gauge sheet steel stamped out in a fashion that resembles a chain-link fence. Ironmongers stock this sturdy material in large sheets and they can cut out a section to fit any door. The material has to be framed for mounting.

Even if the door itself is secure, intruders can still enter the building by loiding the spring latch. (The term "loiding" is derived from the first plastic, celluloid.) I find that I can use a credit card to loid my way into the lobbies of half the apartment buildings I visit. To prevent such entries the doors should be equipped with jimmy-guards.

Unfortunately, some lobby doors can't be equipped with jimmy-guards. These are the glass-paneled doors with very narrow stiles, the metal portion that frames the glass. If it becomes apparent that many intruders are entering the building by loiding, the only solution is to replace the door with one with a wider stile that permits mounting of a jimmy-guard.

Double-Cylinder Locks

The rim lock on the front door of my apartment has a second cylinder. This double-cylinder arrangement means that the key is needed to get out of the apartment. I had this special lock installed because my apartment is vulnerable to entry through the kitchen window, which faces the fire escape. Any burglar who breaks into my apartment through the kitchen window while I am away would not be able to exit through the front door. He would have to retreat through the kitchen window, which would most likely prevent him from taking any of my bulky valuables, such as my TV set or electric typewriter. He might try attacking the rim lock itself. But I had it installed with nonretractable screws.

However, there is a great danger associated with double-cylinder locking arrangements: in the event of a fire, a family can be trapped inside if they can't find the key. For this reason, I always insert the key in the inside cylinder whenever I enter my apartment. This procedure also makes it unlikely that I will leave the apartment without taking my keys with me. If you have any children at home too short to reach your rim lock, I urge against double-cylinder arrangements.

Securing Sliding Doors

Sliding glass doors, such as those that commonly lead out to a home patio or an apartment terrace, require special treatment. The simplest way to hold a sliding door closed is to cut a piece of 2-by-4 lumber that fits snugly between the inner half of the door and the opposite frame. It is dropped into the channel in which the door slides. The Schlage Lock Company makes a special device for sliding doors known as the Charley-Bar. It costs only $5.36. Usually mounted about halfway up on the outer door, it swings down into position into a bracket installed on the inside edge of the inner door. Unlike the piece of 2-by-4 mentioned above, it is quite visible to any potential intruder. Schlage also makes a simpler sliding-door lock called the Mitey-Lok that costs $2.35. Similar locks are made by Loxem and Stanley. Of course, if the intruder is determined, he can smash the glass in the door. If your sliding door can be smashed by an intruder without alerting any neighbors (many upper-level apartments in luxury buildings have been entered through sliding or conventional doors by burglars who lower themselves from above onto the terrace), it must be protected by a metal gate, as discussed later in this chapter.

Another way to prevent entry through sliding doors by smashing of the glass is to install high-security glazing (see discussion of this much more costly glazing later in this chapter).

Peepholes

Every entrance door to a home or apartment should be equipped with a peephole for viewing of strangers. Don't depend on a chain to keep them out. A good shove on the door will snap most chains or pop the short screws that hold them in place. Peepholes come in many shapes. I recommend the kind with a lens that calls for drilling of a small hole a half inch in diameter or less through the door. The peepholes that call for the cutting of larger holes weaken the door and provide a good beginning for a burglar to cut a hole large enough to reach in and turn the deadbolt knob and doorknob. It only costs about $5 for installation of a proper peephole.

Care and Handling of Keys

My most important recommendation to secure doors—and yourself—is not to carry too many keys. There are many good reasons why women in particular should not carry a multiplicity of keys. If a woman burdens herself with a key chain loaded with keys, she will naturally carry this weight (as much for vanity's sake) in her purse rather than in a pocket, where they would be far more secure from both accidental loss and snatching. Because of a new form of robbery, carrying many keys lowers your personal security. In New York, some muggers now follow their victims into buildings and hide while they are opening their doors. As soon as their intended victim has his or her door open, the mugger rushes up and shoves the person through the door, slamming the door behind him. The victims are mostly the elderly, but some are young women. My stepfather's very aged father was attacked in this manner. If you can open your door quickly, you are much less vulnerable to this form of attack. (Some muggers get on the elevator with their victim, observe which floor button their victim pushes, get off on the floor below and run up the stairs to wait in hiding.)

Because of the growth of this form of robbery, I recommend the type of security system in which the arming/disarming control (see Chapter V, "Electronic Security Systems") is inside the home or apartment and is equipped with a delay mechanism that permits the occupant to disarm the system before the alarm sounds. This approach has two advantages: less time spent groping for keys at your front door; and in the event of attack, the alarm will sound automatically after a few seconds, most likely driving away the robber.

There's a very simple way to cut down on the number of keys you carry: have a locksmith install cylinders accepting the same key into all your locks—front door, back door, garage door, security closet, liquor cabinet, etc. And if the cylinder is one of the pick-resistant types with hard-to-duplicate keys, you don't have to change the cylinders or the pins in the cylinders every time you lose a domestic. (However, changing of cylinders or pins under that circumstance still makes sense.)

If your front door does require more than one key (the common situation), and you don't install duplicate cylinders in both locks (two good lock sets are sufficient), make it easy to tell one key from another. A simple way is to wrap the head of one key with colored vinyl tape. Or take a file and serrate the edge of the head of one key. If you are forced to carry many keys, for home and office, the Swiss make a clever plastic "differentiator" that fits over the head of the key covering the edge with a bumpy rim. My locksmith carries these handy rubbery items in a variety of colors for only twenty cents apiece. Of course, one should never add a tag bearing one's address, license plate or phone number to one's key chain. Yet some naive persons do this, trusting that an honest person will return the keys in case of loss. (The person who returns lost keys may not be a Good Samaritan; he may be a thief who retains a duplicate set for future use.)

I have some other recommendations with regard to keys. For apartment dwellers, unless you have complete trust in your super or building manager—and the members of his family—don't leave copies of your front-door keys with him. Your lease or local laws usually require that the landlord or his agent be granted "access" to your apartment. One good reason for this law is that it facilitates entrance by firemen in case there is a fire in your apartment. In practice, firemen rarely wait for the super to show up with the key. If smoke is coming out of an apartment, they will knock down the door or smash through the fire-escape window. If one of their ladders is tall enough to reach an apartment from which smoke is pouring, they use the ladder itself to smash through the window.

Because leaving your keys with the super will rarely protect your door from firemen, I do not recommend that you turn over copies of your keys to him. What I suggest is that you leave copies with trusted neighbors or relatives or friends who live nearby, write their names and phone numbers on a sheet of paper and give this document to your super.

Another way to make your key available to the super yet assure you greater security is to seal the key inside an envelope and then dribble ordinary wax from a candle on the seal, writing your name in the wax before it hardens. This procedure, recommended by Myril Zion, one of the very rare fe-

male master locksmiths,* would make it very difficult for the
super to enter your apartment without your knowledge. Before giving your key to the super in this form, ask him where
he keeps all duplicate keys. Some supers make no effort to
keep such keys secure. (If a burglar breaks into the super's
apartment, he would be tempted to steal the keys and then
use them quickly.)

Master Keying

There is a concept called master keying of which you
should be aware. A master key is one that opens a number
of locks that take different keys. There are various levels of
master keying. In a commercial building, one level of master
key could open all doors on one floor. The next higher level of
master key opens all doors in the building. Master keying is
most commonly applied in hotels and in commercial construction. If your apartment lock can be opened by a master key, I
recommend that you change the cylinder—then give a duplicate key to a neighbor and tell the building manager who
has that key.

Pushbutton Locks

There is one way to avoid carrying any or fewer keys: install
pushbutton locks on your front door. Pushbutton locks come
in two varieties: mechanical and electronic. Some mechanical
pushbutton locks cost as little as $20, while the electronic
versions cost up into the hundreds. Pushbutton locks are generally used in situations where high security is required,
sometimes in homes, rarely in apartments. Some are activated
by a combination of insertion of a plastic identity card and
a unique code associated only with that card. There is also
a variety of special lock that is only actuated by a plastic ID
card without any pushing of buttons.

* A master locksmith is a locksmith with at least twenty years of experience.

The least costly pushbutton lock made is the Preso-matic, which costs only $20 (plus $1 for shipping and an extra $1.50 for a second set of "combs" to change combination). Although installation of this well-recommended lock is advertised as taking only "minutes," one locksmith who has installed many estimates that while it takes a professional about twenty minutes, the average home handyman would need three hours. The distributor claims it would take only ninety minutes for a home handyman. To install a Preso-matic, you would require a brace with a one-inch bit or a hand drill with a one-inch hole saw.

Because of the many combinations possible, these special locks have the reputation of being unpickable. Not so. There are two ways in which a burglar can defeat them. First, he can observe—sometimes from a surprisingly great distance, especially if equipped with binoculars—the sequence of buttons pushed. Even if he doesn't recognize all the buttons, he may learn enough to open the lock after a few attempts. Secondly, the burglar may wipe the buttons clean, then wait for the occupant to open the lock. When the burglar returns, he can tell by the fingerprints just which four or five of the ten or so buttons were pushed. He doesn't know the sequence, but he can generally figure this out in a few tries. To defeat this kind of lock-picking, some expensive pushbutton locks offer a clever feature: a delay following each unsuccessful attempt, plus an automatic alarm if more than a set number of failures to open occurs. Trouble is, what if a code-bearer fails to work the lock because he is rushed or slightly inebriated?

Padlocks and Hasps

Most of us have occasion to use padlocks. The variety of models of padlocks equals and perhaps surpasses conventional locks in number. Padlocks should be chosen with as much care as other locks, especially since overspending on padlocks can actually lower security. How so? Simply because a massive padlock locked onto a flimsy hasp can be used by a burglar with a crowbar to twist off the hasp in seconds. A smaller padlock won't provide a large enough gap into which a crowbar or heavy screwdriver can be inserted.

My message is clear: don't waste money on a good padlock if the hasp is not of comparable strength. And don't waste a good hasp on a flimsy door, especially one with exposed hinges. Good hasps are expensive, as much as $10 a set. But they are more than worth it.

For good security, a padlock should have a heat-treated shackle, which makes it resistant to bolt cutters and steel hacksaws. A good high-security padlock is made by Master Lock Company. If you think you need pick resistance in a padlock, buy one that accepts a Medeco or other pick-resistant cylinder. Sal Schillizzi, chairman of the New York Association of Locksmiths, recommends the Abloy padlock of Finnish manufacture. A particularly massive device, it requires an unusual key that most likely can't be duplicated.

To avoid losing the key to a good padlock, buy the key-retaining kind that holds the key in the open position. These locks offer an unusual security feature for commercial use. When not in use they can be hung open on a nail near the door or opening they secure. At the close of the work day, an executive, trusted employee or guard can lock the door and retain the key, secure in the knowledge that some dishonest employee has not duplicated the key during the day or substituted his own matching padlock (to return later that night, pilfer whatever is protected by the padlock, then reclose the door and relock it with the original padlock).

Shrouded padlocks are a growing trend in padlock manufacture. These are high-security locks, costing from $20 to $25 apiece, with a cavity in the top of the lock into which the shackle retracts on locking. Edwin Toepfer indicates a certain insecurity in padlocks of this design. Although the shackle is not exposed to cutting by a tungsten carbide-coated hacksaw or even an acetylene torch, the padlock does not swing freely, a highly useful characteristic of unshrouded padlocks. This means that they provide a convenient leverage point at which a burglar can direct a sledgehammer to rip off the hasp.

Toepfer is the designer of and now the sole source for an unusual padlock. It incorporates a counter that tells how many times the lock has been opened and closed. Toepfer sells these locks at $40 apiece to race tracks who use them to make sure that no one has visited the stables or kennels during the night. However, they could be used to detect pilferage—say of a liquor closet at night—where it is necessary for a domestic to retain the key. Toepfer's address is Edwin Toepfer Company, Milwaukee, Wis. 53204.

Protecting Windows

I classify windows into two types: accessible and reachable. Accessible windows are those at ground-floor and porch levels or those facing fire escapes, windows that a burglar can attack easily with tools or use force against. Reachable windows are those that a nimble burglar can reach with difficulty, but which he would not be in a position to attack with ease or with both hands.

There are more reachable windows than you imagine. In New York, aggressive burglars have actually scaled the creviced front walls of brownstone buildings in daylight to enter open windows at the second level. (They grab some valuables and leave the building so quickly that even if they

are observed and the police are called, they are not caught.)
Many apartments have rear windows facing other buildings
only four or six or eight feet away. Burglars will stretch
ladders or planks across the gap and walk across. Or they
will inch along a ledge Harold Lloyd fashion and enter an
open window from an adjacent window opening out from
the corridor of the building. Some amateurish burglars attempted to enter the apartment of some relatives of mine
in this way, but woke the occupants, who screamed. The
burglars retreated quickly without losing their footing. Some
burglars enter top-story apartments by lowering themselves
from the roof on a rope and opening an unsecured window.

It takes little to make a reachable window secure. Most
of the reachable windows will be in older buildings with
double-hung wooden windows, the familiar kind that go
up and down. These windows are commonly equipped with
the pivoting lock that can only secure the window in the completely closed position. This is not satisfactory. So many of
these wooden windows are warped or fit into their frames
so loosely that the two halves of the locking mechanism either
don't mate or can be forced quite easily from the outside with
a knife blade.

A popular substitute for the pivot lock is the forty-cent
wedge lock, which is mounted on the top of the lower half of
the window so that the rubber tip is forced against the
wooden frame of the upper half of the window by a threaded
bolt. This lock is unsatisfactory on no less than four counts.
First, the rubber tip mars the paint on the window frame.
After a time, the rubber tip falls off or wears thin, and bare
metal is turned into the window, gouging it in a most unattractive manner. Secondly, the locking action tends to warp or
loosen the window even more. Thirdly, when the window is
locked in the fully closed position, the threaded bolt is ex-

posed to attack from the outside by a small, pistol-type hack-saw, which can cut the bolt in less than thirty seconds. (Wedge locks are actually more secure when the window is locked in the partially open position, which makes the bolt harder to reach even with a longer hacksaw blade.) Finally, the wedge lock, by spreading the two halves of the window, lets in a lot of cold air in winter, which would raise your heating bills.

A better way to secure reachable windows is with a carriage bolt or tenpenny nail that fits through a hole in the lower frame and into a cavity drilled in the upper frame. The window can be secured in a partially open position by drilling a second cavity higher up in the frame of the upper window. A carriage bolt is not as exposed to attack by a hacksaw, and because it is much thicker than the bolt on a wedge lock, it will take longer to cut through. For added security, simply install two carriage bolts in each window, one on each side.

In general, burglars will not break windows to enter homes and apartments. They fear that the noise will attract attention, and they fear cutting themselves on the glass left in the frame. Of course, once they shatter a pane in the window, they can reach in and unscrew a wedge lock or pull out a carriage bolt securing the window. There is an improved wedge lock, costing about seventy cents, that offers more deterrence against the thief who breaks one pane of glass to reach in. Although it only takes one hand to lock this type, it takes two hands to unlock it: a second hand is required to hold down a little locking button.

For protection against thieves who are not afraid to break the window to enter your home, various window locks are available. They are mounted on the top of the lower window and lock into holes drilled in the upper window, providing ventilation in the locked position. They cost from $3 to $5 apiece. If you install them on windows through which you might have to exit in case of fire, hang the keys on a cup hook in plain view, but out of reach of any burglar who breaks a pane in the window. To make double sure that your family can exit from that window in case of fire, install a second cup hook and hang a duplicate key on it—in the event someone drops the first key in a panic.

Thus far I've assumed that burglars who enter through windows will be forced to break them if they are properly secured. Not so. It does not take much skill to use a glass cutter plus a short length of adhesive tape to silently remove a small segment of glass from a windowpane. Glass cutters cost about $1. Locking windows into place will greatly impede the burglar equipped with a glass cutter, and two carriage bolts are more effective than one—because this forces the burglar to cut two holes.

Protecting Accessible Windows

It takes much more to protect accessible windows. Street-level windows in most older apartment houses and brown-stones are protected by iron bars or grills. However, they must be tested for strength. They should be able to withstand the attack of a strong man using a crowbar. If they break loose (they are not likely to bend) due to rusting or deteriorated masonry, obviously they have to be replaced. Unfortunately, there are few ironmongers left. New Orleans is one of the few cities with many active ironmongers. A leading fabricator of custom grillwork is Reeves Ironworks, 3900 Gentilly Road, New Orleans, La. 70129.

The alternative is to install the accordion gates and other bars developed for fire-escape windows, which usually are not equipped with protective gates by landlords. Unlike permanent bars and grillwork, which are always installed outside the window, gates should be installed on the inside. This means that they must be retractable or removable without too much difficulty—if you ever want to wash those windows or exit through them in an emergency.

For windows through which no access in case of fire is required, the accordion or scissor gate is satisfactory. To make an accordion gate more secure, it should fit into steel channels mounted at the top and bottom of the frame. Otherwise, the gate can be bent back, providing access for a man to enter. Burglars use a length of pipe to bend the members of the gate outwards. A strong man can do this with his hands.

Extra bracing may be required to strengthen the gate. J. Kaufman Ironworks in the Bronx, New York, makes a model of the accordion gate called the Invincible that has both extra bracing and upper and lower channels. Depending on the size of the window, locksmiths will charge from $60 to $80 for an Invincible gate, which includes installation.

An even more substantial gate than the Invincible model is made by Frank Klein & Son, Inc., 625 West Fiftieth Street, New York, N.Y. 10019. (212–247–7585). The Sentry model gate slides back and forth in heavy steel channels extending across the entire top and bottom of the window frame (it does not swing out at all). However, it is more expensive. For example, a Sentry gate that fits a seventy-two-inch-by-thirty-six-inch frame costs about $100 installed. Models are also available for patio or terrace doors ten feet high and higher. Depending on width, such gates can cost several hundred dollars. To make them more inconspicuous, they can be ordered in colors to match the background colors, but decorator colors cost at least $25 extra. The Kaufman and Klein organizations are prepared to ship gates to all parts of the country, if you can't find a local source. However, if you do order gates by mail, take great pains in measuring the dimensions of the opening to be protected.*

If you install an accordion gate yourself, or order one installed, make sure that the frame of the window is sturdy enough to hold the gate in place against attack. Installing a gate in a deteriorated frame is a waste of money. A friend of mine called me over to see what a burglar had done to her accordion gate while breaking in. The gate was mounted in a fire-escape window with a rotted frame. The burglar had obviously braced himself against part of the fire escape and pressed against the gate with both feet (the window had been left open). He shattered the frame, forcing the gate back far enough to enter.

If the frame is weak, the bolts securing the gate must extend right through the frame into the masonry behind it. This calls for a masonry drill, lead plugs and screws at least three inches long. I installed an accordion gate in this manner. It took me three hours.

For accessible windows through which access in case of fire is required, I can only recommend the Protect-A-Guard gate made by J. Kaufman Ironworks. This gate, which, unlike all other accordion gates, does not require padlocks to secure it, was invented by two New York City firemen in collaboration with a civilian inventor. These firemen had been shocked by the deaths by fire of a family trapped when they could not find the key to an accordion gate protecting a fire-escape window.

This patented gate is opened by turning a small swivel knob, which is enclosed in a small box-like enclosure with

---

* J. Kaufman Ironworks offers a useful twelve-page catalog that includes instructions on measuring for window guards. To obtain a free copy, write to this firm at 1685 Boone Avenue, the Bronx, N.Y. 10462.

a door. There are so many members to the accordion that even in the extended position covering the window the gaps between members are too small for a hand to reach through to get at the knob. Even if the burglar extends a coat hanger through the gate, it can't turn the swivel knob. The Protect-A-Guard is the only gate approved by the Board of Standards and Appeals of the City of New York for installation on fire-escape windows. If a New York City fire inspector or building inspector finds a gate other than a Protect-A-Guard on a fire-escape window, he will issue a violation against both the landlord and the tenant.

In spite of the law and the danger involved, I find that most New York locksmiths are reluctant to install Protect-A-Guard gates. Some claim that the lighter-weight steel members can be bent easily by burglars. Others cite the higher cost of installing the approved gate. In the event that you follow this bad advice and install a conventional gate over a fire-escape window, be sure to hang duplicate keys to the keyed-alike padlocks in plain view—but out of reach of any burglar behind the gate.

High-Security Glazing

Although the risk of burglary through fire-escape windows is high, I find that many apartment dwellers are reluctant to install gates over fire-escape windows because of their unsightliness. There is an attractive alternative. At least three manufacturers of plate glass make a laminated glass that resists breakthrough—but not shattering. Primarily used in windows of jewelry shops and for display cases containing valuable merchandise, this laminated glass consists of three layers. The outer layers are ordinary glass, but the inner layer is clear, strong vinyl, bonded to the glass in its liquid state.

Protecting Doors and Windows

A representative of the Amerada Glass Company recently offered me the opportunity to try and break through a large pane of their Secur-lite glazing. I used a baseball bat and struck the pane with all my might (I'm six feet four inches tall, weigh 190 pounds and play tennis all year round). On the first blow, the outer pane cracked. On the second blow, the inner pane cracked. After five or six blows, I had exposed a small portion of the vinyl about the size of a dime. The Amerada representative told me that I could then have used a sharp knife to make a small hole in the plastic sheet. However, cutting a hole even large enough for a hand to reach through would take at least thirty minutes because the particles of glass clinging to the plastic would stop the knife from moving more than a fraction of an inch between blows of a bat or hammer.

Because so much noise is made in any attempt to break through high-security glass, it is often a better deterrent than an accordion gate. It also costs more. High-security glass costs three to five times as much as ordinary glass. It is also thicker than ordinary glass. This means that you most likely can't install it in your present window frame. So a new frame is required. That's what really adds to the cost of installation.

There is still another alternative. High-strength plastic glazing is now widely used in schools and other buildings and on railroad cars to replace panes of glass broken by vandals. The plastic is polycarbonate, brought out by General Electric under the name Lexan, but now available from some other suppliers as well. I have a mallet made with a Lexan head that I have used to drive nails for over ten years. The plastic has marred, but not broken. Now GE has come out with a mar-resistant Lexan glazing that won't scratch when cleaned with a nylon-bristle brush.

Mar-resistant Lexan at about $4 per square foot in one-quarter-inch thickness is only thirty-five cents more per square foot than ordinary Lexan glazing that scratches easily. For a double-hung window with two panes 32 inches square, 14.25 square feet of glazing is required. You can buy this over-the-counter from a distributor for about $57, plus tax. If you are at all handy, you should be able to putty in the panes yourself in about an hour. Or you could hire a glazier to do it in twenty minutes for a charge of about $10. (Don't go directly to a glazier for materials and installation: he'll charge much more for the materials since he would have to send a man to buy them.) For a total charge of $67, the cost is comparable to that of a Protect-A-Guard gate, assuming professional installation in both instances. The protection is about comparable too. The plastic panes can be popped out of their frames by heavy blows, but this would make a lot of noise.

Casement Windows

Casement windows represent much less of a security problem than sash or double-hung windows. The lever-type locking mechanisms on casement windows can't be opened from the outside unless a pane is cut or smashed. Even when open, casement windows are often too small for many men to crawl through. Nevertheless, accessible casement windows should be made secure. A locking device for casement windows is available from Ideal Security. Called the Casement Window Key Lock (catalog No. SK–260), it is a key-lockable replacement for the standard lever lock. If the holes on the Casement Window Key Lock match those on the present lever locks, then installation is a matter of minutes. Otherwise, new holes must be drilled, which should only add fifteen minutes or so to installation per lock. List price in the Ideal Security catalog is $3.98, but my local locksmith charges $4.20 for this item.

Installing Locks

Other than the simple window locks discussed here, I recommend that all locks be installed by a professional. Locks are not simple mechanisms. If installed improperly, they may jam, which can cause much aggravation plus a bill from a locksmith for emergency service. (Fortunately, one of the most secure of lock sets, the Segal lock, is the easiest for an amateur to install.)

Unfortunately, reliance on locksmiths raises another risk. Only in New York City and a few other areas are locksmiths and "key duplicators" licensed. This means that in most parts of the country a convicted burglar can open a shop, hang out a sign proclaiming himself a "locksmith" and gain the confidence of those seeking security.

What's the risk? An unscrupulous locksmith called in to install a lock set in a home or apartment furnished with expensive objets d'art simply makes an extra key which he retains. He rarely burglarizes the residence himself; he merely sells the key to a professional burglar.

One locksmith told me that most of the break-ins in which there is no obvious evidence of forcible entry are not the work of expert "pickmen." They are mostly inside jobs in which a building employee or domestic turns a key over to a confederate or, and rarely so, the work of criminals who bought duplicate keys from unethical locksmiths. Yet the victims call these thieveries "burglaries" to collect under the provisions of their burglary insurance policies (a tenant's or home owner's policy protects against thefts as well as burglaries). I suspect that much of the current concern over picking of locks has been generated by many false reports of lock-pickings.

Few locksmiths are unethical. If your locksmith is long established and a member of the self-regulating Associated

Locksmiths of America or the National Locksmiths Association, which bonds its members, there is little risk in dealing with him. However, if you are unable to retain a locksmith you trust, or the risk is inordinate because many valuables are to be protected, there's a fairly simple way to avoid the risk of a locksmith keeping a duplicate of your key. Without revealing your name and address, purchase some high-quality lock cylinders that fit your locks from one professional and then hire another locksmith to install them. If the second locksmith doesn't get a chance to read the code for the keys (for example, the code for a Medeco cylinder is scribed on a separate tag), he won't be able to duplicate it at all or without returning to his shop.

If you are ever the victim of a mysterious "burglary" in which there is no evidence of forced entry, you might use this procedure for future protection.

How Locksmiths Charge

I have been deliberately vague about how locksmiths charge. Their charges appear to vary as much as their opinions on which locks and cylinders are most secure. In general, however, the charges are based on time—from the moment the locksmith leaves his shop until he returns. Like coal miners, they believe in "portal to portal" pay, which is a reasonable concept. One way to hold down on charges is to get as much done as possible in a single visit. If your residence requires a visit from a locksmith, survey the rest of your home to find out if other work is needed. Then tell the locksmith about your needs *before* he leaves his shop so that he can bring the required locks and installation tools with him.

Chapter IV

OTHER

CONVENTIONAL

DETERRENTS

Part A · Safe-Deposit Boxes, Safes
and Security Closets

There is only one place in which to safeguard valuable jewelry, stocks and bonds, considerable amounts of cash and irreplaceable papers: a safe-deposit box in a bank vault.

No home or office safe is substitute for a safe-deposit box. No individual other than a multimillionaire can afford to duplicate the protective features of a bank vault against theft. Thick-walled bank vaults are equipped with all sorts of alarms and timing devices to prevent theft. For example, most bank vaults are equipped with microphones that trip alarms on the slightest sound, such as someone attempting to break into the vault.

Of course, there is a certain inconvenience associated with keeping your valuables in a safe-deposit box; they are only available to you during banking hours and never on weekends or many holidays. And you are exposed to some risk when you are taking valuables back and forth to the bank. On the other hand, it would be very difficult for a robber to force you to remove your valuables from a safe-deposit box. Yet time and again armed robbers have forced home owners, under threat of harm or death, to open their home safes.

On balance, there is no question that a safe-deposit box offers more protection than a home safe. Nevertheless, home safes are useful. If you bring some valuable jewelry home, it should be held in the home safe until used, and then re-placed as soon as possible in the home safe until it can be returned to the bank vault. The home safe can also be used to store any cash, traveler's checks or jewelry of lesser value, or stamp or coin collections or documents to which you refer frequently. The home safe can also provide safekeeping for the valuables of any overnight guests in your home. A list of valuables held in your safe-deposit box should be kept in your home safe against the very rare possibility that the bank vault is looted. (In that event, you may turn to the bank for restitution—if you can prove in court that they did not take proper precautions in protecting your safe-deposit box.)

Disciplined use of a home safe will also earn discounts on a jewelry floater.

How to Choose a Home Safe

Because fire is the greatest threat, a home safe should be selected as much for its ability to resist fire as for theft protection. Key-operated document chests that cost as little as $30 carry a Class C Underwriters' Laboratories rating. This means that the contents are protected for at least one hour against a fire that produces a sustained temperature of 1700°F. plus a drop test of thirty feet (in case the floor gives way). The contents of safes with this rating are protected in an unusual way. The insulation when heated actually gives off moisture, enough to prevent the documents from charring, but not enough to soak them. This protective feature, however, only works for one intense fire. If your insulated home safe or document chest has been subjected to intense, prolonged heat, or if burglars in attempting to open the safe have bent the door somewhat (which would permit the expelled moisture to escape in the event of a fire), the depository should be replaced. Of course, in that eventuality, the safe will have more than paid off your investment in it.

Very small shelf safes with moisture-bearing insulation can be purchased for as little as $30. That's for the key-operated model. A three-number combination lock costs $4 more.

Home safes should be bolted or welded to the structure of the building. Or they can be cast in concrete in the cellar or some other place where concrete can be poured. No matter how heavy a home safe, and some costing less than $300 weigh close to six hundred pounds, thieves are resourceful enough to cart them away; they've done this with much heavier safes in offices. Installation costs run from $10 to $12 per hour, depending on locality.

At least one manufacturer of home safes, John D. Brush, Inc., of Rochester, N.Y., provides instructions for do-it-yourself installation of this firm's Sentry line of wall safes. The instructions suggest that the job can be done in "one to two hours." However, I am sure that at least a morning or afternoon is required.

If you purchase a home safe or rent a safe-deposit box for business purposes, the cost is, of course, deductible from gross income as an ordinary business expense. Safes should be depreciated over a ten-year period. If an individual purchases a safe or rents a safe-deposit box, and the safe or box is used to protect tax records, its cost can be deducted from taxable income. If the safe is a low-cost one, its entire cost, including installation, can be deducted in a single year without extended depreciation.

Once you install a safe with a combination lock, you must learn how to operate it properly. Every time you close the safe, you should spin the dial. When you open the safe, don't hold one finger on the dial to aid yourself in turning to the exact number of the combination. Dishonest employees have been known to open office safes by carefully wiping clean the dial of the safe, knowing that the person who opens it will leave three fingerprints on the dial. The fingerprints are not on the numbers of the combination but are displaced by about a quarter turn. To prevent this form of thievery, some dials are equipped with stationary plastic shields.

Try to prevent anyone who does not have the combination to the safe from knowing the location of the safe. Don't let anyone watch you open the safe, even if they are standing too far away to see the numbers on the dial. Some older safes have distinctive emblems in the middle of the dial that help a sharp-eyed person determine approximately which numbers you are dialing. That's why the safes now manufactured have no emblems in the dials. If you own an older safe with an emblem in the dial, paste a round piece of blank paper over the emblem.

Security Closets

A home safe can only be used to protect compact valuables. Yet most homes have other bulkier valuables, such as cameras, sporting equipment, power tools, sterling flatware, and extensive coin collections, that require more protection than a locked closet.

The answer to the problem of protecting bulkier valuables is a security closet. As the name implies, a security closet is a closet with added security: a sturdy door and steel frame, a high-quality lock and a door closer that forces the door shut.

The Schlage Lock Company offers plans for five different versions of security closets to store a variety of valuables. Over the years, over twenty-five thousand such plans have been distributed gratis. Four of the five plans include installation of a two-drawer file cabinet and a wall safe. Aside from these two items, the company estimates that the bill of materials for a security closet runs about $200 and that it would take a skilled carpenter eight to ten hours to install a closet. A home craftsman would take about twice as long. The bill of materials provides for gypsum-board walls and a floor that retards fire for one hour plus a lamp to be mounted inside the closet.

All of these security closets provide for outward-opening doors. This means that the hinges are exposed and must be protected against removal as discussed in Chapter III, "Protecting Doors and Windows."

If you live in a modern "fireproof" apartment building, installation of a security closet is much simpler and less costly. You merely convert one of your present closets. The gypsum-board interior walls and the fire-retardant floor are not required. Assuming that the door to the closet is paneled, all that is required is strengthening, with either a backing of three-quarter-inch-thick plywood or a layer of galvanized sheet steel. The present lock on the door will not be satisfactory, so you must supplement it with either a hasp and padlock or a sturdy rim lock of the Segal type.

To obtain a free copy of the plans, contact the nearest local office of the company, or write to Schlage Lock Company, P.O. Box 3324, San Francisco, Calif. 94119.

Part B · Lighting and Its Control

Because of the enormous increase in daytime burglaries (up 337 percent from 1960 to 1970), which now account for more than half of all residential burglaries, the role of lighting as a deterrent is declining. In addition, automatic devices that turn on lights (and radios) in your absence are no deterrent to professional burglars, who often act on the basis of tips from delivery and other service personnel, or from building employees in the case of apartment dwellers.

Nevertheless, lighting still represents one of the most useful of deterrents. It is effective against casual, not-so-professional burglars, who are far more numerous, and also against those increasingly common demi-criminals, teenage vandals. Lighting acts as a deterrent in two ways: it suggests that a residence is occupied, and it can reveal the presence of intruders, either to those inside the home or to passersby. Lighting is a low-cost deterrent that offers two side benefits: it is so easy to test and to maintain by the home owner himself, unless he is afflicted with acrophobia and is afraid to get up on a ladder to change a light bulb.

If you own your own house, you can add lighting deterrents to your home without limit, as long as you don't violate any municipal regulations. Unlike some of the other deterrents discussed in this book, lighting and its installation rarely detract from the appearance of your home. In fact, brighter lighting, as long as it does not glare, should enhance the appearance, and the value, of your home.

Apartment dwellers are, of course, limited in what they can do as individuals to improve the lighting of the building in which they live. The landlord is responsible for the lighting of the entranceway, lobby, corridors and stairways. However, he is governed by the building regulations of the local-

Other Conventional Deterrents

ity. Because the trend in all local regulations is toward increased lighting, your landlord most likely does not meet lighting requirements, unless the building is of recent construction. As I suggest in Chapter VI, "Apartment House Security," tenants must act as a group to force the landlord to install and maintain good lighting. Rather than wait months for a building inspector to check the level of lighting, and then wait many more months for compliance, I suggest that tenants chip in and substitute higher-wattage light bulbs.

In some crime-ridden cities, it is very difficult to maintain good lighting in apartment buildings because vandals smash the fixtures and the tenants or petty thieves steal the bulbs for their own use or for sale. Vandal-resistant fixtures are needed. Such fixtures with "unbreakable" plastic globes or covers and special hardware to lock them are now widely available. Although the plastic globes and plates are very difficult to break, they will burn and teenagers sometimes burn small holes in them with cigarette lighters.

Consolidated Controls

One of the most useful modifications that a home owner can make in the lighting of his home is to consolidate the controls for all interior and exterior lighting in one place, his bedroom. All of these lights should not be controlled by a single switch: two switches make more sense, one for the interior lighting and one for exterior lighting. In the event of a real or suspected intrusion, few intruders will remain on the premises if they are suddenly bathed in light. Of course, if a loud alarm also sounds off, the intruders will be even more loath to remain. But alarms—especially false alarms, which make up the great majority of all alarms—annoy neighbors, while bright lights shouldn't annoy anyone at night, as long as they don't shine into your neighbors' windows.

The controls for the exterior should illuminate the entire perimeter of your home. If the lights in the backyard don't cover your swimming pool, have an additional light aimed at the pool.

With the development of high-efficiency mercury and metallic vapor lamps that generate so much light (they're used on highways), it should take only four lamps to illuminate the entire perimeter of your home and the entrance for a separate garage. These lamps are also highly resistant to vandalism or accidental breakage. If you don't need such powerful illumination, a good weatherproof lamp that accepts a big incandescent bulb will cost about $25 plus installation.

The cost of central controls will, of course, vary from home to home, but could run into several hundred dollars. As is true for installation of a permanent security system, the cost of the extra lamps plus the installation of the central lighting controls in the home owner's bedroom becomes a "capital improvement" to the home. As I indicate in Chapter IX, "How to Buy Security Products and Services," no sales tax should be charged on such home improvements and the cost of the improvement can be deducted from any capital gains on the value of the home if and when it is sold.

Once a central control for all lighting has been installed, it can then be tied into a security system. Then if an intrusion occurs or a fire starts, all the lights will go on automatically. (Good illumination would help your family to evacuate the home in case of fire.) However, it is important to check to make sure that illumination option on the security system can handle the combined wattage of both interior and exterior lights.

Many of the self-contained anti-intrusion devices discussed in the next chapter include provisions for turning on one lamp, a useful feature.

Other Conventional Deterrents

Automatic Light Controls

All hardware stores now sell one or more of a variety of devices that will turn lights or anything electrical on and off repeatedly in your absence. These devices, which range in price from $8 to about $20, operate in two ways. Most are timing devices for which exact (within fifteen minutes) times of power on and power off can be set. A newer variety are light-actuated. They contain photoelectric cells that sense the *absence* of daylight to turn on interior or exterior lights. One particularly handy version is the Skywatch made by Invento. It screws into the bulb socket of a lamp—outdoor or indoor. Then the bulb is screwed into a socket in the Skywatch. It costs $10.

To protect a home properly when it is unoccupied, more than one timing device may be required. Besides the entrance light, some interior lights should go on. In his *Autobiography*, Malcolm X, writing of his earlier days as a burglar, recommended that the bathroom light be turned on. Many home owners leave a bathroom light on all night when they are home. If a casual burglar sees just a bathroom light on, he may decide to try the next home or apartment.

With the broad application of airconditioning in homes, burglars have learned to listen for the sound of an airconditioner in the bedroom window, or the central airconditioner in a more modern home, to determine if the home or apartment is occupied during warm nights. If they see lights but hear no airconditioner, they may be emboldened to attempt a break-in. This means that the airconditioner should also be controlled during the home owner's absence by a timing device.

Emergency Lighting

Your home should also be equipped with emergency lighting, beginning with flashlights. In the event of a power outage or if power lines are brought down by ice or an errant car, you and your family run the risk of falling down the stairs or over an object because of lack of illumination. The proper protection against a power outage is a battery-operated light that goes on automatically. You've seen these emergency lights in department and other retail stores, where municipal regulations often require their installation. They usually consist of two lighting heads mounted on a large metal box that contains rechargeable batteries plus electronic controls that convert a-c into d-c to charge the batteries. To find out how much they cost in your locality, check with firms listed under "Lighting—Emergency" in the classified phone book. If there are no sources in your town, try contacting Lightalarms Electronic Corp., 288 Scholes Street, Brooklyn, N.Y. This firm, which specializes in emergency lighting, offers two smaller units suitable for installation in a home. One model that will power two 36-watt lighting heads for forty minutes costs $68.40. A second model with greater battery capacity that will keep the lights on for ninety minutes costs $92.30. The batteries are guaranteed for five years. These lights should be mounted so that one head illuminates any staircase and the other the front door.

If your home is subject to an extended power shortage, you could suffer one very unpleasant loss: spoiling of all food in your freezer. To prevent this requires large power generators in standby condition, an investment that is usually unwarranted in private homes.

Part C · Dogs as Deterrents

Dogs are the only form of prehistoric deterrent, besides the threat of physical force, that has survived through millennia.

Other Conventional Deterrents

Because of its sharp hearing and sense of smell, a dog is often a better and more reliable detector of intruders than any electronic device. And a specially trained dog can do what no mechanical or electrical system not equipped with beartraps can: hold an intruder until the police arrive. Dogs also have a built-in noisemaker that will scare most intruders far more than a bell or siren.

Dogs are a unique and unmatchable deterrent. Yet I advise the use of dogs as a last line of defense rather than first. My reason is simple: a dog calls for greater cost in terms of dollars and time and more self-discipline than practically any other form of deterrent. There's another problem associated with dogs: because they are such appealing, loyal animals, one becomes attached to them to the extent that one won't get rid of them when they are too old and feeble to act as deterrents.

Here are some figures on what it costs to maintain a dog as a deterrent. A good watchdog, according to Arthur J. Haggerty, commander of the Army's K-9 Corps during the Korean War, costs from $550 to $850. Food costs from $2 to $15 per week, depending on how finely you want to feed the animal ($2 per week provides an "adequate" diet). Assuming that the dog, which is about eighteen months old when you buy it, has a working life of nine years, here's the cost of the dog over its working career:

$104 / year for food
  10 / year for vet fees
   5 / year for collars and chains
   5 / year for a license

$124 / year or $1,116 for nine years, plus $550 for the dog, or a total of $1,666 (minimal).

An attack dog, one that is trained to corner an intruder, costs much more. Here are some figures for attack dogs:

The food and other annual costs are the same: $1,116. However, Haggerty asks that all of his dogs plus owners return for a "refresher" training course once a quarter. This costs $15 per quarter, or $60 for the year. That's $540 over the useful life of the dog. Since attack dogs cost at least $850 (some go for as high as $5,000), the total minimum cost of an attack dog is $2,506. In addition, the owners have to be trained to handle these animals. At Captain Haggerty's School for Dogs, the owner training course is made up of twelve one-hour periods, taken one or two times a week.

For the total sums worked out above, which represent the *minimal* costs, not the maximum, one can purchase a safe, build a security closet and install an excellent electronic security system instead of the watchdog, and alternatively, a really superb security system for what one might spend on an attack dog. (Even if one buys a watch or attack dog, the safe and security closet are still required because they do what no dog can do—protect valuables against fire.)

Of course, the dog still has to be walked at least once and perhaps twice a day. However, if you don't have the time to walk the dog, you can buy a dog exerciser called a Jogadog. Haggerty claims that dogs willingly "walk" on the continuous moving belt driven by motor for the required five to ten minutes per day. The machine costs $600.

Incidentally, if an attack dog is left alone for any extended period, it can feed itself and quench its thirst with a self-feeder and a special attachment that goes on a faucet. These cost from $15 to $20.

There are other problems associated with dogs. If an attack dog corners an intruder while the owner is away, the police will not be able to call it off. They will have to find the owner and bring him back—or shoot the dog with either a tranquillizer bullet or a real bullet.

All of my figures are based on the dog living at least into its tenth year. If the dog becomes ill and dies when it's only a few years old, you have to start all over again.

In view of the high costs and time demands of trained watch and attack dogs and other problems associated with dogs, I believe that they should not be considered as substitutes for the electronic security systems discussed in Chapter V, but as special deterrents in homes where electronic systems are not adequate. Such homes are those that are quite isolated from neighboring homes, where even the loudest electronic siren would bring no help or where the police are so far away that it would take them many minutes to respond to an alarm signal sent automatically over the phone lines. There are also some crime-ridden cities where the police respond so slowly or reluctantly to calls for help in certain neighborhoods that burglars or other intruders are not afraid to enter premises protected by security systems. A big watchdog might appear to be the only solution in such a neighborhood.

Some dog owners tell me that the reason they bought a big dog was to protect them when walking in the street, and that home protection is secondary. On the surface, this appears to be a good argument in favor of dogs as deterrents; after all, you can't take your electronic security system with you when you're away from home (not yet, that is, although some manufacturers of electronics are working on portable signaling devices). My reply is that the people who need street protection the most—the elderly and women—are the very ones who may not have the strength to handle a big dog.

Recommended Breeds

If you believe that you have a real need for a guard dog and are prepared to devote the time, money and self-discipline required to make the dog a successful deterrent, there is much that you need to know about these animals. First, there is the question of the kind of dog. The experts say that there are many breeds suitable as guard dogs. Even toy dogs make good watchdogs, particularly for older people who can't handle a big dog, because they are quite alert and make a lot of noise. However, certain breeds are considered more suitable than others. Not too surprisingly, the German shepherd heads every expert's list. Other big dogs temperamentally suited to guard duty are female Dobermans, rottweilers, Bouviers, bull terriers and giant schnauzers. Personally, I am turned off by Dobermans, female as well as male. In the rare instances in which a dog turns on its master, the breed involved is so often a Doberman. Haggerty suggests that female dogs are better with children, but that males make better watchdogs.

Dogs trained as attack dogs operate in the following manner. They will bark to chase away anyone who attempts to enter a fenced-off or walled-in area that they are guarding. (There can't be any holes or breaks in the fence, otherwise the dog will get out. Once it gets out, it is not trained to return. It won't attack anyone outside the guarded area, but it might be run over by a car.) If the dog uncovers an intruder in the guarded area, it will corner him and hold him until the police or the handler arrives, which could be many hours. If the intruder attempts to run away or attacks the dog, the dog will attack. The attack consists of biting and holding the intruder's right arm, but the dog will attempt to grab any part of the intruder's body if it can't get the right arm. If the intruder then freezes, the dog will cease its attack.

I can attest to the fact that these dogs are very powerful. Wearing a heavy protective sleeve over my right arm, I "provoked" one of these dogs as it was held on a very short leash by a husky handler. The dog, a male German shepherd, grabbed the sleeve with its teeth and shook my arm violently. If the handler hadn't ordered the dog to let go, I suspect that my arm would have been dislocated at the shoulder.

Haggerty urges that attack dogs only be handled by responsible adults, at least twenty-one years of age, preferably twenty-five or older. Under no circumstances should these dogs be handled by children. Nevertheless, Haggerty urges that these dogs live in the homes of their owners even if there are children. The dogs can be handled by more than one person in the home: they are not "one-man" dogs.

Even though these dogs will only attack on command or attack an intruder, the owners should carry liability insurance. Coverage against any injuries caused by dogs is a normal part of any home owner's or tenant's policy. Nevertheless, one should check one's policy for any "animal exclusion" provisions.

If you buy a female guard dog, the problem of the dog becoming pregnant arises. The solution is to keep the dog away from all male dogs during its season. The dog could also be spayed. Some experts believe that a spayed dog is not as effective, but Haggerty says that no experiments have ever been conducted to prove that a spayed dog is any less effective.

Dogs trained as watchdogs merely bark at intruders. If the intruder tries to run away or harm the animal, the dog may bite him instinctively. However, the dog is not likely to bite hard enough to hold the intruder. Haggerty actually trains his attack dogs to bite hard.

In time, the dog will become old and feeble, no longer able to function well as a guard dog. What to do? At first, you might want to bring in another young dog to perform its guard duties. Because these dogs have excellent temperaments, the two dogs will get along. (These dogs even get along with cats.) However, after a time, the older dog may grow so feeble that you can't take care of it. One solution might be to have the dog put away. However, I suspect that you will have grown so attached to the faithful animal that you couldn't have the creature put to sleep.

Haggerty's solution is to "retire" such animals to one of his kennels. He is prepared to board such retired guard dogs for about $4 per day. I am sure that other kennels will do the same.

Problems in Buying Guard Dogs

The growth in crime seems to be matched by the number of people selling guard dogs. Just as many poorly qualified if not unethical people have been attracted to the business of making and selling burglar-alarm systems (see Chapter IX, "How to Buy Security Products and Services"), some of those selling guard dogs are sure to be fly-by-nights selling poor merchandise. One has to take as much care in selecting a source of guard dogs as a source for a security system. More so perhaps, because no electronic security system is going to bite an innocent person—or a member of your family. Don't buy a watch or attack dog because it appears to be a bargain. In the end it may cost you much more in lawsuits and aggravation.

I've noticed one very significant characteristic of well-trained watch and guard dogs: when not on duty they are docile, friendly animals, wonderful pets. Never buy a dog that's supposed to protect you and your family because it's so vicious. True guard dogs are vicious only on command; an untrained but vicious dog is a danger to all.

Chapter V

ELECTRONIC
SECURITY
SYSTEMS

Home security is now a big business. As a result many hundreds of companies, ranging from billion-dollar corporations to garage operations, have been attracted to this growing market. The particular type of product that is easiest to develop and sell is electronic. Why? Mainly because the electronics involved are rather simple. The plain fact is that it takes a lot less time to develop an electronic system than a new pick-resistant lock cylinder for doors. Electronics is still glamorous, which means that buyer resistance is often lower. In addition, profits are likely to be higher because an electronic system that costs $500 is most likely easier to sell than a lock plus cylinder costing $50. The dealers commonly mark up electronic security systems by one hundred percent, sometimes as high as one hundred and seventy-five percent.

The entry of so many companies into the business of selling electronic security systems makes it harder for the buyer to make a decision. He is faced with so many claims, some of them conflicting. How to discriminate among all the claims and purchase an electronic security system that does a good job and also represents good value is covered in Chapter IX, "How to Buy Security Products and Services."

In this chapter, I describe the various categories of electronic security systems, what each offers and also some representative examples of each.

The most sophisticated electronic security systems protect against more than burglars: they also guard homes and apartments against fire and provide panic buttons against intruders. This greater range of protection makes a lot of sense. For home owners, fire is a much greater economic threat than all criminal threats against homes and a much bigger killer than criminals. In 1970, out of 12,200 Americans killed in fires, 6,500 died in fires in homes. In comparison, only 29 percent of the 15,810 Americans murdered in 1970 were killed by criminals; most died at the hands of relatives or acquaintances. And of the 4,600 or so felonious homicides in 1970, only a fraction occurred in homes. (Many hundreds involved so-called gangland slayings in which criminals were murdered by other criminals.) So you stand far more risk of death from fire than at the hands of criminals while at home.

For this reason it makes sense for home owners to choose a security system as much for its efficiency in detecting fires as for antiburglary features. For those who live in so-called fireproof apartment buildings where the landlord's insurance covers the structure, the prime emphasis in selection should be on protection against burglary, with fire protection going piggyback on the primary consideration. However, there are many living in apartments in "old-law" apartment buildings and converted brownstones that are far from fireproof. For these apartment dwellers, fire protection is an important consideration.

Electronic Security Systems

Electronic security systems consist of the following: detectors, noisemakers, control mechanisms and a means of arming and disarming the system. Some systems also offer the option of communicating the alarm signal to someone at a central monitoring station.

Fire and Smoke Detectors

Detectors of fire and smoke range from the unsophisticated and inexpensive to the sophisticated and comparatively expensive. The simplest of all is the thermal detector. Usually set to close at 135°F., these contact-type switches can cost as little as $2.50 apiece. When mounted in normally hot spaces, such as the attic or furnace room, they are set to react at a higher temperature.

Rate-of-rise detectors are actuated if the temperature in a room goes up too fast. Often the rate-of-rise detector is combined with the thermal detector. Prices for rate-of-rise detectors are about $4. When combined with thermal detectors, the units cost about $5.

Smoke detectors are especially useful in detecting the smoke from a nearby fire before the temperature rises. They are based on photoelectric cells on which a light beam is directed. When smoke obscures the light beam, the voltage from the cell falls, setting off an alarm. Obviously, smoke detectors should not be mounted in kitchens. They cost about $120 installed.

The most sophisticated of all fire detectors is the ionization detector. This device reacts to the products of combustion, sounding an alarm long before any smoke can be seen or the temperature rises. In homes, they should be mounted in the passageway or area leading to the bedrooms. Ionization detectors cost about $150 installed.

Fire detectors are not usually installed by themselves, although many manufacturers now offer self-contained fire-detection systems (see section at end of this chapter). Most commonly, home owners purchase an anti-intrusion system on which fire detection goes piggyback.

Categories of Anti-Intrusion Systems

There are three main categories of burglar-alarm systems: perimeter; space or room; and object. As its name implies, a perimeter system guards the perimeter of a home or residence. This means that it is designed to detect intrusions through doors, windows and skylights. If the property guarded warrants it, a perimeter system can also be designed and installed to guard against intrusions through air-conditioning ducts and through the ceiling and walls and even the roof.

Few homes require detection of intrusion through ceiling, walls and roofing—this is basically for commercial establishments. If a home contains particularly valuable objects in one room, such as painting or statues or silver, which require special protection, a space or room detector can be installed in that one room. These devices will detect the entry and/or movement of intruders. If only one object in the room or home is specially valuable, then an object detector can be connected to it. An object detector can be a simple switch that opens when a painting is lifted off a wall or a statue off a table. In general, room and object detectors are connected to perimeter systems. However, some room alarms are self-contained and portable, even battery-operated, as discussed below.

Local Alarm and Communicating Systems

Fire, perimeter, room or object detectors can activate two types of alarms: local and/or communicating. A local alarm means simply that a noisemaker—siren, bell or buzzer—mounted outside or inside the residence (if the latter, loud enough to be heard outside) is actuated by the various forms of detectors. Communicating alarm systems inform the police, fire department, guard service or some nearby friend or relative that an intrusion or fire has been detected. Communicating systems can also warn of other emergencies, such as an overflowing boiler or a malfunctioning deep freezer. Usually, communicating systems are combined with local alarms.

Communicating systems can be based on two forms of communication: a leased line on which nothing but emergencies are communicated or an automatic dialer that uses the conventional switched telephone network system to report the emergency by recorded message. The leased line is the most expensive form of communication, unless the line is shared by many homes, a growing trend. The automatic dialer can use the phone line, but this lowers its reliability since burglars have been known to call up a home equipped with an automatic dialer to tie up the line so that no emergency message gets out. Also, if someone is at home in an upstairs bedroom using the phone and a fire is detected or an intruder enters downstairs, no emergency message goes out—unless the automatic dialer is equipped with a feature that lets it take over the phone line. (At the end of this chapter I discuss a brand-new means of communication just coming into being.)

Police Ban Automatic Dialers

There is still another objection to automatic dialers set to call the police. In many cities, there are so many automatic dialers in use and the detectors to which they are linked generate so many false alarms that the police phone switchboards have been overwhelmed. As a result, the police or municipal authorities in many large and small cities have banned phone alarms. The police in these cities will not respond to recorded emergency messages. Before considering any of the home security systems that include automatic dialers, check with the police in your locality. A ban on such dialers may exist or be under consideration. Even if there is no ban on the dialers, the police may indicate informally that recorded messages do not get priority. If such is the case, reject the system if the automatic dialer is an integral part of it; only consider the system if the automatic dialer can be left out.

There are two approaches in which automatic dialers make sense. First, if the recorded message goes to some central monitoring station which then has the option of calling the police. Or the dialer could arouse a nearby friend, relative or neighbor, who could then rush over to your home and decide whether or not to call. Why should there be any question about calling the police? Because there are certain climatic conditions under which many false alarms occur. These are heavy rainfalls, lightning storms and high winds. Heavy rains and the winds that often accompany them can rattle windowpanes and doors sufficiently to set off alarms. Lightning can induce false signals in the phone lines. The central station operator or whoever the dialer calls should have enough experience with the system to recognize the high probability of a false alarm.

For example, on one occasion when I was inspecting a central station, a violent rainstorm occurred. An alarm was received from nearly every subscriber to the service. Yet the monitor at the station did not call the police. He calmly waited a few minutes for the storm to abate, then restored service. Every alarm was false.

Even when the possibility of a false alarm is high, the station or person called should nevertheless check your home if the system does not reset itself. If they see evidence of an entry, or a strange car parked near the home, the police should be called immediately.

In some small towns, a leased line direct to a noisemaker and/or indicator panel in police headquarters may be installed. If there is always someone on duty in the room in which the alarm is mounted, this arrangement can be most efficient. Of course, as soon as a number of commercial establishments and wealthier residents ask for installation of alarms in police headquarters, the police will have to ban them.

If you own a well-equipped vacation home in a remote location, it makes sense to install a communicating system— and you may be able to convince the police to permit an alarm in headquarters. Again, if many owners of vacation homes in the area demand the same, the police will be forced to withdraw this privilege. An alternative for owners of vacation homes concerned about the rising level of vandalism of such homes is to band together and install a sound- or other monitoring system (see discussion of sound-monitoring systems in Chapter X, "Security on the Job"). This has been done by vacation-home owners in the lake region of Wisconsin.

Details of Perimeter Systems

Perimeter systems require the mounting of a detector on every "reachable" or "accessible" opening in a home or apartment. (As I indicated in Chapter III, "Protecting Doors and Windows," agile burglars can reach upper-level windows that home owners might consider immune from entry.)

By far the most popular form of detector for doors or windows is the magnetic switch. There are no external moving parts to a magnetic switch. One part contains a magnet and the other part (the one with the two connection points) a reed switch. The magnet holds the two contacts on the switch together. When the magnet is moved away, the switch opens, actuating the control electronics.

Magnetic switches of this variety are quickly attached, but some home owners might find them unattractive. In addition, a burglar—or an employee—could conceivably short out the exposed connection points, thereby defeating the detector.

At least two companies have developed magnetic switches in a form that makes them easy to conceal. Sentrol, Inc., makes a magnetic switch in the form of a thin cylinder one-quarter inch in diameter and one inch long containing the switch. The magnet half has the same dimensions. To install, one uses a quarter-inch drill bit to simply drill a hole a bit over one inch in depth in the movable portion of the opening. The magnet is inserted into this hole and covered up with wood putty. The switch half is inserted into a matching hole in line with the magnet. Since the wires have to be brought out, this hole has to be much deeper. There are no exposed connection points to short out.

Ademco, a leading supplier of systems and parts, has developed a magnetic switch in the form of a thick wafer one-half inch in diameter. The two halves are mounted in holes cut with a half-inch hole saw.

If you want magnetic switches of this new variety for improved appearance and greater security, just ask for them from your supplier. They will add very little to the total cost of your system.

Simple contact switches are also used as detectors on doors and windows. A contact or magnetic switch might not be suitable for a skylight because the burglar may break the glass without disturbing the switch. More appropriate is installation of the metallic tape or foil commonly seen on windows of jewelry stores. If the glass is broken, the tape is torn and the circuit opens, actuating the alarm.

Pressure Detectors

Doormat detectors are the most widely used form of pressure detector. Made in the form of a rectangular doormat, these flat detectors include a number of switches placed between rubber laminations. When anyone steps on the mat, a switch closes, activating a normally open alarm circuit. Doormat detectors are most commonly used in commercial establishments, but they can be used in homes to protect closets containing valuables, art objects or safes. They cost about $50 apiece installed.

A newer form of pressure detector from Detectron Security Systems, Sag Harbor, N.Y., is much less conspicuous than a doormat detector, which must be hidden under a rug or doormat. Detectron's Pulsor is less than three inches long. It contains a piezoelectric element that provides a signal whenever it is stretched. When firmly glued to the *underside* of the floor area to be protected, the Pulsor is completely hidden from an intruder. Yet any footstep on the floor above generates a signal. Pulsors can also be used on the undersides of flat roofs, ladders, fire escapes and porches. Unfortunately, the signal-carrying cable from a Pulsor can't be wired directly into control electronics. It requires a signal processor, which costs about $100 installed. However, the processor can handle up to sixteen Pulsors. To equip a summer home with ten Pulsors plus associated electronics would cost from $300 to $400.

Variety of Space Detectors

There are a number of different detectors that tell if someone has entered and is moving about a room. The simplest is the photoelectric beam. Formerly, this detector consisted of a visible light source aimed at a light detector. Intruders could spot the light and avoid it. Today, infrared light, which is invisible to the human eye, is used. The light sources can be tiny semiconductor (solid-state) devices about an eighth inch in diameter and drawing very little current. The detectors are also very small, so small, in fact, that they can be mounted in an ordinary power outlet. At least two manufacturers produce semiconductor infrared detectors mounted in power outlets so they are inconspicuous. They are: Alarmatronics Engineering, Inc., Newton, Mass., and Optical Controls, Inc., Burlington, Mass. List price for a light-source-and-detector pair is about $125. The Mini-Sentry detector produced by Alarmatronics comes in a battery-powered version that the manufacturer claims will operate for one year on a standard six-volt alarm battery. The Mini-Sentry is also made in an a-c-powered version with battery standby.

Infrared detectors are useful in guarding a bank of windows where a detector pair is less expensive than mounting magnetic switches on each window.

Infrared detectors can also be installed outdoors to protect your home, or warn if some children are climbing over a fence to use your pool. The beam of the infrared source can be turned around corners with mirrors so that only one source and one detector are required. The light source should be mounted high enough so that the beam is not broken by any stray animals. These detectors are set so that birds or falling branches do not set off an intrusion signal. The infrared detectors used indoors have a range of about seventy-five feet, which means they would rarely be suitable outdoors. The manufacturers supply models with a more powerful infrared light source that can be detected as much as a thousand feet away.

The detectors based on walking through an infrared beam

are so-called active systems: they require the generation of the infrared energy. A new kind of infrared detector is passive in the sense that it depends on detection of the infrared energy given off by all living objects, including man. The military has used passive infrared detectors for years. Now a California company has brought out a commercial version to guard rooms. The manufacturer is Advanced Devices Laboratory, Inc. An installed detector would cost about $400.

Other space detectors are based on filling the room or portion of a room to be guarded with an invisible field of energy. Ultrasonic detectors fill the space with ultrasonic energy, sound waves of a frequency somewhat beyond the upper limits of the human ear. If the sound pattern is disturbed, an alarm signal is generated by the detector. Ultrasonic energy bounces off the walls, so it is confined to the room or area guarded. The range of an ultrasonic detector is based on the capacity of the ultrasonic transducers inside the detector. The bigger—and more expensive—the transducers, the greater the range. However, few ultrasonic detectors have a range greater than twenty-five feet. Ultrasonic detectors have one big disadvantage: unless equipped with special circuitry, they can be actuated by sharp noises, by pets and by a sudden blast of air, such as from a space heater or airconditioner starting up.

A less serious disadvantage of some ultrasonic detectors is the possibility of annoying those people with super-sensitive hearing, those who can hear higher-frequency notes. Some ultrasonic detectors operate at frequencies just above the audible range. Children and in particular young women may be able to hear the annoying sound made by the detector. In addition, some men, who don't actually hear the sound, may get headaches from it. To avoid this problem, only consider ultrasonic detectors that operate at 22,000 cycles per second or above (the upper limit is about 40,000 cps). Dogs will most likely avoid any room containing an operating ultrasonic detector, but that's an advantage.

A rival to the ultrasonic detector is the microwave or so-called radar detector. This type of detector produces a field of microwave (very-high-frequency) radio energy. If the field, whose "shape" can be adjusted so that it does not reach right down to the floor, thus eliminating false alarms due to cats and small pets, is disturbed, a signal is generated. One of the problems with the microwave detector is that the energy it produces goes right through nonmetallic walls. This means that someone walking about in an adjacent unguarded room may set off the detection signal—unless the range of the system has been properly set. On the other hand, this ability to detect through walls could be very useful. A room could actually be protected by an unseen detector in the next room or in a closet. Or a single detector at one end of a home could guard the entire house, assuming it has sufficient range.

Microwave detectors have one big disadvantage: they can be activated by a fluorescent lamp going on. This means that any microwave detectors must be installed so that the light from any fluorescent lamps in the same area does not fall directly on them.

Up until last year, microwave detectors were much more costly than ultrasonic detectors. Now, however, a new low-cost way of generating the high-frequency energy has resulted in microwave detectors that cost no more, or even less, than ultrasonic detectors.

One solution to the false-alarm deficiencies of both ultrasonic and microwave detectors is offered by Bourns Security Systems. The new coincident-trip detector, Model RA-3, includes both an ultrasonic and a microwave detector. Only when both detectors operate simultaneously is an intrusion signal generated. This self-contained alarm unit costs $340.

Still another form of field detector is the capacitance detector. It is a simple wire that generates a harmless electromagnetic field of limited range, only a few feet. If someone approaches the wire, he changes the field pattern, triggering a signal.

Arming and Disarming

There are two ways of arming or activating a security system: by key or by a pushbutton control. Key arming—and disarming before entering your home—is less costly, but raises the possibility of defeating the system in case a key gets into the wrong hands. Also, if a member of the family who doesn't have a key, say a child who has been away at college, returns home, he or she will have to wait until a key holder returns to get in.

Pushbutton controls depend on remembering the proper sequence of buttons to push. They are more costly, but usually more flexible than key controls: it's possible to change the code number easily. However, they are subject to the same disadvantages as pushbutton locks for doors (see discussion of these locks in Chapter III).

Most desirable is an arming/disarming arrangement that includes a time-delay feature, which permits installation of the control box *inside* your residence. The advantages are threefold: no exposure to weather; no chance of vandalism; and less time spent fumbling with keys or pushbuttons at your entrance door (the advantages of which I explain in the section on "Care and Handling of Keys" in Chapter III, "Protecting Doors and Windows").

Panic Buttons

Many security systems either come equipped with panic buttons or this feature can be specified as an option. Panic buttons come in two forms: permanently mounted on a wall or on the control console that is mounted near one's bed, or in a remote-control form, similar to a TV channel changer, with a range of about one hundred feet. Because intrusion into occupied homes and apartments is so very rare, I consider panic buttons more of a reassurance to the timid than a significant deterrent. However, there is one circumstance in which panic buttons make sense. If you have an elderly or infirm parent or other relative at home and that person is often left alone, a panic button can be used to summon aid if the person becomes too ill to operate the phone or falls down and is unable to crawl to the phone. Remote panic buttons cost about $50.

Noisemakers

Everyone has heard the noisemakers most commonly used in security systems—false alarms set off bells or horns that can be heard for two or three blocks at night when there isn't much traffic. The great majority of security systems are equipped with bells, which are low in cost and very reliable. The bells come in various sizes, from three inches in diameter up to about twelve inches. They meet the needs of most home owners.

However, if your home is so far away from others that a bell can't be heard, then you would need a siren. Sirens are made in two ways: mechanical and electronic. The mechanical sirens contain a metal cylinder that is spun by a motor at high speed, creating the sound. The electronic sirens, which are a newer development, contain no moving parts, which means they should be more reliable and less subject to weathering. Called the Earsplitter or the Curdler, some of these electronic sirens can be heard over a mile away. These powerful noisemakers cost about $100.

The self-contained security systems discussed later in this chapter include noisemakers related in principle to electronic sirens. These are tiny, low-cost loudspeakers that make enough noise inside a residence to scare an intruder, but which can't be heard very well outside.

What Does the Control Electronics Do?

Decision-making ranging from the elementary to the sophisticated can be designed into the control electronics incorporated in electronic security systems. In the lowest-cost systems, the controls operate in two modes: "normally open" and "normally closed." The latter is by far the most common. A series of switches are tied to the controls and receive energy when the system is armed. If an intrusion opens one of the switches, it is the *absence* of a signal that tells the controls to sound an alarm. The normally open mode does just the opposite: no energy flows in the circuit until an intruder steps on a doormat detector, for example, at which point energy flows and the controls tell the noisemaker to sound off. The systems one step above the most simple can accept signals from both normally open and normally closed detectors.

False alarms are a very serious problem with all security systems. The control electronics can be upgraded to include enough intelligence to ignore false signals, such as those that might be induced by a nearby stroke of lightning or some sharp electrical transient on the power line.

If a very large home or an estate with several buildings must be protected, the occupant wants more than just an alarm: he also wants to know where the emergency condition originated. Indicating the nature and location of the emergency calls for a substantial increase in sophistication. In theory, it would be possible to wire each detector directly to the control electronics; then there is a positive indication of the location of the emergency, which can be displayed on some sort of panel. However, this direct approach calls for a lot of wiring, which is not only costly, but could also be unattractive. In practice, it is far more desirable to include some sort of address code in the signal generated by each detector and enough intelligence in the controls to interpret this signal correctly. Such systems are available and they permit a large number of detectors to be wired in series in a loop with only two wires. However, a little code generator must be attached to each detector. A low-cost supplier of such systems is Pulse Dynamics, Inc., Pennsauken, N.J.

There is still one more important type of decision that can be designed into the controls. After an intrusion signal triggers an alarm, the alarm need not sound indefinitely. If the intruder hasn't departed after a few minutes of clanging, he will never leave. It would be most helpful if the alarm ceased. Otherwise, you will merely be irritating your neighbors, the very people you are depending upon to respond to an alarm. Some systems include provision for automatic resetting of the system to the alert stage after a set period. The AR-421 system, made by Metrotec Industries, Plainview, N.Y., resets after ten minutes. I recommend this feature highly.

Some of the manufacturers speak of their control mechanisms as "computers." Although a small amount of logic may be built into the controls, they are hardly computers. In fact, there can be a penalty in purchasing too much electronics in a control mechanism, because the more parts and complexity, the more chance of something going wrong.

Wired or Wireless Interconnection?

Originally there was only one way to connect the various kinds of detectors to the control electronics of a security system: by wire. The lightweight wires were either strung along the baseboards or moldings as inconspicuously as possible, which many home owners may nevertheless find unattractive, or they were run behind walls, which requires a lot of labor and extra-length flexible extensions for drills. The latter method is more reliable—as long as the insulation is not on the diet of rodents. Another way to conceal the unsightly wires is to cover them with a molded two-part plastic or metal channel, which is purchased in long sections. First, the base of the channel is attached to the wall along the path of the wiring. Then the wiring is laid in this channel. Afterward, the outer mating section of the channel is snapped over the wires. Of course, the channels have to be painted to match the walls.

To speed up installation and also eliminate all unsightly wires, at least a half-dozen companies now offer wireless techniques for sending signals from detectors to the control electronics. Two approaches are used. In one, tiny transmitters are attached to the detectors (in several such battery-operated transmitters, the fixed half of a magnetic switch is actually incorporated in the transmitter). In another approach, the high-frequency signal is superimposed on the 60-cycle power lines through a power outlet. The control electronics, which receives its power from the same lines, also receives the signals through the lines.

Most of the wireless systems have ranges of about five hundred feet. However, greater ranges of up to one thousand feet and even farther away can be ordered. This means that remote buildings, such as boathouses, barns, hothouses or tool sheds, can be protected without stringing wires, which are unsightly, expensive and subject to storm damage. In addition, an auxiliary alarm in a neighbor's home can be actuated—very handy if the protected home is vacant for an extended period.

Installation of a security system is much quicker by the wireless approach. Despite the inherently higher cost of the parts of the system to cover the cost of the tiny transmitters, the total cost to the home owner may be less because of low installation charges. For example, many installers will charge about $50 per "opening" (i.e., per window or door) for a wired detector. However, by wireless methods, the charge per opening can be as low as $30, and it will most likely drop as more and more manufacturers offer wireless systems with transmitters imported from the Orient.

On the other hand, a wireless system makes greater demands on the home owner. If the signals are broadcast and not sent over the power lines in the building, the transmitters usually operate on batteries. The batteries must be changed every three to six months. In time, the transmitters may fail or require adjustment (it would most likely be cheaper to replace them).

Another disadvantage to wireless systems is that detectors linked in this fashion can't be checked automatically by the control electronics at frequent intervals because the transmitters are one-way. This is a simple task if detectors are wired to the control electronics, assuming that the controls are capable of such monitoring.

In addition, you must receive signed assurances from your supplier that the transmitters are broadcasting at a frequency assigned by the Federal Communications Commission for this purpose and also that no neighbor has been assigned the same frequency. By using various coding techniques, suppliers can install wireless systems in adjacent homes using the same frequency, yet they will not interfere with each other. (In the very rare eventuality that two wireless systems interfere with each other, this becomes apparent very quickly so that corrective action can be taken.)

Can You Mix Components from Different Suppliers?

An interesting possibility for anyone whose home is equipped with a sophisticated security system is attaching a very effective new detector from one supplier to a system supplied by a different manufacturer. Can this be done? If you own your own system, there is no reason why you can't. The only obstacle is electrical compatability. Since most of the systems operate at 12 volts, all you have to be sure of is that the new detector operates at 12 volts, or matches whatever voltage your system operates on.

Remember that there is a great deal of "private labeling" in the security field. This means that electrical compatibility is the norm. For example, the ultrasonic detector in the American District Telegraph (ADT) home security system is made by Bourns.

Major improvements in security systems will come in detectors. In time, some new microwave intrusion detector or a new smoke detector will be available. If you want this new detector—or if your system doesn't have that kind of protection at all—it makes sense to add it on. But first check with your local supplier to make sure that addition of the new component will not void your warranty or maintenance contract. If there is any valid opposition from your supplier, ask him to obtain the new detector and install it. He will most likely do so to avoid friction with a customer. (Unfortunately, the detectors in wireless systems cannot be mated with the control electronics supplied by other manufacturers.)

Installation of Alarm Systems

There are three ways in which alarm systems can be installed: by the dealer; by you; or by an electronic technician hired to install one of the do-it-yourself types. If the property you are protecting is costly, it makes sense to let a professional do the job. However, installation costs are high, particularly if you want the wires concealed for improved appearance and reliability. The wires that run to the various detectors can be strung along baseboard moldings, but this type of installation is less secure: the wires may be damaged or severed by children, pets, painters, vacuum cleaners or floor polishers.

A professional installer is equipped with the snake-like extension drills that enable him to run wires leading from windows and doors but concealed behind walls. However, as I indicate in Chapter IX, "How to Buy Security Products and Services," there are some tax advantages gained when a security system is permanently installed in a home, and these in effect compensate somewhat for the high installation charges.

The Do-It-Yourself Approach

If you are a handy person, you should be able to install your own security system—and save hundreds of dollars. The parts for security systems are available in some specialty electrical shops in big cities, or you can take the simpler step of buying a kit. The kits are sold in radio-parts and hardware stores or by mail order. The lowest-priced one I know of costs only $34, but it doesn't include magnetic switches.

The most costly kit available comes from Crown Instruments, Inc., Portland, Ore. The Crown Security Alarm System includes two combined rate-of-rise and thermal fire detectors, three door-window magnetic switches, a combination lock to arm and disarm the system, an alarm horn, plus other required electronic components. The kit costs $249. It can be supplemented by additional magnetic switches at $4.05 each, a photoelectric smoke detector for $67.50 and an ultrasonic motion detector for $74.00. The manufacturer claims that it would take the "average" home owner "one weekend" to install the system. However, a "skilled handyman" would only need 6.5 hours. The system operates at 12 volts, stepped down by transformer, so that in the event of a power outage, the system would be powered by the 12-volt battery included in the kit.

Kits for security systems are even being sold through direct-mail solicitation. Along with its charge statements for purchases of gas and oil, the Shell Oil Company encloses a brochure and order form for a Security Alarm System made by Puritron, an appliance manufacturer. The kit, which costs $49.90 (payable in ten equal monthly charges) plus $2 for shipping and handling, includes four Ademco magnetic switches, two hundred feet of wire, a control box and an auxiliary horn for outside installation. An interesting aspect of the offer is the "thirty-day free trial." If you are not satisfied after thirty days, you can send it back. However, if dissatisfied, are you supposed to rip out the two hundred feet of wire?

To find out what it takes to install your own system, I installed an On-Guard burglar alarm in my parents' ground-floor apartment. Listing for $50, this kit is available in Lafayette and other radio-parts stores. It includes four sets of magnetic switches, a panic button and exit-entry switch (to arm the system while at home) and a large bell plus control electronics (battery operated) mounted in a sturdy steel box with a tamper-proof switch that sounds the alarm if anyone tries to open the box, which is held closed by sheet-metal screws. The kit also includes several hundred feet of twisted wire plus mounting hardware.

The box is designed to be installed outside a home or apartment. To avoid drilling a hole through the wall of the entrance vestibule and also to make the system more secure and less liable to vandalism, I added a Monroe time-delay to the system. By inserting this ten-second delay in the bell circuit, the box could be mounted on the side of a wooden kitchen cabinet. In addition to the $6 for the delay module, I had to buy a carbide-tipped masonry drill bit for $5, a 12-volt battery for $3, and spend a few cents for self-tapping screws to mount one pair of magnetic switches on the entrance door, which is made of hollow steel. Unfortunately, I had to go to seven different stores before I found one that sold the right size battery. Even though the bell is inside the apartment, it is loud enough to be heard in the street outside. For a total cost of $64 the system is a good buy.

It took me about five hours to install the system, which protects the kitchen window and the front door. I estimate that it would have taken me another two hours (plus two more magnetic switches) to add protection for the remaining four windows in the apartment (the small bathroom window can't be opened).

If you are going to install your own system, I recommend that you do it *before* repainting your residence. Otherwise, you should expect to do a bit of retouching and you would most likely want to paint the gray switches to match the background color.

Examples of Security Systems

Suppliers of security systems range from billion-dollar corporations down to garage operations. One of the heartening developments in the field has been the entry of very large companies with substantial field-service forces. Unfortunately, even the largest of these corporations has found the business too tough. For instance, Honeywell, Inc., one of the big factors in security systems for industry, withdrew in 1971 from the home-security business after only a year of effort. There's a lesson in Honeywell's failure: the less time a company has been in the business, the less likely it will stay in this competitive field.

Westinghouse. The Westinghouse Electric Corporation has developed an attractive security system sold through franchisees. The outstanding feature of the system is its ability to communicate emergency signals to a central station maintained by the franchisee for the territory. As soon as the central-station monitor (who may only be a girl at a phone-answering service) receives an emergency signal, he is automatically connected to a microphone in the home where the signal originated. If the monitor decides it is a true emergency, he calls the appropriate municipal force—police or fire department or ambulance service. Or the occupant of the home may simply tell the central station that the indicated emergency is a false alarm or that he was simply testing. This desirable ability to indicate false alarms avoids "crying wolf" to the local police.

Available detectors include door and window switches, active infrared detectors, ionization detectors and an ultrasonic detector. In addition, the system includes some optional features against intruders: a panic button mounted near the front door to be pushed if some stranger tries to force his way in and a remote panic button that sends a radio signal from a little hand-held box back to the control box from a distance of up to 100 feet from the home or anyplace within the home. (As I indicated earlier, I can't work up any enthusiasm for this remote-control panic button, which is also offered on most competitive systems.) The Westinghouse system includes a control panel usually mounted near the owner's bed. It displays the nature of the emergency in very clear lettering and also provides a warning signal in case the occupant is asleep.

A most interesting aspect of the Westinghouse system is the way it is sold. If a home owner is not able to pay for the system, which averages $1,200 in cost but can easily run over $2,000 with various options, the system can be leased on a sixty-month (five-year) basis. At the end of the lease, the cost of which includes maintenance and central-station service, the home owner has the option of buying the system at 40 percent of list price. If you sell your home before the five years are up, the lease and purchase option are transferable to the new owner. If you pay for the system outright, the monthly charge for central-station service is about $15.

American District Telegraph (ADT). The home-security system marketed by ADT is of interest mainly because it is offered by ADT. A listed company, ADT is the largest by far of the companies offering central-station alarm services (at one time it was the major element in a near monopoly since broken up by court order). ADT has about 150 branches all over the country plus installers and service. More importantly, it can offer a proven central-station service as a supplement to its home-security system. This is significant to those who want to protect homes with many valuables. In addition, this service can be obtained on a short-term basis to protect a home while you are on an extended vacation or away for the summer or winter.

As long as your home is within thirty miles of an ADT central station (the great majority of American homes come within the ADT market area), you can obtain central-station alarm service on a pro rata basis per month plus a special charge of $50 for the first month. Year-round, this central-station service costs the home owner $105 and up (depending on where you live). If you want guards to appear each time there is an alarm, this added service costs $100 per year, plus $25 for the first month.

The features of the ADT system are otherwise quite similar to those of the Westinghouse system. However, ADT offers a pushbutton entrance control instead of a keyed one. Installation charges for the ADT system range between $500 and $1,000 depending on features.

Novar Electronics. "Sound discrimination" is the basis for the various anti-intrusion systems and devices made by this small outfit in Barberton, Ohio. The units are in effect programmed to respond to unusual sounds. Instead of turning on a noisemaker, the systems turn on all lights to which they are connected. However, a noisemaker can be attached to the devices, and a new portable, self-contained unit includes a very loud horn as well as floodlights. However, when installed in a home, the unit is set off by the movements of the occupants. So the $198 portable unit is in effect only applicable to an unoccupied home. The main system offered by Novar doesn't need much installation. It simply goes into a switch box in place of the present on-off switch for the lights in a room. As long as the windows are closed, the unit will only respond to unusual noises in the room. If the unit is installed near the front door, it will turn on the lights when the home owner opens the front door. This can be very reassuring. Novar claims that as of late 1971 there were twenty-five hundred of these units installed. They cost only $129 plus installation.

Self-Contained Security Systems

In the past few years, a number of self-contained security systems that include detectors, controls and noisemaker all in one package have come on the market. Each unit usually detects only one form of danger: intrusion, fire or possibly flooding. Most are battery operated, some draw their power from the power outlet and one even operates by winding like an alarm clock.

By far the greatest number of these self-contained units

are antiburglary devices. Most mount right on the front door or windows of a residence. They range in price from $5 up to about $100. The alarms are usually set off if someone opens the door or window. However, 3M Company manufactures an alarm that sounds off if someone merely tampers with the door or attempts to pick the alarm. It also includes a panic button. 3M's Lock Alarm ranges in price from $60 to $90 depending on features, plus installation.

Because all but one model of the Lock Alarm comes with its own lock cylinder, it should be installed by a locksmith. However, many of the other self-contained door alarms can be installed by a handy person.

Don't confuse 3M's Lock Alarm with a product called the Lokalarm. The latter is made by Mannix Industries, Westbury, N.Y. Selling for about $100, it offers an "instant relocking mechanism" that shoots a cylindrical deadbolt into place if anyone tampers with the lock or attempts to force the door to which it is attached. If your door is equipped with a good rim lock of the Segal variety, as I recommend in Chapter III, I don't see any need for the Lokalarm, especially if your home is also equipped with a security system. However, if you want to add an alarm to a rim-lock-equipped door, you can buy one for about $40.

Among door alarms, the one that is particularly easy to install is the P-S-C Apartment Alarm. Made in two parts, it fits over the top of an entrance door the way saddlebags are mounted on a horse. The outside part includes a set of push-buttons that enables those with the right combination of numbers to disarm the device. Arming is done from the inside with a key. A panic button is included that prevents the noisemaker from sounding off as long as it is held in the "open" position. If someone attempts to break off the outside part, the noisemaker goes off. The supplier recommends that the Penlite battery be replaced every six months. Sold door-to-door by girls, the device costs $89.50, including battery.*

The ultrasonic space detectors that I mentioned earlier in this chapter are also made in self-contained form. All of these units include a detector plus noisemaker as well as a time-delay feature and an outlet for activating a lamp. This is to permit a home owner entering a darkened room containing an armed ultrasonic detector to walk over to the box and disarm the alarm before it starts to wail. An intruder entering the same room would be stopped short by the light and then supposedly flee when the alarm blares ten, twenty or thirty seconds later.

But what if the burglar does not flee? If he knows how these simple self-contained alarms work, he will use the delay to unplug the unit, or if he can't find the plug, simply yank the unit out of its connections. To avoid this possibility, ultrasonic units can be ordered with built-in battery power supplies (which also keep the unit working during a power outage). For still greater deterrence, the unit can be mounted up high out of reach, with the arming control mounted in some concealed place within reach. Prices for such simple ultrasonic systems range from a low of $90 (Decatur Electronics, Inc., Decatur, Ill.) to several hundred dollars.

Bourns manufactures an ultrasonic alarm in the guise of a stereo bookcase loudspeaker that also includes an alarm. The model ACA-150 costs $180. These portable ultrasonic detector-alarms are designed so that their internal alarms

---

* This alarm closely resembles a predecessor called Comput-O-Larm that was introduced in late 1969 at a price of $40. The manufacturer was then located in Manhattan. The maker is not listed in the 1972 Manhattan phone book and I have not been able to track down this firm. Nevertheless, in late 1971 the Comput-O-Larm was still stocked in some New York department stores and selling for as little as $35.

can be made silent and the output from the detector transferred to an overall home-security system.

Several of the ultrasonic units contain features that permit communication of the alarm signal many hundreds of feet if not miles. Northern Electric's Ultrasonic Intruder Alarm, which lists for $150, can be equipped with an accessory alarm that receives its signal over the power lines. This $75 option can go into a neighbor's home many hundreds of feet away—as long as both homes are on the same local power lines. The Northern Electric unit is also unusual in that it comes in two parts: transmitter and receiver (in all other self-contained ultrasonic units the intrusion signal is returned to the same container housing the generator of the ultrasonic field). By this means the coverage of the system has been extended up to forty feet, around corners too.

An automatic phone dialer has been incorporated with an ultrasonic detector in a unit offered by Acron Corporation. The Acro-Guard, which sells for around $500, can also accept signals from fire detectors—and will then call the fire department too.

For several months, I tested the self-contained ultrasonic alarm marketed nationally by 3M. I set it up in my living room to guard against any intruders who might enter through the bedroom windows and attempt to exit through the front door, or, conversely, those who might enter through either the front door or kitchen window and attempt to rifle the bedroom.

I found the unit quite reliable for this period. The delay was sufficient to permit me to prevent the alarm from wailing after the unit turned on a table lamp. The range of the unit varied with the weather. On very humid days, the unit could detect motion through an open arch into the foyer. On dry days, its outer range shrank back into the living room. Space detectors are designed to detect motion. Even when set for "maximum sensitivity," I found that the 3M alarm exhibited a tolerance for very fast or very slow motion. In other words, if I dashed from the foyer into the bedroom or if I walked extremely slowly, the alarm would not go off. This means that an intruder aware of the installation of one of these units—or any other space detector with the same characteristics—could pass it without setting off any alarm.

The alarm was loud enough to startle visitors who did not expect it. However, every one of my visitors who heard it suggested that the alarm really wasn't loud enough. It could be heard in the hallway of the building outside my apartment, but not very clearly. However, an auxiliary noisemaker for outside mounting can be added for $20. At the price of $100, the unit appears to be a good value in security, but far from foolproof. A 3M representative told me that the unit will soon be offered in a version that looks like a book. This means that once the alarm goes off an intruder won't be able to find the unit as quickly (assuming it is nested among many other books) and disarm or unplug it.

Soon low-cost self-contained security systems based on microwave fields will be available. Although they will not generate false alarms due to flapping curtains, airconditioners turning on, etc., they will not be foolproof. The range of the units must be adjusted carefully so that they do not detect anyone walking around outside your residence, unless you want to detect outside intruders too.

The least costly anti-intrusion alarm of which I am aware is a $5 device for windows made by Mannix Industries. The manufacturer claims that the battery lasts one year.

Self-Contained Fire Alarms

Since fire is the greater threat, it is no wonder that several companies have developed self-contained fire detectors plus noisemakers. The most complicated of these units is the Fireguard made by Three B Electronics, Brooklyn, N.Y. It combines heat, smoke and flame detectors. The manufacturer claims that the device will detect flames up to one hundred feet away. It lists for $149.50, with options for an $18 dry battery or a $60 rechargeable battery unit.

Two companies make self-contained battery-operated fire detectors that depend on ionization detectors (see earlier reference in this chapter to fire detectors). Both have UL approval. The BRK Detector made by New England Home Security Company costs $175, while the Ademco Combustion Products Smoke Detector sells for about $100. The former employs two separate sensing mechanisms, and both must be activated before an alarm is sounded. Because one mechanism depends on the deposition of smoke particles on a resistance grid with a glass surface, the glass must be cleaned at least once every six months for the unit to operate. The Ademco unit has one attractive feature: as the battery weakens, the unit beeps with increasing frequency, warning the home owner to replace the battery.

The Vigilert Smoke/Fire Alarm, made by Lutron Electronics, combines a photoelectric detector with a thermal detector set to actuate at 135°F. Costing only $50, it is powered by a-c, which means it can't be mounted too far from a power outlet.

If $150, $100 or even $50 appears to be too expensive, you should be aware of some less sophisticated detectors that cost much less. At only $8, the Wilkinson fire alarm is an English product imported for many years by Firewarning, Inc., 919 Third Avenue, New York, N.Y. 10022. A wind-up mechanical device that does not, of course, require batteries or electrical outlets, it emits a loud alarm-clock-like noise that I could hear clearly about forty feet away through a closed door. The alarm is set off when a fuse inserted in a linkage melts—at 125°F., which is about ten degrees lower than the alarm point on most other thermal detectors. The device, which is only three inches in diameter, can be hung high up on a wall, where the temperature is higher. An indicator tells if the alarm needs rewinding. It will sound off for one minute on a single winding. The alarm comes with one internally mounted spare fuse; additional fuses cost forty-four cents apiece.

At about the same price various companies supply an imported thermal detector-alarm that plugs right into a power outlet. The disadvantage of these devices is that they must go where the outlets are mounted, which is usually in a baseboard and rarely more than four feet off the floor. In general it makes sense to mount fire detectors as close to the ceiling as possible.

Over the next few years a number of manufacturers will undoubtedly introduce other self-contained detection devices. They offer two big advantages: little or no installation cost and mobility—they can be removed and remounted in other parts of your residence or in a new residence if you move.

Avoid "Crying Wolf"

Once you've installed a noisy burglar or fire alarm, invite all neighbors within earshot to come over and study the system and listen to the alarm. Try to get them all to come at once (opportunity for a party?) so that you don't have to warn each of the others that you are merely demonstrating the system (avoid false alarms, otherwise your neighbors might think the system is "crying wolf" during an actual emergency).

In the event that you or some member of your family set off the alarm by accident, immediately call all your neighbors (or call them the next morning if it is late at night) and indicate that it was a false alarm.

The Future of Security Systems

There are many millions of homes and apartments in the United States now wired for cable television via community antenna (CATV) systems. To obtain good reception, many millions more will be wired in the coming years. For a long time electronic experts have recognized that the high-capacity cables that carry TV programs into homes could also bring other services in—and out. Among these services is security.

Here's how it would work. Alarm signals would be sent back over the coaxial cable to a central monitoring station, where a printout would tell the operator on duty just which subscriber's home is reporting an emergency condition and the nature of the condition. The operator would then call the appropriate municipal service: police, firemen or ambulance. In addition, the central station would automatically check each subscriber's security system at regular intervals (in one approach as frequently as every five seconds) to make sure the system is functioning properly.

At least four companies have already developed the central-station equipment required by the CATV system to provide security services. These are: Advanced Research Corp. (Atlanta, Ga.); Holmes Communications Corp. (New York, N.Y.); Hughes Aircraft Co. (Culver City, Calif.) and Scientific Atlanta (Atlanta, Ga.). Undoubtedly, more will get into this business. (For a description of the Holmes system, see discussion of Holmes apartment-house system in Chapter VI, "Apartment House Security.")

Unfortunately, few CATV systems can utilize the equipment because they were constructed with one-way amplifiers, which is all that is needed to distribute TV programs. However, the Federal Communications Commission has decreed that all new CATV systems be equipped with the two-way amplifiers needed to return emergency and any other signals from subscriber homes. In addition, by 1975 all existing CATV systems must convert over to two-way amplifiers. This will pave the way for a high-grade central-station alarm system for residences that does not depend on the overloaded telephone system.

Don't hold off installing a security system in anticipation of a security service via cable TV. Some sort of interface equipment will most likely be available that will convert signals from your present security system so that they can be accepted by the cable.

Chapter VI

APARTMENT

HOUSE

SECURITY

The best way to introduce you to the subject of making apartment houses secure is to contrast a secure building with a "defenseless" building. The former is characterized by a sense of community. The tenants know each other, visit each other, their children play together—in the hallways and in front of the building—and they move about the building freely. The building, even if old, is well maintained. If there is an unusual noise in a corridor, apartment doors pop open and people look out. The special mark of a secure building is the attitude of the residents toward strangers; strangers will have questions such as this one directed at them: "Can I help you find whom you're looking for?"

A defenseless building is characterized by a sense of isolation. Each tenant retreats into his apartment and ventures out as infrequently as possible. The lobby, hallways and staircases are deserted. A stranger could enter the building and wander about without a single person accosting him. Even if newly constructed, the building will wear rapidly, perhaps showing signs of vandalism. All of the apartment doors are equipped with two or three locks. If someone is attacked in a hallway, no one even bothers to call the police.

No need to ask which kind of building you would prefer to live in. How to create a secure building is the thrust of this chapter. In part, new locks and other hardware are often needed. But the prime ingredient is still that scarce commodity, self-discipline—plus another essential human characteristic, leadership. Without these, a massive expenditure on security hardware sufficient to turn the building into an apparent fortress will not make it secure. With leadership stimulating self-discipline in each resident of the building, it doesn't take much to make the oldest of buildings very secure.

Tenants Association Essential

Before a multiple dwelling can be made secure, the tenants must band together and form an association. Even if there is no present security problem and no concern that criminals will ever invade the building, it makes a lot of sense to form a tenants association. Few landlords pay much attention to the complaints of individual tenants, especially in those cities in which desirable housing is scarce. But even in New York, with its great shortage of desirable apartments, tenants associations are able to force the toughest of landlords to correct deficiencies such as poorly maintained elevators, infrequently painted or cleaned lobbies and hallways, burned-out lighting, surly, drunken or inefficient building employees, and inadequate garbage collection. In other words, a tenants association can do a lot toward making a building more livable, one in which the tenants can take pride and not be ashamed to invite guests into.

The Nature of the Threat

Before going on to describe just what a tenants association can do to make a building secure, I will define the nature of the criminal threat to apartment buildings. For most buildings, the criminal threat consists of a very rare burglary that all those except the victim shrug off. At the other end of the spectrum is a state of sheer terror.

Indoor mugging is far and away the major contributor to such terror. Muggings are only one form of indoor crime, but they are the ones that terrify more people. Rapes are comparatively rare and, like most indoor murders and assaults, involve acquaintances or members of the same family and take place inside of apartments.

On a quantitative basis, indoor mugging does not loom large. In 1970, for the first time the New York Police Department began compiling "Robberies, indoor, residential," as a separate category (so it can't be compared with previous years, but it is surely way up). The *reported* number was 15,451, which includes indoor purse-snatchings. That's less than 10 percent of the number of reported burglaries and about 16 percent of the reported car thefts. The "reported" is important. There is good evidence that the number of unreported muggings may equal or exceed that of reported cases, whereas in car thefts, for example, it is believed that far fewer than 10 percent of incidents are unreported.

The impact of muggings is another matter. A car theft is an annoyance; a burglary is a shock; but a mugging is a trauma. All muggings are accompanied by display of weapons or threats of violence. One mugger, dissatisfied with what he found in his victim's purse, threatened to carve his initials in her face. So she fished another $5 out of her brassiere.

It's hard to come up with a qualitative picture of the indoor mugger. Analysis of arrest reports shows that he's a slightly older criminal than the outdoor mugger and more successful in evading arrest. One police official told me that, contrary to popular belief, the mugger is not commonly a drug addict. He finds that the drug addict, debilitated by his habit, tends more to larceny from stores and burglary from apartments.

There is no racial or ethnic breakdown available on those arrested for mugging. But the police in New York don't hesitate to indicate privately that most of the muggers are from minority groups. Many if not a majority of the victims of muggers are themselves black or Puerto Rican. Because of despair or doubt that much would be gained, it is apparent that many blacks and Puerto Ricans never report that they have been robbed—especially if they were not harmed physically.

Although there are no organized gangs or "syndicates" among muggers, experts who have interviewed confessed or convicted muggers are convinced that there is a grapevine among them. Once an attractive building is found defenseless, the word soon circulates among muggers—and burglars too.

A most interesting theory about indoor muggings comes from Oscar Newman, an architect, and his staff of sociologists and psychologists who are studying apartment-house security under a federal grant. They find that often a transient relationship is set up between mugger and victim, that frequently the victim implements her (most of the victims of muggings are women) victimization by in a sense "cooperating" with the mugger. The investigators believe that the mugger is encouraged by this cooperation, and when given a choice, always chooses the cooperative victim. The act of cooperation or "acquiescence" takes various forms: the victim holds the front door open for the mugger; or on finding a suspicious-looking young man waiting at the elevator, opts to enter the elevator with him despite her apprehension; or when an elevator door opens revealing a suspicious-looking young man, enters the elevator instead of letting it pass. Nearly all the women who had been mugged said that despite their apprehension they did not avoid the confrontation because, as one put it, "It would have been an insult to the man."

On the assumption that the majority of apartment dwellers are more concerned with deterring than insulting the potential mugger, what can be done to make apartment houses secure against muggers and purse-snatchers, and therefore, much more secure against the rare rapist and the many who burglarize apartments and mailboxes?

Let's first put limits on one obvious deterrent, the police. Does the automatic and near universal cry for "more police" following a mugging make any sense? Of course, more police would help. Yet it is obvious that more police will not be appointed. And if municipalities can't pay for the big raises commonly demanded by their uniformed employees, the number of police may actually decline through attrition.

However, even if the number of police were increased, it would have little effect. At least five and maybe more men have to be added to the force to produce one *visible* patrolman. The mathematics of it are simple. In most cities, there are twenty-one tours in a 168-hour week. Since each patrolman stands only five eight-hour tours a week, we need at least 4.2 policemen to man a given beat during the week. When vacations, sick leave, supervision and court appearances are factored in, it is obvious that about *six* men have to be added to cover one outdoor beat. And even if the police all patroled *indoors,* how could the small fraction of men on duty at any given time cover all of a municipality's multiple dwellings?

The police, at least in New York, are starting to pay more

attention to the indoor mugger. As part of his plan to make the police more effective, Commissioner Patrick V. Murphy has assigned six or more plainclothesmen to each precinct head (normally, plainclothesmen are part of the independent detective force). Some precinct commanders have assigned walkie-talkie-equipped plainclothes teams to buildings notorious for muggings. And they have made arrests. It only takes one or two arrests of muggers to produce a dramatic drop in muggings in a building, which would confirm that there is indeed some form of grapevine among indoor muggers.

The Security Evaluation

Now that I have demonstrated that reliance only on the police is not sufficient to make a building secure, what steps should a tenants association take to make their building secure?

First, the association has to enlist the support and cooperation of each tenant in the building. Meetings and frequent bulletins are essential. However, even if everyone is cooperative, the tenants in a building will not raise its level of security if they don't know what to do. The tenants association has to prepare a list of security rules and issue a copy to each tenant and each new tenant who moves in. A model set of such rules has been appended to Chapter II, "Commonsense Measures."

However, preparation of these rules is difficult if the authors are not aware of the strengths and weaknesses of the building in regard to security, and such knowledge can be gained only from a survey of the building by a professional trained in security. In most parts of the country, it is very difficult to find such a professional. One of the few places where professional evaluators are available is New York.

Free security evaluations are performed by the New York Police Department. In most parts of the city, that means waiting for the small Premises Protection Squad to send a man around. And since the primary function of the squad is to advise commercial establishments, you might have to wait a long time. But if you happen to live in the Twenty-fourth Precinct of the West Side (86th to 110th streets, Riverside Drive to Central Park West), it's very easy to obtain an evaluation. The innovative precinct head, Deputy Inspector Richard Di Roma, has set up teams of evaluators who will appear within a few weeks after a request. They follow up with a report to any tenants association in the building. Other precinct commanders are emulating Inspector Di Roma. Hopefully, this concept will spread to other cities.

To find out what such an evaluation is like, I accompanied Patrolmen William Allison and Charles Fornuto as they conducted an evaluation at 318 West 100th Street. Robert Sandoval of the tenants association there had requested the evaluation because two elderly women had been mugged simultaneously by three young men when they went down together to check their mailboxes one afternoon in January, 1971.

The evaluation was quite thorough. Working from a detailed checklist, we began on the roof. The required steel ladder from the next and slightly higher building onto the roof encouraged any potential intruders. The two metal doors that led from the roof into the fire stairwell had sturdy "eye" hooks fastening them from the inside. However, Allison indicated that slide bolts were better and that the knobs should be removed from the outside of the doors to make them even harder to pull open.

The roof-level stairwell was quite dark, which was a matter of concern to those on the top floor. All the other stairwells were comparatively well lighted.

Apartment House Security

Because the irregularly-shaped corridors provided several places of concealment, Allison recommended that concave mirrors, similar to those installed on elevators, be mounted at strategic points in the corridors and lobby so that anyone who attempts to conceal himself would be revealed.

The basement was a special problem. The super lived on that level, so he blocked the basement elevator door after 8 P.M., which was good. However, he and his wife claimed that the moist air from the laundry was very objectionable, and therefore insisted that the door to the laundry could not be left open. Result? The women in the building were afraid to use the laundry, which had unbarred windows opening out on the backyard. Aside from the unbarred windows, the basement was fairly secure. To my surprise, Allison gave the building a "fair" rating, claiming it was "like Fort Knox" compared to many other buildings in the precinct.

Several weeks later, Inspector Di Roma appeared with Allison before a meeting of the tenants. The articulate inspector fielded the standard demands for more police with explanations of what the department and the Twenty-fourth Precinct in particular were doing to improve security.

Di Roma pleaded with tenants to report all crime so that he could find out where to place his forces. Later, Allison told me that at a prior meeting with tenants of another building he had been informed that several women in the building had been molested, yet no reports of sexual crime had ever been received. After talking to the assembled tenants, he found that no less than fifteen women had been molested or raped and that everyone knew the offender, a fellow tenant. Allison marched them all down to the precinct house, got them to fill out complaints, and arrested the man, who was subsequently convicted.

Allison's strongest recommendation at 318 West 100th Street, that a tenant patrol be set up, was shelved. But many of his other suggestions were implemented. The tenants association initially collected $5 per apartment. Out of these funds, they bought heavy slide bolts for the roof doors. The outer knobs were removed too. It would have cost only $120 to move the mailboxes from the dark alcove out to the bright lobby. A metal "lip" was installed on the entrance door so that the lock can't be forced with a knife. The association wrote to the landlord asking that the intercom be upgraded and that the rotting fire hoses be replaced (one of Allison's offhand, nonsecurity suggestions). Next to come were bars on the laundry-room windows.

One of Allison's recommendations would be hard to implement. He suggested that the tenants approach the landlord with an offer to share the cost of nonmandated security measures. I've spoken to several landlords with small holdings about such arrangements, which they rejected. They claimed that they are either losing money on their buildings, especially rent-controlled apartments, or not making enough to justify any further investment. Bitterly, they spoke about the increasing rate of abandonment of residential buildings, now totaling into the thousands.

The best security devices in the world are useless if the tenants don't respect them. Can anything be done about a tenant who, for instance, persistently allows visitors in the front door without checking through the intercom? Moral suasion is the only real answer. In New York, there is an involved procedure by which tenants can organize and petition for the eviction of a tenant who is a great nuisance. It's a rarely applied procedure—usually only for noisy or unruly tenants, never yet for those who violate security regulations. However, merely going around and collecting signatures on a petition might scare some nuisances into following the rules.

How do you arrange for a security evaluation if you don't

live in New York City? I would start with the local police. Even though few police departments have formally organized premises protection squads, many experienced members of the police force will have done enough investigating of crime in apartment buildings to be in a position to offer useful suggestions.

If the local police can't help, I suggest that you contact one of the major industries in town. Nearly every large company has a director of security or security officer. Often he is a former policeman, FBI agent, commander of military police or some form of retired "peace officer." Perhaps a tenant in the building works for the company in question, which would simplify arranging for a visit. The security expert will most likely volunteer his services, but if he charges, the fee will probably be a bargain.

If neither of the above sources proves fruitful, an alternative is a local master locksmith. In anticipation of landing some business, the locksmith would most likely not charge a fee. However, if he does, it would probably not exceed $10 per hour. Since locksmiths are in the business of selling locks and related hardware, the tenants association has to consider any locksmith's recommendations in this light. Nevertheless, I suggest that most of his recommendations will be reasonable both in concept and cost.

"Standard" Security Requirements

There is still another source of security evaluators. Every municipality has a building code—and inspectors to enforce it. If a tenants association can induce the local building department to send an inspector to go over the building, he will most likely uncover many and varied violations.

Because building codes began to evolve long before security was delineated as a problem or when the problem was much less critical, security generally receives scant and scattered treatment compared to such other serious requirements as fire protection, overcrowding and adequate heat and light. Actually, enforcement of the building code and other city regulations could lower security. For example, the closing down of polluting incinerators in certain cities now forces many tenants to carry their garbage down to the basement, where they are loath to go. On the other hand, this does permit locking of the incinerator closets, in which muggers sometimes lurk.

Because of the codes' necessary emphasis on danger from fire, the building inspector may insist on fire-protective features that also lower security. The inspectors look for locked doors on roofs and padlocked gates on windows leading to fire escapes. In New York, if they find the former, they remain on the premises until the lock is removed—even if they have to call the police emergency squad. If they find the latter, they will issue a violation to both landlord and tenant.*

Building inspectors can also be expected to make many positive recommendations with regard to security. Depending on the building codes in your locality, here are some of the items checked by building inspectors:

• A lockable building front door with a key issued to each tenant.

• A peephole in each apartment front door—and sometimes in the back door as well.

• Well-lighted front entrance, lobby and corridors.

• A mirror in one corner of the elevator that permits someone outside to tell if a suspicious-looking person has hidden

---

* To avoid the latter violation, tenants should install the only security gate approved in New York by the Board of Standards and Appeals for use on fire-escape windows. (See discussion of gates for fire-escape windows in Chapter III.)

in an obscure corner of the elevator (few elevators these days are large enough for anyone to hide in).

• A good lock on the front door of each apartment.

• A hollow metal front door that resists fire for some specified time (at least an hour), but which also resists break-in.

• A buzzer-door-opener system.

In New York, new buildings must be equipped with a phone intercom to the front door. Older buildings are not even required to have a bell-and-buzzer system. Outside, there must be two lighting fixtures. Inside, the lobby, hallways and interior fire escapes must be lighted by at least 10 watts' worth of incandescent bulb per twenty-five square feet.

Because security is rarely one of the priority aspects of building inspection, it's essentially futile to attempt to force your landlord to put in the required level of lighting in hallways and lobby. The practical solution, according to one police expert, is for the tenants to band together, chip in a few pennies each and replace present inadequate light bulbs with ones of higher wattage. A rare landlord might discover the switch and then return the building to its former low light level (because his electricity bill has gone up). If this happens, the tenants can invite building inspectors in to slap a violation on the landlord.

New York City's administration apparently makes it easy to report building violations for security—or any other reason. All one has to do is call WO 4-3000. It's supposed to be manned 168 hours a week. In wintertime, however, New Yorkers should not expect any action on a security violation: the three hundred "inspection units" (one man per unit mostly, but two men in the ghetto areas to protect each other) are overloaded with complaints about heating violations. According to an expert study, New York needs at least twelve hundred building-inspection units to halt urban blight, much less get around to security. Now, due to "administrative delays," it may take up to three months before anything happens after a violation has been detected by an inspector.

The same expert study of manning requirements for enforcing building codes reported that no major city in the United States has enough building inspectors to prevent urban blight.

Written Recommendations

No matter who is the source of the security evaluation, make sure that the expert's recommendations are presented in written form. If the expert is volunteering his time, it makes sense for one member of the tenants association to take down each of his recommendations, type them out and then present the document to the expert for approval. Even if the expert as a matter of routine prepares written recommendations, his verbal comments and suggestions should be noted down at the time and written up. For one reason or another, the expert may take weeks to present his formal recommendations. In the meanwhile, the tenants association could be putting some of his suggestions into force.

Tenant Patrols

Only a small minority of buildings can afford doormen or guards, and few neighborhoods will join in an effort to support the uniformed street patrols that are now so common in Manhattan. Practical alternatives are tenant patrols or the electronic equivalents of doormen.

To find out how to organize a tenant patrol, I went to the top expert on tenant patrols, Charles J. Owens, a very articulate ex-housing project manager, who has been assigned by the Housing Authority to the full-time job of organizing tenant patrols in all 173 projects housing over 600,000 New

Yorkers. The deficit-ridden Authority just can't afford any more Housing Police.

Owens and his two "consultants," William Byrd, the black tenant who invented the patrols, and Edwin J. Kaufman, another tenant, meet with interested tenant groups and try to find a "concerned individual" to appoint as tenant supervisor for the project. The Housing Authority can offer what few tenant associations in privately owned buildings can: money. These supervisors earn $2.50 an hour for up to twenty hours of duty per week.

The supervisors then organize other interested tenants using noncash incentives such as brightly colored jackets, identification buttons, certificates of service, award dinners and even clubrooms. As Owens put it, "We're trying to duplicate the small-town volunteer fireman's association."

To find out how a tenant patrol operates, I visited De Witt Clinton Houses in Spanish Harlem early in 1971. The supervisor then was a self-confident Puerto-Rico-born machinist named Henry Cintron. A widower with four children, Cintron was also head of the local tenants association and was the local scoutmaster. Those on duty usually patrol in pairs (at Van Dyke Houses a tenant patrolman on duty by himself was mugged). Mostly, the tour of duty consists of sitting at a bridge table in the lobby of the building. Each desk is equipped with a visitor's book and a plug-in phone paid for by the Housing Authority. All strangers are asked to sign the book. Some patrols start by searching the enclosed stairwells before they go on duty in the lobby. In several projects, the patrol also checks the parking lots occasionally to make sure no one is tampering with the cars.

Most of the on-duty tenants that I saw were middle-aged housewives. Cintron told me that they were the most dedicated. And when a man joins the patrol, it's usually at the urging of his concerned wife. Many retirees take their two-hour shifts with the younger tenants. In one project, an octogenarian is a member of the patrol.

Chief Dan Daly of the Housing Police told me that he welcomes the tenant patrols. Nevertheless, there has been some friction. Some patrolmen think the tenant patrols are "spying" on them, while some members of the tenant patrol criticized the Housing Police. As one tenant said, "We don't see much of the Housing Police. They have girl friends in the project, and they stop off for a cup of coffee, a beer, a little love!" Also, tenants complain that once a tenant patrol is organized in a building, the Housing Police spend less time in it (perhaps because the crime rate usually drops sharply where there is an effective tenant patrol).

Tenant patrols are like that childhood game in which for every two steps forward, you risk taking one back. For every two or three patrols that Owens sets up, one disbands. And that's what happened at De Witt Clinton Houses. By late 1971, the once-effective tenant patrols in some of the buildings had all but disbanded.

So far, far fewer than half of the buildings in housing projects have patrols. Nevertheless, the concept of tenant patrols is reaching out. Tenant associations in some of the many private projects in the city have called Owens for advice,* and he has also advised housing authorities in other cities. In Stuyvesant Town, a large privately-owned housing project in lower Manhattan, tenants formed a volunteer auxiliary police force that patrols the grounds in uniform. They have been effective in cutting down on indoor crime as well.

The Electronic Equivalent of Doormen

If a tenant patrol can't be started up or kept up in a building, then an alternative is the electronic equivalent of door-

---

* If you want to call Owens for advice, his number is (212) 433–6030.

men or guards. Unfortunately, the economics of electronics are lagging way behind the technology. One of the few professionals to come up with cost-cutting techniques is David Kaye, engineering vice-president of L. J. Loeffler, Inc., a long-time New York City manufacturer of apartment-house intercoms. He has invented the BPT system of superimposing voice communications on the aged, inadequate wires that carry the signals for the old-fashioned bell-and-buzzer systems for opening entrance doors.

Installations of BPT systems should run about $35 to $40 per apartment, which includes the handset, and only take a few weeks per building. Unfortunately, installations usually run 30 to 40 percent higher and take much longer because tenants don't cooperate. They have to either be present to let the installers into their apartments, or leave their keys with the super or a neighbor.

If viewing could be added to voice communication, then the door-opener intercom would obviously be a much better electronic doorman. Back in 1961, Bell Television (no relation to the Bell Telephone System) introduced the Watchdog TV system, which added a closed-circuit television (CCTV) to the standard voice intercom. The first installation was at 415 Argyle Road in Brooklyn. The camera was mounted over the buzzer board in the lobby, and each apartment was equipped with a box containing a small TV receiver, simple controls and the two-way voice communicator.

For a few years, Bell made good headway with the system. About thirty installations were made, mostly in New York and its suburbs, but also in Boston, Chicago and San Juan. Loeffler's Kaye conceived a worthwhile advance: he put the TV viewing tube on a constant trickle current which kept it warm. This meant that as soon as the visitor pushed the buzzer button, the picture appeared instantly in the apartment. (As a result, the Loeffler arrangement came to be known as the "mother-in-law system" because the occupant could see who was downstairs without the guest realizing he was under surveillance—and then not open the door.)

Although Loeffler sold six of its CCTV intercoms, not one was installed in New York City proper. Another supplier, Auth Electric Company, couldn't sell a single one, and withdrew from the business. By this time it was apparent that there were deficiencies in Bell's Watchdog TV system. Because it doesn't use solid-state components, it requires frequent service. I examined one of the Bell installations closely (by coincidence, one was in the building next door to the one in which I live). The system went in in 1964. The first problem was the orientation of the camera: it was mounted vertically over the buzzers, which meant that the viewing mirror was facing upwards at a 45-degree angle. As a result, dust could collect on the mirror. The mirror I saw was filthy. I observed the monitors in two apartments. Both had the original TV picture tubes. Although the picture tubes lit up, they were in such poor condition that any visitor was unrecognizable. The system had not been maintained for years. However, the voice portion still worked and the tenants relied on that.

Unfortunately, CCTV intercoms now have a poor reputation in the real-estate community, particularly in New York. This is unfortunate because the CCTV approach has one great advantage over voice-only systems: the occupant of the apartment is forced to see who is signaling for entrance. It is apparent that many apartment dwellers, especially younger people, automatically push the door-opener whenever their apartments are buzzed without checking the identity of the visitor, and this makes for poor security.

If you are in a position to push for installation of a door-opener system (either as a resident of a cooperative or condominium or as a member of a tenants association), try hard for CCTV. The cost per apartment—from $200 to $300 initial installation plus $5 to $6 per month maintenance depending on the number of apartments—may seem high (it would be even higher if there is no master antenna in the building) but the added security is well worth the price. There are at least three sources available: Loeffler; Holmes Video Surveillance Corporation, New York, which took over Bell Television; and a small firm in Canoga Park, Calif., named DJC Electronics. Guido Danek, vice-president of Holmes Video, told me that if and when his company reintroduces the Watchdog TV system it will be completely redesigned with trickle current on the TV picture tube and one more desirable feature: automatic shut-off of the picture after thirty seconds to save the tube.

For the majority of apartment buildings, installing a CCTV or even a voice-only intercom means working out some equitable arrangement with the landlord.* Fortunately, there is an approach by which a good voice-intercom system can be installed that puts little or no burden on the landlord. The major phone company, the Bell System, and the next largest, General Telephone and Electronics, both offer an intercom door-opening system based on the phones now in apartments. It calls for installation of a handset plus buzzer system at the entranceway. Signals from the entranceway handset go back to the local exchange, then bounce back to the apartment queried. If the apartment phone is in use, a distinctive beep is superimposed on the conversation. The

---

* In New York, landlords can be "forced" to install a voice intercom if 51 percent of the tenants vote for it. However, landlords have been slow to install this useful deterrent because they claim that it takes so long for the Rent Commission to approve the rent increases that reimburse them for the investment in the intercom.

tenant then asks his caller to hold, pushes one of the little buttons on which the handset rests and is automatically connected to the visitor. To let the visitor in, the tenant dials 4 on his phone, then resumes the outside conversation.

General Telephone has been quite successful with its Enterphone: there are over 150 installations. The Bell System has far fewer. In New York, the Bell System intercom has mostly been installed in housing projects. I went back up to the De Witt Clinton Houses to see one. Despite their low incomes, the tenants of these eight buildings voted overwhelmingly for the intercom, even though it costs each one $2.85 per month extra. (That's over 5 percent of the rental of some of the apartments, which shows how concerned these residents are about security.)

Certain benefits were immediate. Because the mailboxes are now behind a locked door, thefts of welfare and Social Security checks have stopped. (This is a neighborhood in which U.S. postal drop boxes at street corners are broken into at Christmas time.) Also, thefts of light bulbs in hallways have practically ended. In the six months prior to installation of the intercoms, eight thousand light bulbs had to be replaced in the entire project, which meant a lot of wasted maintenance manpower. Missing light bulbs also mean lower security.

The installation at De Witt Clinton Houses revealed unfortunate deficiencies in the system. First, it took many months for the system to be debugged. Complete dependence on a single source of maintenance could become a big deficiency. It often took days for individual phones to be put back into service. Sometimes the entire system went out and stayed that way for days. During the extended strike of phone repairmen in New York State, the system deteriorated rapidly. (If the phone company in a town has a poor reputation for service, I would not recommend installation of a door-opening system based on the phones in apartments.)

When the tenants of a building are disciplined in using a reliable voice intercom system, it is very effective in eliminating most intruders. But it's a rare building into which an intruder can't make his entry merely by pushing one call button after another—until some tenant releases the front-door lock without inquiring. Once inside, the mugger can wait for his victim in many convenient spots: the mailbox alcove, the laundry room, incinerator closets or the stairwells. But the automatic elevator is far and away the most convenient place for a mugging: after the crime is completed, the victim is carried up and away while the mugger makes his escape down the staircase.

Making Self-Service Elevators Safe

Of course, those who live in the increasingly rare buildings with manned elevators are safe. But then they have to be concerned that all visitors are forced to use the elevators: one-way doors on fire stairs are the best and usually legal means.

Making automatic elevators more secure is not too costly. Being drawn down to the basement is what rightfully scares many women, and modifications to prevent this cost only a few hundred dollars, according to Ronald Vent, president of Serge Elevator Company, New York. Assuming that all other entrances to the basement are properly locked or barred, best by far is a key-actuated switch in the elevator that permits only key holders to get down to the basement. At one building with this arrangement, across the street from Columbia University, the residents, students and faculty members, don't hesitate to do their laundry in the middle of the night. (In many new luxury buildings, this problem does not arise: there's a laundry room on every level.)

Other modifications include a twenty-four-hour clock that can be set to eliminate basement stops after certain hours and a key stop that permits a building employee to eliminate basement stops. I live in a building in which the doorman who goes off duty at midnight stuffs a rubber insulator into a relay to inactivate the basement stop. (Later in this chapter I discuss still one more useful modification of elevator controls.)

At Stuyvesant Town, the elevators have been modified in one intelligent way: only passengers can signal stops on the way up. This means that those muggers who operate by entering elevators on the second or third landing can't board ascending elevators. This arrangement is an inconvenience for those who want to ascend from some level above the lobby. They have to go down to the lobby first.

Mounting cameras in all elevators for CCTV to be viewed by the doorman or on a monitor outside the elevator at lobby level has been done in many so-called luxury buildings. These systems, which cost in the thousands, are resented by some tenants who consider them too much like Orwell's "Big Brother."

Fake TV cameras simulating expensive CCTV installations in elevators have been mounted in some buildings. The fakes are also used at front entrances. These empty block boxes, which are widely used in department stores in combination with the real thing to deter shoplifters, cost as little as $50 each installed. They may have some deterrent effect, until a mugging takes place.

There is still another low-cost way to make self-service elevators more secure. Earlier in this chapter I mentioned Newman's studies, which indicate that women often sense that they may be mugged yet find it difficult to back out of the situation. If women could be provided with some valid excuse for getting off an elevator whenever a suspicious-looking young male boards it, they might be able to avoid many of the muggings that now take place in elevators.

A helpful deterrent for such situations is to mount a bulletin board next to the elevator entrance in the lobby and also at each landing. The opportunity to "check the bulletin board" is all many women may need to avoid staying in the elevator with the anxiety-arousing man. Of course, if he then steps out to remain with the woman, it's time to scream—and loud.

Making Mailboxes More Secure

Some muggers catch their victims unaware when they are opening their mailboxes. If the mailboxes are in the outer unlocked vestibule, outdoor muggers may invade there to trap their victims.

Moving the mailboxes behind a lockable door (or installing a lockable door between the street and the mailboxes to prevent burglarizing of the boxes) causes problems. How does the mail carrier get to the boxes? Often, he merely pushes the super's button or some button until he is let in. That in itself could lower security. Muggers know that the carriers do this and use the cry "postman" to gain entry into a building—then lie hidden until the housewife comes down for her mail.

To eliminate random pushing of intercom buttons by mailmen, Key Keeper boxes have been installed in the outer vestibules of many buildings. A Key Keeper is a heavy steel box, mounted in the wall or door frame, containing the door key attached to a wire on a retractable reel. The door to the box can only be opened by a special key that fits every Key Keeper box on the carrier's route. But if a bold mugger were to take that key away from a carrier . . .

Doormen and Uniformed Guards

If you can afford to live in a building with one, the prime security measure is still a doorman, or at least a guard at the door. A doorman should be more effective than a guard provided by a service because the former gets to know the tenants and their frequent visitors and will be more alert to intruders. On the other hand, if the doorman is often away from his post walking dogs, hailing cabs, collecting bets or moving cars from one side of the street to the other, then a guard who does not perform those little extras is a better deterrent.

Highly effective is a doorman who is required to announce all guests and deliveries. Unfortunately, this strong deterrent is often difficult to sustain, according to real-estate leader Edward Sulzberger, president of Sulzberger-Rolfe, Inc., because both tenants and their visitors resent being stopped by the doorman. "Why should the doorman intercept tenants of the building? Doesn't he recognize them?" I asked. Sulzberger replied, "You have to be a genius to differentiate many tenants from Bowery bums in dress, appearance and behavior!"

In some buildings, announcing of guests has been opposed vigorously by singles who want their overnight guests to remain anonymous.

Elevator operators in addition to doormen are, of course, nearly perfect deterrents against the muggers who operate in elevators. If there are no doormen but the elevators are manned, then one-way doors should be installed on the fire stairs (opening out at the ground level and roof, opening in in between) to force all visitors to use the elevators. This is a rather inexpensive modification, costing in the hundreds, and, contrary to wide belief, rarely violates the codes. (But before advocating one-way doors on fire stairs, I suggest that you check with your building department on local codes.)

Doormen and guards are no guarantors of security. Without trying very hard, I found two attended buildings in New York of the "better" variety that have attracted many muggers: Sutton House and a Mitchell-Lama co-op * on Columbus Avenue in Manhattan. The former, at 415 East Fifty-second Street, was once one of the most desirable addresses in the city—until it was hit by a rash of muggings and burglaries. Two doormen were supposedly in attendance a good part of the time, but they did not check strangers entering the building. A particularly blatant example of this occurred one Saturday afternoon in June, 1970. A young mugger bought a $2 bunch of flowers at a shop right in the building, told one lackadaisical doorman he was delivering flowers and proceeded without hindrance into an elevator where he was joined by a twenty-one-year-old coed. He stopped the elevator on a floor, pulled out a switchblade and demanded her money. She screamed, he grabbed her purse, which contained $8, and fled down through the basement.

The coed was the daughter of Mr. and Mrs. John H. Collins III. Shocked, the Collinses organized a drive to raise the security of the building. They circulated a petition and sent it to the owners, Goldman & DiLorenzo. They also sent copies with all 239 signatures (out of 290 apartments) to Representative Edward I. Koch and City Councilman Carter Burden. Congressman Koch called the owners and Councilman Burden called *Park East,* the community newspaper. *Park East* described the conditions in the building in its October 1, 1970, edition. Mrs. Collins also called the building-employees

---

* These are cooperatives for middle-income families set up under the Mitchell-Lama Act in New York State. They are not permitted to have doormen.

union about the ineffective doormen, but claims she got little encouragement.

The times favored the Collinses. They don't know if it was the recession or all the bad publicity, but for the first time since its erection over twenty-one years ago, Sutton House had vacancies. Within months, Goldman & DiLorenzo gave the building nearly all that the tenants asked for: two alert doormen around the clock; a guard at the back delivery gate whenever it is open; relocation of the switchboard one hundred feet so that it now stands at the front entrance; a new super; a resident building manager (result: no more drunken doormen); and a locked garage door. Muggings and burglaries have ended at Sutton House.

Poor architecture, not poor guards, is the problem at five-year-old 100 West Ninety-fourth Street. Although this high-rise Mitchell-Lama co-op fronts on Columbus Avenue, the entrance is on Ninety-fourth Street through a tightly gridded steel gate that opens into a roofed-over gazebo with the phone intercom on one wall. After the second locked metal gate opens, one takes twenty or so steps through an open plaza before making a right-angle turn into the lobby.

When muggings erupted in the building in late 1970, the tenant-shareholders voted to hire a guard, the $3-per-hour cost ultimately to come out of their pockets. Other than in summer, the guard can't be stationed in the exposed intercom area, so he remains in the lobby, supposedly observing the locked gate through a mirror.

It didn't work. Muggings actually increased after the guard was authorized, with some muggings taking place while the guard was on duty from 4 P.M. to midnight. Before 4 P.M., truants from the local junior high school slipped in to congregate in the deserted stairwells. Empty glassine envelopes told that they were shooting drugs.

One possible solution was recognized by the tenants: extend the lobby to enclose the intercom. But this would cost $15,000. They also considered some sort of closed-circuit television intercom system using Channel 6 on the receivers in each apartment, but rejected this as too expensive. (In the past, attempts to use home TV sets as monitors for TV cameras mounted at entranceways have failed. If the set isn't on, the tenant has to wait what seems to be an interminable thirty seconds. Also, the set is never near the intercom phone.)

Not far away from 100 West Ninety-fourth Street, guards are being used in an unusual way. West Ninetieth Street between Central Park West and Columbus had been plagued by burglaries and indoor and outdoor muggings. Most of the buildings on the block are converted brownstones with too few tenants in each to support guards. So the active block association has gotten the residents to chip in for a uniformed billy-swinging guard who patrols the street from 4 P.M. to midnight. It's been very effective. At least a dozen block associations on both the east and west sides of Manhattan have done the same.

Walkie-Talkies for Guards

Electronics has still another role to play in countering indoor (and outdoor) terror. Walkie-talkies have been used since 1970 by guards at some of the large complexes of Mitchell-Lama co-ops in the Bronx. In 1971, guards and doormen at some Manhattan buildings were equipped with walkie-talkies set to the same Citizens Band frequency as a transceiver manned by a civilian volunteer each evening at the Twenty-fourth Precinct house. The volunteers relay all messages for help to the police. Apparently, it's faster than calling the police emergency number, 911. The volunteer operators are members of City-Wide React, a group organized by a psychologist, Dr. William S. Wahlin.

Collective Security Systems

Many apartment dwellers have and will install security systems, mostly anti-intrusion but sometimes with fire detection as well. Good! However, such systems can be made far more effective if every tenant shares the cost of installation and maintenance, particularly so if the emergency signals can also be brought to the attention of some human monitor such as a doorman, super or building manager.

Collective security systems are available, both for new and existing construction. Both the Auth and Loeffler companies manufacture anti-intrusion systems for new construction in which the alarm signals are displayed on a large console. Over twenty new luxury apartment buildings in New York are equipped with Loeffler's Guard Alarm system in which a concealed switch on the entrance door of each apartment tells if the door has been opened. (These are all buildings of modern construction with interior fire stairs, so there is no need to install detection switches on windows.) All of these large buildings also have doormen, and the alarm signals are displayed on a large console at the doorman's station. In practice, the doorman knows each tenant by sight, which means that as each one enters or leaves the building, the doorman can set the alarm condition for each apartment—"on" as a tenant leaves, "off" when he returns. In the event of an alarm the doorman can either send another building employee up to investigate or call on a guard service to send an armed guard to check the apartment.

One of the few installations of Auth's Intruder Alarm is at the four-hundred-unit Trylon Plaza apartment building in Washington, D.C. This building does not have doormen, so each tenant has to arm the system by key before leaving. The alarm signal is displayed on a console in the apartment of the building manager. The Intruder Alarm is quite inexpensive (for new construction, that is): only $40 per apartment for a building with as few as thirty-four units.

Installing a collective security system for each apartment in existing construction could be quite expensive. The major cost is in pulling wires throughout the building, a time-consuming and messy procedure. Fortunately, there is a reasonable alternative. Holmes Communications Corp. has developed a collective system that uses the same signal cable that carries TV signals into apartments from either a master antenna on the roof or a community antenna system (CATV). Fire as well as intrusion can be detected and the system also offers a panic button. The emergency signals are displayed on a large console. If the building has a doorman, the console is mounted at the doorman's station, otherwise in the super's or building manager's apartment.

If doormen are not on duty twenty-four hours, the system obviously is not a very reliable one: one can't expect the super, the building manager or members of their families to monitor the console twenty-four hours a day. So Holmes offers a worthwhile option: by adding a leased phone line, a local guard service can be signaled. The console would remain on the premises in a locked room, but the guard service would have the key to the room. This option would cost about $3 a month extra per apartment.

The total cost of the Holm-Com system is reasonable: for a hundred-unit building, about $180 per apartment for installation plus $15 per month per apartment for maintenance. The more apartments in the building, the lower the costs. The basic system handles up to five hundred apartments. Beyond that number, control of the system is taken over by a minicomputer. The computer-controlled system can handle thousands of apartments in a great complex. The Holm-Com system offers one valuable feature that would be hard to duplicate in a system that goes into a single apartment: automatic checking of the detectors in each apartment every five seconds. If the system senses that the detectors, arming or interface equipment in any apartment is not functioning properly, this condition is also displayed as an emergency.

"Defensible Space"

Most of the measures that I have detailed so far are designed to make existing buildings more secure. I've implied more than once that it is easier to make new buildings more secure by design, particularly in providing electrical cabling for security devices. Yet the opportunities to make new buildings more secure are balanced by less obvious pitfalls that can make a newly constructed building *very insecure*.

The close and complex relationship between architecture and security is the special study of the New York University Project for the Improvement of Security in Urban Residential Areas. Headed by architect Oscar Newman, the project has been supported by about $600,000 in federal funds spread over three years.

Newman has developed a concept called defensible space. His thesis is that the residents of a building can be stimulated to claim natural "territorial rights" to a building and the space around it. They assert these rights by "challenging" strangers, not in an obnoxious way, but by the simple device of asking, "Can I help you find whomever you're looking for?" Or, "If you'll tell me whom you're looking for, perhaps I can help you find them?" When people develop this challenging spirit, muggers and other intruders stay away, Newman claims. He doesn't believe in turning buildings into fortresses, much the opposite: he says that self-policed buildings are more livable and satisfying to the residents.

Newman came up with his powerful concept during his five years as a faculty member at Washington University in St. Louis. In association with anthropologist-sociologist Lee Rainwater, he began studying the infamous Pruitt-Igoe public housing complex. Pruitt-Igoe is to public housing what Tacoma-Narrows is to bridges—a total disaster! Designed by the renowned Minoru Yamasaki (the architect for the World Trade Center), Pruitt-Igoe was hailed at its opening in 1956 as an innovation: high-rise living for the poor. Yet within months it became apparent that something was very wrong with the design and placement of the forty-three buildings. The twelve thousand blacks living in them were not developing—and never did develop—any sense of community or belonging. Soon the buildings were overrun with robbers, burglars, pushers and street gangs. Pruitt-Igoe became an anarchy instead of a community. Tenants moved out as quickly as they could, even if they had to pay much higher rents for shacks.

Today, most of Pruitt-Igoe has been abandoned and boarded up, and soon all the buildings will be vacant. With one notable exception, perhaps. One building is fenced in; the fencing was put up to protect the tools and materials of construction workers repairing the building. The tenants pleaded that the high fence be left standing. That building is far more secure—and experiences less vandalism—than any of the others.

The Pruitt-Igoe phenomenon has surfaced in some New York City housing projects, notably in Van Dyke Houses in the Brownsville ghetto. To prove that it's the peculiarities of the architecture of Van Dyke Houses that is to blame, Newman studied another project, Brownsville Houses, just across the street. A complex of three- and six-story buildings opened in 1947, Brownsville is essentially a mirror image of high-rise Van Dyke in all aspects of population, including density. Yet the rate of muggings (robberies) in Van Dyke is 264 percent greater than in Brownsville—except for the nine three-story buildings in Van Dyke. In those, the crime rate is much lower. So most of the crime is concentrated in the thirteen high-rises, which are each fourteen stories high.

There are other important architectural differences between Brownsville and Van Dyke besides building height. The main entrances to the Brownsville buildings face the street, while the Van Dyke entrances are all off the street (so residents regard the walkways at night as among the most dangerous portions of the project). The streets around Brownsville profit from the on-street entrances and are much safer. The long corridors at Van Dyke contrast with short corridors at Brownsville.

At Brownsville, the cruciform shape of the buildings, plus their rather close "packing," has encouraged the residents of each building to assert territorial rights over certain portions of the common grounds. At Van Dyke, the more abundant grounds are not associated with any one building.

The crime rate is not the only significant measure of the sharp contrast between Brownsville and Van Dyke. Although the latter is newer, was designed for wear and with better materials, it requires far more maintenance than Brownsville. For instance, the breakdown rate of elevators at Van Dyke is 245 percent higher than for the older elevators at Brownsville. Also, wasteful turnover of apartments is six times higher at Van Dyke.

Newman and his staff are doing much more than identifying the design elements that make for higher crime and vandalism: they have been allotted over $2 million by the

Department of Housing and Urban Development (HUD) to apply their proposed solutions at four New York housing projects. They started with a $500,000 tenant-approved modification of Clason Point Gardens, a low-density project made up of barrackslike two-story buildings in the Bronx. The money was spent on: resurfacing the institutionlike cinderblock walls of the buildings to make them look like the private-family homes that surround the project; fencing in much of the project to limit severely the number of public paths through it (the tenants wanted a twelve-foot fence, but Newman got them to agree to a six-foot fence); low fencing behind each building to create backyards shared by eight to twelve families; creating little front yards with low brick walls; providing recreation and "congregation" areas for various age groups; and much better lighting for the remaining public paths.

Newman favors medium-density construction, but he concedes that high-rise construction is here to stay. Fortunately, he is sure that there are relatively low-cost ways to make existing high-rise construction much more secure and he is spending over $400,000 in HUD funds to prove his point. At the Bronxdale project, he is directing an extensive modification that should provide the tenants of the twenty-eight seven-story buildings with a strong sense of territory and ownership. First, the grounds will be reorganized to create subdivisions of two or three buildings. Low walls topped with fences will be built between buildings to limit access to a few points. CCTV cameras will be installed about the grounds, with their signals fed into the police room. To avoid any implications that the Housing Police are playing "Big Brother," the monitors will be observed by a salaried tenant.

All the lobbies will be modified to make them more "viewable" and to accept the $2.85-extra-per-month phone inter-coms supplied by the telephone company.

Finally, two clusters of three buildings each will receive special electronics. One cluster will have CCTV cameras mounted in the lobby and elevators. By means of a $5 adaptor, TV sets in each apartment will be modified to accept signals from the added cameras plus those cameras observing the grounds enclosed in that cluster. When a visitor buzzes an apartment on the intercom, the tenant can view him on Channel 3; mothers can observe their children playing in the central playground on Channel 10; and watch and listen to them in the elevators on Channel 6.

The other cluster will test Newman's original concept of the "audio window." Since the tenants strongly rejected Newman's original proposal to build narrow little windows into each apartment next to the door, he came up with the idea of an electronic equivalent. The audio window is a two-way "hearing aid" that enables residents to listen in on the corridor immediately outside their apartments and also to push a button and talk to those in the corridor. To simulate the effect of short corridors, these audio windows would be linked in groups of three or four so that any time one resident talked, his adjacent neighbors would be aware of but not hear the faint conversation. (Newman is still debating whether or not to add a cut-off button so that the neighbors can't listen in.)

In addition, residents would be able to listen in to the elevators and the elevators would be modified so that passengers could call out and be heard not only by any residents listening in on their intercoms but also via small loudspeakers mounted on each level over the elevator doors.

Another electronic modification should improve security in the project. At present, tenants in housing projects must call a central number to attract the local housing patrolman. At Bronxdale, the tenants will be able to call the local police room directly. If the man or men are out on patrol, an electronic device will transfer any local calls to their walkie-talkies.

After a year passes, Newman and his associates will analyze the crime statistics for Bronxdale, interview the tenants and then try to figure out what's best not only in terms of security but livability as well.

New high-rise construction can also be made much more secure, according to Newman, and at no great cost differential. He strongly opposes the conventional double-loaded corridors, those with apartments on both sides. Single-loaded corridors, open in milder climates and glazed in harsher climates, are inherently more secure. Any intruders are quickly spotted from the street or facing buildings. Extremely long corridors, single-loaded or double-loaded, dissipate any sense of community. To paraphrase Robert Frost, short corridors make good neighbors.

To make corridors even more secure, Newman suggests that each apartment have a very narrow window facing out on the corridor. If that is not done, he suggests the audio window as an alternative.

Staircases are a big problem. The old-style open staircases are more secure than the enclosed ones now required by law. (Newman has found that enclosed staircases are often the scene of those rapes by strangers that occur in high-rise apartment houses.) To make enclosed staircases more secure, he suggests that they exit into the lobbies near the front door and that they be equipped with one-way doors.

Watching Newman in action is an experience. I arranged for him to make an evaluation of 100 West Ninety-fourth Street. To impress the building's security committee, headed by Mrs. Gerald Pape, Newman entered the building through a basement door, using a credit card to loid the lock, and then came up behind the committeemen assembled at the front door. Then he asked each of the four committee members to station themselves at a different entrance, with a promise to meet them in five minutes at a designated apartment. Then he went outside. Sure enough, he was waiting for them five minutes later without having passed any of the committee members.

In Newman's opinion, the building was a "security sieve." He made recommendations, the total cost of which would run well below the $15,000 required to extend the lobby to enclose the gazebo as discussed earlier in this chapter. Here are three of his suggestions that could well be applied in many high-rises:

• Reset the timing on the garage doors so that they close in ten instead of ninety seconds.

• Adjust one of the elevators so that it can only go from the garage to the lobby and back and set the others so that they can't reach the basement. This would be a justifiable inconvenience to those who bring in a lot of groceries in their cars.

• Put key stops in the elevators so that the guard can stop an elevator and bring it back down in case someone slips past the guard or fast-talks him into allowing him entry. (This was the measure that led to two arrests at 560 Riverside Drive for "trespassing" and ended all muggings in that once vulnerable building—in which Newman himself formerly lived.)

Newman obviously made a strong impression, because two of his recommendations were accepted within days: adding a guard from 11 A.M. to 4 P.M. and making both guards direct employees of the building (Newman doesn't think highly of the low-cost guard services on which buildings depend). In addition, plans to hang drapes in the lobby have been dropped (while he was in the building he noted that the head of the "decorating committee" was measuring for drapes) since Newman urges high visibility both ways for lobbies.

In time, many of his other and more costly recommendations will be put into effect. The building is on its way to becoming a secure place in which to live. In contrast to five muggings in February, 1971, there have been no muggings and teenage truants no longer shoot drugs in the stairwells since the extra guard was hired.

Later, Newman spoke to me about the lessons of 100 West Ninety-fourth Street. He was motivated to make a proposal to the Justice Department that it organize "security clinics" for police and other experts so that they could do for thousands of buildings in other cities what he had just done in one hitherto defenseless building.

What are the chances of wide implementation of Newman's well-documented concepts? Some architects are already aware of them, and many more should be soon through the planned publication of *Defensible Space* by Newman.

Mayor Lindsay, high police officials and many other leaders in New York City have observed Newman's very persuasive slide presentation. In his speeches, Simeon Golar, chairman of the City Housing Authority, continually uses Newman's catchphrase "defensible space."

Because Newman is a consultant to HUD and the Justice Department, his ideas may be forced on some of the architects who design public housing or housing that is subsidized by government. When Newman is brought in early on a project's design, he claims that he does not have too much trouble convincing the principal architect to modify his plans to improve security. However, when asked to advise on completed plans, his suggestions, not too surprisingly, are resisted strongly. Ultimately, Newman's concepts will influence all American architects: he's been asked to write the section in the National Building Code on security.

Security for Brownstones

High-rises are not the only multiple dwellings with serious security problems. What about the many thousands of brownstones and other smaller apartment houses? Eight, twelve or even twenty tenants are just not enough to sustain a tenant patrol, and the cost of a doorman or guard would be prohibitive. The "mother-in-law" intercom would also be quite expensive, but at least it is within reason for some buildings—perhaps an initial installation charge of $400 to $500 per apartment, plus maintenance of $5 to $6 a month per apartment.

Oscar Newman recommends his audio windows for brownstones; intruders might draw attention merely by entering and are very likely to draw attention if they attempt to force open an apartment door or attack a victim in the corridors or staircases. Since an audio window works two ways, residents could inquire ("What's going on out there?") without even leaving their apartments. An installation of ten audio windows in a brownstone would cost about $50 per apartment, according to Newman's electronics consultant, Arnold Goldberger.

An effective deterrent for a block of brownstones is to hire a street guard through a block association as indicated earlier. Drawing on his investigations in St. Louis, Newman offers still another approach. There, residents of brownstones formed associations and literally purchased the streets from the city to form superblocks with limited access. In place of the standard grid pattern, they created serpentine street patterns within the superblocks that eliminated all through traffic. Crime dropped 50 percent.

Buying up streets is obviously a complicated legal maneuver. But blocking of streets may not be that difficult to arrange. In New York, it is done regularly on commercial thoroughfares such as Nassau Street and Madison Avenue.

The prime example of effective blocking of a residential street is on St. Mark's Avenue in the infamous Bedford-Stuyvesant section of Brooklyn. "A very bad block" before 1967, according to Wendell Rice, who had a lot to do with its restoration, the block is now so desirable that thirty to forty applicants show up for each rare vacant apartment. Funded mostly by the Astor Foundation, the restoration consisted of eliminating through traffic, building a plaza in the middle of the block with play equipment for children and benches for adults, providing diagonal parking space at either end and installing fifty bright street lamps.

The results have been spectacular. Crime has dropped off sharply, and landlords, who were abandoning properties on the block before, are now investing in them. The St. Mark's project has been copied to a limited extent in New York and also in other parts of the country. So it can be done.*

The means by which indoor terror can be countered are apparent: if meaningful deterrents are to be created, it will have to be done largely by the residents themselves acting as a group. There are many courses open, and all or most should be applied: taking advantage of available municipal services to bring in police evaluators and building inspectors; badgering landlords or boards of directors into eliminating

---

* In New York, to find out how to block off a street, begin by calling the Deputy Traffic Commissioner at EM 1–8000, extension 216.

violations and adding recommended security devices; chipping in to pay for those the landlord won't pay for; voting to put in a modern intercom with the knowledge that its cost will be borne by the tenants; hiring guards, either for inside the building or out on the street; setting up a tenant patrol; and most important of all, getting all the tenants to cooperate, especially by not letting uninvited strangers into the building. Vigilance, but not vigilantism.

Happily, this country is peppered with "concerned individuals" such as Cintron, Byrd, Dr. Wahlin, Sandoval, Mrs. Pape, Mr. and Mrs. Collins and many thousands of others who have what it takes to get their neighbors to band together. The result could be termed a healthy self-policed state. There is no other way.

Chapter VII

CHOOSING A HOME
WITH SECURITY
IN MIND

Part A · Security as a Factor in Choosing, Building
or Rebuilding a House

Security is important but not the factor of highest priority in choosing or building a house. First comes livability. If you sacrifice comfort or enjoyment or the opportunity to relax to any significant degree to gain security against criminals, you and your family will be so unhappy that ultimately you will sell your new home to find one in which you can live in peace.

After livability, the item of highest priority is security against fire. As demonstrated in Chapter V, "Electronic Security Systems," fire is a far greater threat to life, limb and property than the criminals who prey on houses and their occupants. If an older house represents a significant fire hazard, don't buy it—or be prepared to spend a lot of money modernizing the electrical power distribution system, replacing the heater and adding fire-detection devices. No matter how "fireproof" the materials of construction, check the quality of the fire department in any community to which you contemplate moving. Professional fire departments are generally superior to volunteer fire fighters. Measure the distance of your home to the nearest fire plug. If it is many hundreds of feet, then firemen would lose precious minutes in coupling extra lengths of hose to bring water to the fire. Remember, a few minutes of action can make the difference between a partial loss and a total loss.

It's easy to find out how much of a risk you are buying: distance to the nearest fire plug as well as the quality of the fire department are all factored into the rate you pay for fire insurance. Before buying a home, ask your insurance broker to quote rates on the new location.

If there are any children in your family, the quality of local schools is certainly a primary factor, outweighing security. However, the need for children to travel back and forth to school raises security problems that will be discussed later in this chapter.

All of a community's services should be considered by any home seeker: libraries, recreational facilities, hospitals and the rapidity with which ambulance services respond to a call for help. Besides fire protection, there are other services that relate to security. Obviously, the main one is the police department. Is the police force honest, efficient and *mobile?* Ask how frequently it patrols the street to which you are considering moving. How quickly does it respond to a call for help? Is the switchboard at headquarters adequately manned, especially at night, or does it take what seems to be hour-long minutes before someone answers a call at police headquarters or your local precinct house?

Even if you are satisfied that the police are efficient, what is the level of crime in the community? Avoid communities with high crime and vandalism rates, not just to lower the chance that you and your family will be victimized, but also because the value of your property could decline in proportion to the increase in crime and the fears that result.

Are the streets well lighted at night? Good lighting does drive street criminals away, most likely to concentrate elsewhere. But good lighting is not effective if the town's maintenance department doesn't replace burned-out bulbs.

Frequency of street cleaning is significant too, and for more than appearance. Sloppy streets are not only unattractive, but they invite intruders, just as a poorly maintained apartment building does. More importantly, a community that tolerates dirty sidewalks and streets is one that does not take any pride in itself.

In winter, rapidity of snow removal is significant. If the sanitation department can't cope with a heavy snowfall, you may not be able to get to work. More importantly, neither fire trucks, police cars nor ambulances will be able to respond to an emergency. And the police won't be able to patrol in cars, which in most communities means they won't patrol at all. If you choose a home site at the end of a long dead-end street, there is less chance that it will be cleared quickly.

Regulations against overnight parking of cars are very desirable. Then any intruders in parked cars attract attention from cruising police vehicles.

Carefully check into the history of catastrophes in the community. Avoid communities or neighborhoods with a history of brush fires, mudslides, earthquakes, flooding, tornadoes or hurricanes. Many of these catastrophes are not covered in ordinary home insurance policies, so you risk far greater economic loss than any burglar can inflict, aside from the risk to life and limb. I am amazed at the fatalistic attitude of otherwise rational individuals who will buy a home in or not move out of an area that is repeatedly devastated by brush fires, flooding or earthquakes.

Devastating earthquakes, incidentally, are not limited to California. The National Earthquake Information Center in Rockland, Maryland, claims that in addition to California, fifteen states could suffer "major destructive earthquakes." These are: Arkansas, Maine, Massachusetts, Mississippi, Missouri, Montana, Nevada, New Hampshire, New York, South Carolina, Tennessee, Utah, Vermont, Washington and Wyoming. The rest of the country, except for parts of Alabama, Florida and Texas, have a "reasonable expectancy" of earthquakes. Those who live below dams in areas subject to earthquakes take the greatest risk. During the great earthquake that struck Southern California in February, 1971, the Van Norman Dam in the San Fernando Valley came close to rupturing. Had this broad earthwork structure given way, thousands of homes would have been washed away. Few if any were covered by earthquake or flood insurance. Earthquake insurance is readily available, costs about the same as fire insurance, but it generally includes a 5 percent deductible.

Proximity to an Airport

Check also on proximity to airports—or plans to build an "international" airport or upgrade an existing airport for small planes to one that can handle big jets. Besides the air and noise pollution, there is also the remote but distinct danger of an airplane crashing into your home. (Damage caused by falling aircraft, and errant vehicles too, is covered under the most basic of home owner's policies.) The value of homes directly under the flight path of big jets can drop sharply. Some years ago I rented a summer home on Long

Island that was under the flight path of planes departing from JFK Airport. Frankly, the noise was frequently intolerable.

Blackouts and Brownouts

Investigate the reliability of the local utilities. If the power company can't handle peak loads in summer, causing brownouts or even blackouts, then you could suffer the discomfort of no airconditioning or the substantial loss of everything in your freezer. Obviously, your electronic security system won't work during a blackout if it doesn't have standby batteries, and it may not work at all or not very well when the voltage drops due to a brownout.

Check also into the reliability of phone service. Poor phone service is a discomfort at home and a disaster in business. Any security system that depends on communications over phone lines would be limited by erratic phone service. However, the community may offer cable TV service, which could lead to an excellent alternative to dependence for security on the phone service (see discussion at the end of Chapter V on the coming thing in security systems).

Secure Communities

In all parts of the country, we can see the development of planned communities in which "security" is a strong selling feature. These communities, usually retirement towns, are fenced in and offer twenty-four-hour guard service at the gate. Obviously, they are more secure than the average community. However, I would caution against weighing security too heavily in the decision to buy. First, you and your spouse or your family must really like the notion of living in an artificial community, not one that grew out of historical or economic necessity (except for the profit motive of the developer). You must accept the constraints set up by the developer; you must decide that it is desirable to live in a completely homogeneous community in which everyone is very much like his neighbor. If that pleases you, then the strong security is a plus.

Neighborhood Factors

Community factors are primary. Next, consider the immediate neighborhood. Privacy is desirable, unless you are so far away from any neighbors that they are not likely to hear or respond to calls for help. Very hilly streets are usually quite attractive, but they also make it more difficult for emergency vehicles to reach you, especially in winter.

The position of the house on the street affects its security. Because of higher visibility, a corner house is inherently more secure than one in the middle of the block or at the end of a dead-end street. Because dead-end streets are likely to receive less coverage from patrol cars, and passersby are rare, houses on such streets are especially attractive to burglars. A home on a curving street is less secure than a home on a straight street because of its lower visibility.

Does the rear of your home face a highway? I would reject such a location because of the noise, smell and pollution. It is also less secure. Some friends of mine in Westchester County live in an attractive home whose rear faces a major parkway. Twice burglars have pulled well off the highway, parked where passing county patrolmen could not see them easily from the highway, and worked their way through the shrubbery to burglarize this home successfully.

Speaking of major highways, make sure that there are no plans under way to run a major highway through the neighborhood. Aside from the undesirable ambiance, the existence of such a highway would most likely depress the value of any homes near it. Unless, of course, the land on which these homes stand has been rezoned for commercial purposes.

Check on any plans to widen the street. If the street is to be widened just a few feet, the municipality would reclaim only a few feet of lawn that belongs to it, which has been cultivated by those who live on that street. But a major widening may call for moving of all homes back a dozen feet or so. All home owners would be compensated, but not enough to make up for the inconvenience.

Proximity to public transportation is important—baby-sitters and other visitors may not own cars, and your children may be too young to drive (unless you or your spouse are prepared to chauffeur them about on all occasions). But check the route between the nearest bus or trolley stop and the home site. If it skirts a park or darkened or deserted streets, that's a point against that home site.

If your children are old enough to drive, you face another great hazard: the strong chance that they will be hurt or killed in a car accident. The death rate in motor vehicles for drivers fifteen to twenty-four years of age is close to twice that of drivers twenty-five to sixty-four years of age, and 40 percent higher than for drivers in the age group from sixty-five to seventy-four years, according to the National Transportation Safety Board. A survey made in Minnesota in 1969 showed that more than 60 percent of fifteen-to-twenty-four-year-old drivers killed in accidents had measurable amounts of alcohol in their systems.

These distressing statistics should impel any parents to investigate the attitude of any community into which they are considering moving toward reckless driving by youths and the illegal availability of alcohol to minors. The way your children behave behind the wheel of a car is mostly determined by the way you have brought them up. However, stern enforcement of speeding regulations by the police and the closing down of bars that serve underage customers helps to cut down on the toll of deaths in cars among youths.

According to the study by the National Transportation Safety Board, a federal agency, driving or riding in cars with other young drivers has become "the greatest hazard to survival which American youths must pass successfully to reach adulthood."

Favor communities in which "recognized" driver training courses are given in the high schools (completing such recognized courses earns substantial discounts on auto insurance). There is a correlation between the offering of such courses and lower driving deaths among youths. Though there is no proof that the courses themselves help youths to drive with greater care and responsibility, communities that offer such courses apparently encourage the proper attitude toward driving.

The makeup of the population of the neighborhood is important. The presence of many families with young children is practically a guarantee of a strong community spirit plus concern for and willingness to demand good service from the municipality. On the other hand, an aging population may be less energetic in asserting its rights and prodding the police, fire and sanitation departments to stay on the ball. But you will have to pay a penalty for a population with a high proportion of young children: higher taxes for schools.

Check into the prevalence of "block-busting" tactics by unscrupulous real-estate brokers. Block-busting, which has been declared illegal in many municipalities, is forced desegregation of a street that nearly always results in the hurried departure of all white families. The result is a return to segregation—a street inhabited by none but blacks or other minority groups. No one gains but the brokers. The white families sell out at prices well below what they might have gained before the block-busting. The newly arrived families are deceived in three ways: first, they pay more for the houses than they are now worth (with the brokers pocketing the difference); secondly, they soon find that they have moved into exactly what they paid dearly to leave, a seg-regated community; finally, they are often burdened with high mortgage payments they can't meet, so they lose the houses, which are then bought up at bargain prices by the brokers—for sale to another round of victims.

Criminals can thrive in the turmoil and destruction of com-munity feeling created by block-busting.

The Building Itself

After weighing all the community and neighborhood fac-tors, you must, of course, consider the house itself. Again, I stress that livability and fire resistance come ahead of security from criminals. Once you and your family have satisfied your-selfs on those, you can consider the following aspects, either in selecting an existing house or building a new one (some of these also involve protection against fire):

Architectural style. Although two-story and other multi-level designs offer more security because fewer openings are exposed at ground level, the ranch-style house offers far greater ease of exit in case of a fire—no one can be trapped upstairs. Because a ranch-style house is more spread out, there is a somewhat greater risk of burglary while the house is occupied—intruders could enter one portion of the house without disturbing those asleep at the other end. However, usually, only professional burglars are cool enough to break into an occupied house.

Entranceway. The entranceway should face the street or at least be highly visible from the street without any intervening shrubbery. At least two bright lights should be mounted above the entrance door (in case one burns out). The entrance and rear doors, and the door between the garage and house if the garage is attached, should meet the tests, standards and specifications detailed in Chapter III. After the closing, change all lock cylinders immediately. You don't know how many duplicate keys are in circulation.

Garage. Two lights should be mounted over the garage entrance. If the garage is separate from the house, the path between the garage and the house should be illuminated. If there is a rear exit to the garage, the door should be sturdy and equipped with a deadbolt lock or slide bolt. The driveway to the garage should not be so steep that you will have difficulty in either getting out or in during winter when snow falls or ice forms. Aside from the inconvenience, you may need to move a member of your family during an emergency. To make sure that the driveway is traversible, it may be equipped with buried electrical heating elements (you can add these at a cost of several hundred dollars). The garage may be equipped with an automatic electronic door-opening mechanism. Although some may argue that this convenience enhances security because you don't have to get out of your car at night and expose yourself to a concealed intruder, I believe this device lowers security. Too many of these devices are actuated by radio transmissions from low-flying aircraft and other random electromagnetic disturbances. Once your garage door is open, in your absence, a burglar would be able to attack the door between the garage and house with less chance of exposure. If you favor this convenience, consider mounting a remote door-opening control lock on a post outside the garage that you can reach from the driver's seat. (Ultimately, this form of wired door opener is cheaper because there is no transmitter to remove from one car and install in its replacement.)

Check to make sure that at least one of your cars, preferably the more desirable one, fits inside the garage. In cold or very damp weather, it makes sense to park at least one car in the garage to avoid all starting problems in the event you need to move a member of your family because of an emergency. Also, should a rash of car thefts occur, you should garage both cars, or the more valuable one in a one-car garage, and then block the driveway with the others as discussed in Chapter VIII, "Protecting Automobiles and Other Vehicles."

Landscaping. No trees should be planted so close to the house that an intruder climbing one could get into an upper window or drop onto a roof section that leads to an accessible window. No shrubbery should be planted so close to the walls that an accessible window is obscured from view. Remove from the side of the house any trellises and vines capable of supporting a climber, even an undersized teenager bent on vandalism.

Access to site. The site should be laid out so that a fire truck could be driven around to the rear of the house, either to put out a fire in the rear or a brush fire in the backyard.

Roofing material. If there is any hazard from local forest fires, the roofing material should be noncombustible, such as slate shingles, or treated in a manner that retards fire. If there is any risk of such widespread fires, the home should at least be equipped with outside hose connections and a heavy hose (not a garden hose) so that the roof and walls can be wet down quickly, And, of course, you should check carefully to make sure the roof does not leak.

Electrical distribution system. Overloaded electrical cables are one of the leading causes of fires. In the event that the electrical cabling must be updated, you should consider combining the electrical job with the installation of a security system. Both jobs require cable pulling, and it makes sense to avoid the inconvenience twice. It's also cheaper to do it simultaneously. At the same time, the added outdoor lighting and the concentrated lighting controls detailed in Chapter IV, Part B, could be incorporated in the rewiring job.

Security system. With increasing frequency, houses up for sale will be equipped with an electronic security system. Review Chapter V on desirable features of these systems before taking the present owner's assertion that the system is "foolproof" or "the best you can buy." In particular, if the system has been in service for more than five years, it is most likely obsolete in one or more respects. However, there are probably many salvageable aspects of an older system, such as the magnetic-switch detectors, cabling and noisemaker. Replacing the controls and moving the control box inside (by adding a delay feature) may not require a large expenditure. If the system is on rental or for lease, find out if the contract is transferable. Also check out the reliability of the dealer who services the system. Remember, a functional fire detection system can earn discounts on fire insurance.

Termites. Examine any wooden structure closely for evidence of damage from termites. Undisturbed termites working slowly can do far more damage than a burglar who moves quickly. "Dry rot" is another progressive form of destruction to which wooden homes are subject. (Many banks require an inspection for termites by a professional before issuing a mortgage. The charge is nominal.)

Additional fire protection. Every home should be equipped with at least one fire extinguisher in the kitchen, and an optional extinguisher in the basement if it contains an oil or gas heater. Mount fire extinguishers in plain view near the exit to the room, so that the extinguisher can be reached even if the fire starts in that room. Don't buy one of those little cans of extinguishing fluid that sell for a dollar or two.

Instead, buy a substantial extinguisher, but not one that is too heavy for a woman or older child to lift out of its wall mount and operate. Once you buy the extinguisher, show the other members of your family how it works. If you buy or build a home with more than one level, it makes sense to buy a chain or rope ladder for each upstairs bedroom. Typical prices for chain ladders are $18 for the fifteen-foot length (second-floor window) and $30 for the 25-foot length (suitable for a three-story-high widow).

Buried phone line. A buried phone line is not only more attractive than an overhead line, it is also far more secure. The professional burglar, aware that a home is protected by an automatic dialer, will cut an exposed phone line (although the better automatic dialers will signal an alarm if the line is cut). A house with a buried phone line rates an extra point. To bury a phone line, the phone company will charge several hundred dollars.

Professional Inspection

The nonsecurity factors listed here, plus many others, should be checked by a professional before you buy any home. Such inspections are performed on a fee basis by services throughout the country. These services retain experienced inspectors, usually licensed professional engineers with special experience in homebuilding, who are available on very short notice. Most of these services can be reached at any hour of the day or night. They will provide an experienced home inspector within twenty-four hours. If you call in the morning, the inspector will generally complete his thirty-minute to ninety-minute inspection before the end of the day. First, you get an oral report, followed up by a written report within three to five days. Usually the inspectors work alone, but you may be present if you so desire. Charges for this valuable service are one-tenth of one percent (0.1 percent) of the sale price of the home for those selling for $100,000 and up. Below that price level, charges are based on the size of the home, its proximity to the inspector and its price. However, the charge is rarely below $40. Look for these services under "Building Inspection Service" in your classified phone book.

Adding Security Features When You Rebuild a Home

If you restore or rebuild or add on to an existing home, you have an opportunity to incorporate many of the recommendations made here. It is certainly cheaper to add security features while building or rebuilding than at a later date. In particular, it is much easier to conceal or camouflage the wires from window and door detectors during construction than afterward. (Don't forget to increase your insurance coverage to protect your added investment.)

Special Considerations for Brownstones

Reconversion of brownstones and other town houses back into private homes is an increasingly common activity in New York, Philadelphia, Washington and many other older cities along the Atlantic Coast. These buildings, some of which are well over one hundred years old, were converted decades ago into rooming houses or small apartments. Although the basic structure may be sound, the rest of the building may be in such sad shape that it must be gutted before reconversion can begin. The cost of conversion can range up into the many tens of thousands.

Often, these four- or five-story buildings are not completely converted to one-family occupancy. Usually only two levels are retained by the owners, while the remaining floors are converted into luxurious apartments. Therefore, the owner has to consider such obvious security measures as voice intercoms, a secure front door, key keepers, audio windows, elevator controls and sprinklers on the staircases. He becomes the landlord, who is often the villain of Chapter VI, "Apartment House Security."

However, the prime security measure to be taken by those who buy old brownstones for reconversion is to check the credit of their contractor. All too often the small contractors who handle such conversions are poorly financed themselves. When they go bankrupt, the home owner will have to engage a new contractor, yet be stuck for bills incurred by the original contractor. I have friends who have experienced such catastrophes, and it resulted in added costs of tens of thousands, aside from delays of many months in moving themselves and their prospective tenants into the buildings.

Before buying or moving into an old brownstone, check the following security feature: the strength of the iron bars or grills on the ground-level windows, which may be tested by using a crowbar in the same manner as a burglar would. Since nearly all town houses are attached, it is easy to gain access to the roof from adjacent buildings. The roof doors should be secured from the inside by sturdy slide bolts. The original doors to each apartment will most likely be made of wood. Unless these doors are the sturdy doors manufactured decades ago, they will not withstand attack. They should be replaced with metal doors, even if these modern doors and frames are less attractive or do not blend with the architectural style.

Security in Proportion to Risk

The thrust of this chapter is obvious. Security must be factored into the decision to select, build or rebuild a house in proportion to the risk. Where the risk is low, security is definitely a minor factor. However, if the risk is high, protecting against every eventuality could greatly raise the cost of your home and might even result in neglect of that greater danger, fire. In addition, construction of a "fortress" may result in a home that is so unattractive, uncomfortable and repellent to visitors that it soon palls on the occupants.

Part B · Security as a Factor in Choosing
an Apartment

Security is now becoming one of the important criteria in selecting a building in which to rent or buy an apartment—particularly if you are a woman living alone or only with small children.

In preparing the chapter on "Apartment House Security," I addressed present tenants of a building. Nevertheless, a reading of Chapter VI should provide many hints, suggestions, recommendations and even outright fiats on selecting a new apartment. You don't want to move into a building—particularly if purchasing a cooperative apartment or condominium—and then discover that the building is suffering an epidemic of crime. Living in the building could become a nightmare. And your investment in the cooperative shares or condominium could decline sharply, assuming you could even find someone to take the undesirable apartment off your hands.

The obvious way to find out about the level of crime in a building is to talk to some of the present tenants. However, they may be reluctant to level with you: they don't want the building to gain a reputation for insecurity. If you don't believe that the tenants you approach are being candid, try some of the employees, such as the doorman, guards or elevator operators. Another good source of information is the local police precinct, which should be maintaining records on the level of crime in its jurisdiction. Since few police precincts compile crime records on a building-by-building basis, you may have to obtain an informal opinion, either from the precinct commander or the cop on the beat.

Hopefully, you will obtain a positive report on the building in which you are contemplating becoming a resident. However, even if the building is presently free from crime, it is important to have strong assurances that it will remain so in the future. There are many essentially defenseless apartment buildings that are free from crime because local petty criminals have not as yet become aware that they are easy marks. Once they do, beware! All evidence suggests that there is a grapevine among criminals. As soon as the first criminal finds out how easy it is to burglarize apartments or rob lone women in the building, he will return—and so will his cronies.

The following check list can be used to gain an appreciation of the level of security of a building. It should also tell you if the building is well managed, an important criterion in selecting any residential building.

• Location: Is the building close to public transportation? (Even if you use a car, your visitors, servants or children may still require public transportation.) The route between the public transportation and the building should preferably be direct, well lighted and well traveled. Avoid routes through public parks or narrow side streets.

• The superintendent or building manager should live on the premises. (A resident manager will be concerned for his own safety and that of his family.) Make sure that the super has a phone and that he makes his number known to the tenants.

- Does the building have a tenant association? If so, make sure that it is active and not merely a paper organization.
- Does the building have a doorman? (If you can afford to live in a building with a doorman, do so.) Does the doorman "challenge" all strangers—including you on your first visit? Does the doorman have an intercom by which he can announce all visitors and delivery men? (Check the intercom in any apartment you are considering for volume and clarity of speech.)
- If the building does not have a doorman, does it employ a guard, at least during the more dangerous hours of 4 P.M. to midnight? Since buildings with part-time guards usually have door-opener intercoms, make sure that all visitors and delivery men use the intercom to gain entrance.
- If the building does not employ either guards or doormen, does it have an operable door-opener-intercom system? A door-opener system using closed-circuit TV is preferable by far; voice communication is essential; a bell-and-buzzer system invites intruders.
- If the building does have a voice intercom, perform the following experiment: Push apartment buttons in order and cry "postman." If some tenant lets you in without further inquiry, the system, which depends on tenant cooperation, is not very effective.
- If the building does not have guards or doormen, check the condition of the front door, which should be locked at all times. The lock should be sturdy and not operable by "loiding" (see discussion of loiding under "Front Doors for Apartment Buildings" in Chapter III).
- After making sure that the front door is secure, check the perimeter of the building to determine if there are any other unguarded or easy ways to enter the building, including the roof and fire escapes.

• It is essential that you visit the building at night to make sure that the front entrance is well lighted (many municipalities now require one or two lights at the front entrance; if two, one on either side of the door). The perimeter of the building should also be well lighted. Even better, if there is a fire escape, it should be floodlighted (but this last is very rare).

• If the building has a garage, check its security. If the garage is open to nonresidents (a common arrangement in some large cities), it should have an attendant or at least CCTV monitored by the doorman to protect the garaged cars. The entrance to the building from the garage should be locked at all times. If one or more of the building elevators descend to the garage level, they should be controlled, by keys issued to the tenants, from the basement level. If not, and the building has a doorman, a less desirable alternative is for any elevator ascending from the garage to stop at the lobby level and open—exposing the occupants to the scrutiny of the doorman or guard. Even better is an elevator that only travels between the garage and lobby levels, forcing all passengers to change for another elevator at the lobby. If there is no attendant in the garage, the garage doors should close automatically and rapidly (within ten seconds). Do not consider any building with no automatic or very slowly closing garage doors and no controls on entrance to the building from the garage.

• Check the roof of the building. If the building is adjacent to other buildings, permitting an intruder to walk or jump from neighboring structures onto the roof of the building, then any doors or hatchways to the roof should open outward, secured on the inside with slide bolts or at least sturdy eye hooks. Skylights should be locked. (However, the roof doors and hatches should not be locked by conventional locks or padlocks, which expose tenants to the great danger of being trapped at the roof exits in the event of fire.) Check the roof for dog excreta. This is a sign that some tenants may be allowing their dogs to run up to the roof alone, which means the roof door is left open. If the roof can be reached from an adjacent building, this form of "dog-walking" represents a serious security violation.

• Only consider a penthouse apartment in a building with excellent security at the street level and whose roof can't be reached from adjacent buildings.

• The entrance to the building should be approached directly from the street. Avoid buildings with off-the-street entrances, such as from interior courtyards. The lobby of the building should be well lighted, with no curtains or, alternatively, curtains woven with a very open mesh that permits someone outside to see anyone in the lobby. Direct viewing of the elevators from the outside of the building is most desirable. Elevators that are entered from alcoves are least desirable (assuming that there are no elevator operators).

• The composition of the tenant population is most significant. A building populated largely by young marrieds with small children tends to have much higher security than a building populated mostly by single people, either young or old. The young singles tend to make light of security measures and particularly resent any restrictions on visitors, while older singles are often economically unable to contribute to any cooperative security measures. (However, older retired folks can become the most loyal members of tenant patrols. They are usually the only people in the building who can stand a tour of duty in the late afternoon, before working husbands come home from work and while housewives are occupied with their children.)

• Elevator controls are crucial. In large cities, elevators are becoming the most common scene for muggings. Most preferable are elevators whose circuitry is set so that stops while ascending from the lobby can only be signaled by passengers. (This works a minor inconvenience on tenants who wish to visit neighbors on upper levels: they have to descend to the lobby first.) In addition, descending to the basement or garage can only be signaled by special keys issued to the tenants. If the most preferable arrangement is not in force, a system by which the elevator can't descend to the basement after some reasonable hour is helpful.

• Assuming that you don't plan to equip your apartment with laundering machines, the location of the laundry room is important. Most preferable is a laundry room on each level of the building—an innovation in some new luxury buildings. Next comes a laundry room in a secure area, such as a well-protected basement or the lobby. If the laundry room is located in an insecure basement, check for monitoring of the room by TV or the establishment of a "buddy" system whereby housewives use the facilities in pairs. Downgrade buildings with a laundry room open to the public, particularly at night.

• If mail is distributed through individual mailboxes, check the location of the mailboxes. Least desirable are mailboxes located in a vestibule outside the main entrance door (outdoor muggers and purse-snatchers prey on women—and men too—who stop to read their mail in outer vestibules). Most desirable are mailboxes prominently located in the lobby. In some buildings, the mailboxes are located in a blind alcove, which makes those coming for their mail vulnerable to attack.

• Corridors with the apartments on one side and open on the opposite side, in milder climates, or with glazed-in areas, in colder climates (single-loaded), are preferable to corridors with apartments on both sides (double-loaded), especially if there are facing buildings. If corridors are double-loaded, they should at least be well lighted without hidden alcoves and other places of concealment, such as incinerator closets. Double-loaded corridors that are short are preferable to long corridors.

• Front doors to apartments should be made of steel in steel frames. Doors must have peepholes. If you choose an apartment with a wooden door, be prepared to spend money to back the door with heavy-gauge sheet metal or three-quarter-inch-thick plywood. All front doors should be hung to open inward so that the hinge pins are inside the apartment. If the lock is one of the key-in-knob types, be prepared to supplement it with a mortise lock with a heavy deadbolt.

• Buildings with exterior fire escapes are most vulnerable. Interior fire stairs in many newer buildings are now enclosed. For this type of construction, most preferable are one-way doors opening out at the lobby and roof levels and only inward on all levels in between. In many older buildings, the fire stairs are not enclosed. Preferable are mesh constructions at the lobby level enclosing the fire stairs with a one-way outward-opening door in the mesh. Of course, all forms of fire stairs should be well lighted.

• Does the corridor have any windows facing narrow interior courtyards? Some burglars have used these upper-level windows to enter adjacent apartments through accessible open windows. Apartments facing into such constricted courtyards require extra protection for windows (see Chapter III).

• For apartments in buildings with only two or three stories or apartments on lower levels, are there any ladders or large pieces of wood stored in the interior or back courtyard or tall trees about the building through which an agile burglar could enter an apartment window?

• Fire hoses should be clean and not show signs of rotting. A landlord who neglects protective measures against fire will most likely neglect security aspects as well.

• The appearance of a building can tell you a lot about the level of security and the attitude of the tenants. A dirty or sloppy building, with signs of neglect or outright vandalism, such as broken windowpanes, graffiti on lobby and elevator walls and peeling paint, is to be avoided not only for its unsightliness but also because it indicates that the tenants don't care. Tenants who are not concerned about the appearance of a building are less likely to be concerned about security—or so terrorized that they retreat into their apartments behind doors with extra-heavy locks. A combination of poor appearance plus apartment doors with many locks is a sure sign of low security.

The various security aspects discussed here must be weighed in relation to the level of crime in the neighborhood in which the building is located. If in a large metropolitan center where crime is common, vulnerability on only a few of these aspects should be enough to disqualify a building. On the other hand, an apartment building in a suburban setting where crime is rare may be considered even if somewhat vulnerable—always bearing in mind that an epidemic of crime is unpredictable, and once a building is known to be defenseless, criminals flock to prey on it.

Chapter VIII

PROTECTING
AUTOMOBILES AND
OTHER VEHICLES

Stealing cars is one of the major criminal activities in the United States. Because the dollar cost of the theft of over one million cars each year is absorbed by the portion of your auto insurance policy known as "comprehensive," few Americans feel the full impact of these crimes, beyond the $50 or $100 "deductible" they lose if their stolen cars are not recovered (even if they are recovered, the owners are likely to lose their deductibles because of damage to the cars).

Over one thousand Americans do feel the full impact of auto thefts each year—and never know it. They are the innocents who are killed each year by cars stolen by joyriding youths. Then there are tens of thousands more badly injured or maimed in accidents caused by stolen cars. The FBI reports that the incidence of accidents among stolen cars is an incredible two hundred times the norm.

Fortunately, there is much that you can do to protect your car and its contents against the amateurs who take over two-thirds of all cars solen. Protecting your car against the professional predators is very difficult, perhaps impossible.

There are four categories of thieves who prey on cars: the professionals who steal late-model cars, often "to order"; the other pros who steal cars only for their saleable parts; the juveniles and some adults who steal cars for pleasure; and the drug addicts and others, known as "boosters" or "car clouts," who steal parts and property out of cars. Increasingly, Fagin-like pros recruit from the latter two categories, training young thieves and hard-core addicts to steal cars for them for $200 to $250 per machine.

The first category of pro is the most skillful and systematic of all. They recruit car wreckers who will sell them the identification plates and associated registration papers off late-model wrecks (going price: $300 per set); repaint stolen cars that match the wrecks in all but color; and find customers or transport the car to some other state or overseas where it can be sold without suspicion.

Some pros are brazen enough to call up legitimate dealers and con them out of ignition key numbers, which is all they need to steal cars. Here's how they do it. After spotting a desirable car, they learn the name of the owner. The thief then calls the dealer (his name is decaled on the trunk), claiming that he is the owner and has lost his keys. He requests the serial number of the ignition key, asserting he knows a master locksmith who can make a duplicate. Knowing the serial number, the thief can make a key in less than a minute with a $50 portable tool that is widely available.

Creating false registration documents is easy for the thieves in New York State: in early 1971, a group broke into the Valley Stream branch of the Motor Vehicle Bureau and stole the necessary imprinting machines and rubber stamps. Elsewhere, car thieves merely forge the necessary documents.

Who is opposing this army of full- and part-time criminals? In a sense, all of the nation's local and state policemen, backed up by the many computers now installed in police departments, state police headquarters and motor vehicle bureaus, and the FBI's computers at the National Crime Information Center in Washington. However, most policemen have only occasional contact with car theft. The brunt of the fight against the highly successful professionals is borne by the specialized squads in each of the big cities where car theft is epidemic. These squads range in size from Philadelphia's tiny squad of several men, to New York's undermanned squad of eighteen men plus three sergeants and one lieutenant, to Chicago's comparatively huge squad of one hundred and fifty.

These squads work quietly through supervision of all new- and used-car dealers and auto-wrecking yards. These establishments are usually licensed, which gives the authorities a means of excluding shady characters from what could be ideal outlets for stolen cars and valuable parts.

The auto squad examines all suspect cars and motorcycles to find out if they were stolen. These specialists can positively tell if a vehicle was stolen by comparing the visible VIN, the vehicle identification number which is now mounted on top of the dashboard, with the same number secretly scribed someplace on the frame of the car. The location of the hidden VIN varies from model to model and is changed each year. Only the members of the auto squad have access to the location of the hidden VINs. This carefully guarded information comes through the National Auto Theft Bureau (NATB), the private investigative force of the auto insurers, which receives it directly from the manufacturers.

Unfortunately, many pros soon find the location of the hidden VINs on the most marketable models. At least a dozen rings of car thieves in the United States buy or steal the latest models as soon as they appear to make a microscopic examination of the frames to find the hidden VINs. Or these pros simply buy this invaluable information from the assembly-line employees who scribe them on cars. Then they sell this information to affiliated thieves in other cities.

The hidden VINs are no obstacle to the thieves who specialize in "nose clips"—the front fenders, grill, hood and bumper—which fetch up to $1,900 per set. After removing the nose and any other marketable parts, a surgical procedure taking as little as fifteen minutes, they abandon or scrap the frame.

Car owners can foil or at least impede thieves. Begin by keeping your registration with you at all times. Don't leave it in your car. It's a big help to a thief if he finds the registration inside the glove compartment. For instance, if a car thief is stopped by suspicious police before the car's theft is reported—and on the average, it takes eight hours before an alarm is received—the police will generally let the thief go if he can produce the registration ("Sir, I borrowed this buggy from my brother-in-law").

Here's another good reason for not leaving your registration in your car: it tells thieves your home address. If they steal the car from a public parking lot (which represents up to 12 percent of all thefts in some cities) near a movie theater, for example, they know you won't discover the loss for up to three hours. That's more than enough time to burglarize your home too—and carry away the loot in your car.

Never leave your keys in the ignition when you park—even for a minute. This may sound obvious, yet an estimated 40 percent of all thefts occur because of keys left in place. Also, avoid leaving your keys with parking-lot attendants. Some copy the keys for later theft. Worse still, don't leave your house keys on the same chain: they'll be copied too.

If you have a garage, park your car in it every night. If

your garage is too small for two cars, leave the less valuable one outside overnight. If you do own two cars and can't fit either one into the garage, park the more valuable car closer in and block the driveway with the older car. If you don't have a garage, at least park on a well-lighted street or under the lamppost, preferably on an avenue instead of a side street.

If your car breaks down on the highway, stick with it. Try to get it towed away as quickly as possible. If you leave it alone for a while, especially overnight, don't be shocked if the battery, wheels and tires, carburetor and other parts are missing—that is, if the body of the car is still there. The strippers go to work very quickly. Also, in some localities, you'll be subject to a ticket if you leave your car overnight beside a highway.

Life is now more difficult for car strippers in New York. A recent change in the city's administrative code now makes it possible for the police to arrest car strippers in the act, without waiting for the owner to file a complaint. The conviction rate on this form of crime is a spectacular 99 percent.

Burglar alarms are an excellent deterrent against the amateurs—and may help you to get insurance on the models preferred by the pros. But burglar alarms on cars still don't earn insurance discounts the way they do for commercial burglary insurance. There are two main kinds of burglar alarm systems: those that actuate your car's horn and cost about $15 if you install them yourself; and those that set off loud sirens mounted under the hood. If you install the latter yourself, they only cost about $28 to $30. If they are installed by specialists, the cost runs to $75 and more. If you install a burglar alarm yourself, figure on taking three to four hours. However, one manufacturer of such alarms, PMC/Car Alarm of Los Angeles, claims that his system can be installed "in less than twenty minutes." For a dollar, you can "simulate" a burglar alarm with a metallized plastic part that adheres to the side of your car. It looks like the locks for burglar alarms. A phoney warning decal comes in the same kit: it doesn't fool the pros.

Increasingly, burglar alarms are backed up by a hidden cut-off or ignition-killer switch. These are simple switches installed in the ignition line that must be closed before you can start your car. If you install one yourself, in about an hour, for around $3.50, or if you have one put in by a specialist, make sure that it is not mounted in some easily discovered place such as the glove compartment or under the ignition switch.

Alarms, which are wired to switches on all doors, the hood and the trunk lid (or to the door-operated courtesy lights on some alarms), are circumvented by thieves in two ways. First, they open the hood, knowing they will set off the alarm, but pry off one battery lead in seconds to still it. After disconnecting the alarm, they reattach the battery lead and proceed as usual. Or, they slide under the front end and cut the battery cables. An effective deterrent to these two techniques is hood locks, which cost about $11 per pair.

For those who are unhappy about the drilling of two holes about a half inch in diameter in the hood of their cars to accommodate hood locks, the alternative is a locking system installed from the inside. One version, the Kar-Lok, made by Chapman Security Products, Bayside, N.Y., costs about $50 installed, with a lock mounted near the ignition key. It also grounds out the ignition system. A less costly but also less effective alternative is to chain the hood shut with a heavy chain and padlock that slips through the grill. But unless the chain is especially treated, it can be cut with bolt cutters. Also, this make-do arrangement is not especially attractive.

If your car has a vent flap, some thieves force the flap,

reach in and run down the window, and then climb in through the open window without disturbing the alarm.

To foil this last approach, an improved solid-state alarm is now available. It goes off if there is any significant change in electrical demand, such as turning on the headlights or the ignition. Trouble is, some brands of these alarms are not yet perfected. Before you buy one, check carefully on its performance record. These alarms cost about $5 to $10 more than the conventional alarms.

Truck-type Babaco alarms are rented by thousands of salesmen who carry samples of high-priced merchandise in their cars. Installation runs from $100 to $400 (the Jeweler's Special) and annual rent goes from $35 to $100. This type of alarm is difficult to disable because the battery is enclosed in a locked steel container.

The latest in antitheft systems locks off the fuel supply to the motor. Developed by a little outfit in Fairfied, N.J., called Safetech, Inc., this system is controlled by a five-digit code entered through an eighteen-button keyboard mounted under the dashboard. Even if you leave the ignition key in place, the car can't be started without the code. A thief would have to both jump the ignition and replace the carburetor with its special hardened-steel cut-off valve to start the car. Assuming he had the correct carburetor on hand, switching carburetors would take from thirty to forty-five minutes. That's a substantial deterrent. The system, which costs $160 installed, has a bypass button that can be activated by the car owner, which permits a parking-lot attendant to start the car without being given the code.

The Safetech system, which has been attracting much attention from truckers hard hit by hijackers, is one of the few antitheft devices for cars that has been approved by Underwriters' Laboratories, the nonprofit testing service set up by the insurers. The only alarm system to obtain UL approval to date is a higher-priced system made by Auto-Matic Alarm Systems, Chicago. UL approval is an important but limited endorsement. The limitation is that the UL does not supervise the installation and maintenance of antitheft systems for cars.

When installing or having an alarm system installed in your car, make sure that the arming switch is mounted in a place that can't be reached from outside the car when the hood is closed. This is to prevent a thief from cutting the wires to the switch. Obviously, the switch must be exposed when the hood is opened, otherwise it can't be installed in the first place. However, the switch should not be readily accessible when the hood is opened, otherwise a thief could cut or rip away the wires in a few seconds after opening the hood, thus stilling the siren. Some of the instructions for these systems recommend that the switch be connected either directly to the battery or to the "hot" side of the voltage regulator. I favor the latter connection point to make the system a bit tougher to defeat; the connection to the battery is easier to spot.

A simple way to avoid the problems associated with an outside key-operated switch is to select an antitheft system with a built-in delay. In such systems, the switch is mounted *inside* the car, just as the control boxes on home security systems with delays can be mounted inside the residence.

You can make thieves' work tougher by using the various kinds of special locks that link the steering wheel to either the brake pedal or the gear-shift lever. The former, called Krooklok, costs about $15, while the latter, known as Car-Lok, costs only $4.50. It takes a tungsten-carbide-coated hacksaw to break one of these locks. (But you can buy one of these hacksaw blades in most hardware stores for about $2.)

A variety of locks are also made for various marketable parts of cars. You can buy a battery lock (it also fits the spare tire) for $4 and wheel locks at $10 per set of four. The latter are particularly recommended if you mount fancy magnesium wheels. At up to $200 per set, plus tires, they are worth protecting. Now wheel locks are made in metric sizes for foreign cars, particularly VWs.

Wheel locks can save more than the wheels and tires. To remove wheels, thieves use two jacks at one end at the same time. After they remove one pair of wheels, they usually yank the jacks away, crashing the car down on its axles and causing hundreds of dollars' worth of damage.

Tape decks are very popular with boosters: in 1970, about $50 million worth were stolen from U.S. cars. So many tape decks are stolen in New York that sales have declined as car owners have given up replacing them. You can buy a tape deck lock mount for $11, or you can buy one of the models of tape decks, such as the Craig, that come with built-in locks.

Many believe that the older the car, the less likely it will be stolen. Not so. Many older cars are favored by youths who want to convert them into hot rods. The pros go after older cars for scarce parts. Perhaps for these two reasons, the preferred Pontiac with thieves in 1970 was the 1966 model.

"Stolen" Cars That Weren't Stolen

In the cover article on auto theft in New York City in the April 19, 1971, issue of *New York* magazine, I wrote that the best deterrent to thievery was to own a Rolls-Royce. In all the decades of record-keeping by the New York City police, they had never recorded an "alarm" for a stolen Rolls.

Within a week of publication of the issue, I received a letter from a woman in Bedford, Massachusetts, with a newspaper clipping enclosed. The clipping reported the finding of a 1970 Rolls at the bottom of an abandoned two hundred-foot-deep quarry filled with water. In her covering note she gleefully noted that a Rolls-Royce was not immune to the car thieves of Massachusetts.

I responded in the magazine's letters column that the fact that the car had been "deep-sixed" in a two hundred-foot-deep quarry filled with water with its original license plates still attached proved that there was no market for stolen Rolls-Royces. That's one interpretation. Another is that the owner couldn't meet the payments, so he rolled the car into the quarry (leaving the tire marks that alerted the police to the ditching) and reported the car stolen.

Each year many thousands of fraudulent claims are made for cars reported stolen or destroyed by fire that were either abandoned or destroyed by their owners. Sometimes the cars never existed. These fraudulent claims are a matter of concern for all car owners because if accepted by the insurers, the cost of these claims is ultimately passed on to the other customers of the insurance companies. In other words, false claims represent dollars out of your pocket.

Burning of cars to obtain the insurance money is so common down South that the auto-insurance fraternity refers to the South as the "Fire Belt." Because most car insurers are headquartered outside the South, auto arson below the Mason-Dixon line is referred to as "selling cars to the Yankees." Now the Southerners are teaching their Yankee cousins how to burn cars. A variation is abandoning the machine where it will soon be stripped down to unrecognizability. Burning a car to obtain the insurance is not really very smart. The NATB's agents know all the tricks and can usually tell if the fire was set.

The car arsonist is nearly always an amateur. But another

category of false claimant is quite professional. This is made up of the defrauders who obtain insurance for nonexistent cars, then soon report them missing. If the fraud is not detected, the settlement cost is passed on to the public in the form of still higher theft premiums. This kind of fraud is not too difficult to detect if the con man has taken out insurance with more than one agency, which happens. However, if he is smart enough to limit the fraud to one insurer, he's very hard to catch. The estimate of such frauds in New York alone runs into the thousands.

Selecting a Car to Avoid Theft

The kind of car you buy and how it is equipped can very much affect the chances of its being stolen or "clouted."

Professional and amateur thieves favor certain brands and models of cars. If you don't buy them, your chances of keeping your car are increased. In general, General Motors cars are favored over all others. The pros go for new Chevvies, Caddies and Pontiacs, also Oldsmobiles and Buicks, the more options the better. The amateurs favor older Chevvies and Pontiacs.

Sporty cars are much in demand: Mustangs, Camaros, Corvettes and Chargers. Corvettes are so popular with thieves that this is the only car offered with a factory-installed burglar alarm system. It costs about $75.

Thefts of foreign cars are much lower in volume, mostly because there are fewer of them on the road. Except for the Volkswagen. Only three brands of cars are stolen in greater volume than VWs. The popularity of VWs with thieves is based on their ease of adaptability into dune buggies. VWs are also stolen for parts needed to repair damaged machines. Porsches and Jaguars will also be stolen on occasion—usually for quick shipment to South America.

If you live in one of our great metropolitan centers, especially New York, Newark, Cleveland or Detroit, there's the problem of car clouts and vandals. To cut down on break-ins and vandalism, avoid buying a convertible, station wagon or any car equipped with a vinyl-covered roof or a conventional antenna. Convertibles are too easy to break into, and invite vandalism in the form of slashing of tops. In many cities, station wagons present a special problem: there's no trunk in which to hide property such as luggage, spare tire, clothing, tools or sports equipment. Favor the new radio antennas built into the windshield; the extra charge will ultimately turn out to be much less than the cost of replacing antennas.

If you buy a sports-type car, don't specify fancy magnesium wheels, which cost up to $200 extra per set. Unless the wheels are protected by wheel locks, you'll probably come out some morning and find your car sitting on its axles—most likely with a lot of body damage as well.

When you're out shopping for a used car, favor the newer models with steering-column locks, buzzers that remind you when you've left the key in place, no vent flaps and less accessible interior door-lock knobs. These features really frustrate amateur thieves. (If possible, buy a used car from a dealer. The professionals sometimes brazenly dispose of their wares via classified advertising. If that "steal" you bought turns out to be stolen, you lose all—and subject yourself to the possible embarrassment of a charge of receiving stolen property. However, if a dealer sells you what is ultimately found out to be a stolen machine—or one with an unrevealed lien on it—you can obtain redress.)

Protecting Property Inside Cars

Don't leave valuables visible inside your car. It's an open invitation to car clouts, who are now found in all parts of the nation, including our national parks. Avoid leaving any really valuable property in the trunk: thieves use crowbars to open trunks, or they punch a small hole in the trunk lid with a chisel and pop the lock from the inside with a coat hanger.

A low-cost deterrent to car clouts is replacing the original knobs on the interior door locks with unflanged knobs. Easily grasped from within, the replacements can't be manipulated from the outside by a coat hanger snaked past the rubber gasket at the window's edge. These replacement knobs are a bargain at fifty cents apiece.

Property stolen from cars is covered by your home owner's or tenant's policy. The coverage is limited to $1,000 or 4 percent of the face value of the policy, whichever is higher.

Car owners can do a lot toward stopping the amateurs by merely locking their cars and pocketing the keys. Stopping the pros, who do the most damage in many cities, is another story. That's partly the role of the car makers, but mostly the responsibility of government. The auto industry, under attack by the car insurers for making overpowered and overly fragile products, has managed to pick up some kudos from the insurers for what it's doing to make cars more theftproof. Each of the four major car makers employs design specialists in security who meet regularly to exchange ideas. These are the people who came up with such useful deterrents as steering-column locks, the elimination of flap windows, and less-accessible (from the outside) interior door locks. Although these features deter amateur thieves, they are only mild challenges to the ingenuity of the professionals. For example, within weeks after General Motors introduced its 1969 models with steering-column locks, the pros conceived antidotes. One is to lift up the front end of the car and tow it away (would you be suspicious of two mechanics picking up a car with a tow truck?). The other circumvention is based on a common tool found in all body-and-fender shops, the slam-puller. This is a $16 contraption consisting of a long cylinder on which rides a heavy weight. At one end of the cylinder is a case-hardened screw. At the other end is a flange to catch the weight when it is flung back, creating a jerking force of up to forty pounds. Normally, the slam-puller is screwed into a small hole drilled in dents in parts of the body that can't be reached with a mallet. Car thieves use the slam-puller to rip the steering-column lock out by its roots. The car makers have countered by making the face of the lock even tougher.

The auto industry's security experts are working on new approaches to make their products more theft-resistant. Some show real promise. For example, GMC has developed a push-button unlocking system for the ignition. Primarily designed to make it tough for a drunk to start a car, it could deter thieves too. It was tested at the Medical College of Wisconsin, where a group of medical students first drank enough to become plastered and then failed to operate the pushbuttons in the correct sequence. It is too early to tell if it is practicable. If so, it won't appear for several years because the 1974 models have been designed already. (GMC has a special stake in reducing car thefts: it owns one of the larger insurers of cars, Motors Insurance Corp.)

Right now the police and the insurers are pushing the auto industry to add identification numbers to other major parts besides the engine and transmission. The industry is resisting this pressure, claiming it would cost too much. One suggestion that has a fair chance of adoption is factory installation of hood locks on all cars. (Engine-compartment locks became a $9 option with 1971 model VWs.)

Just so much deterrence can be designed into cars—and

the pros still find ways to steal them. The only real deterrent is a powerful effort by government. That's why the police and the insurers are gung-ho for a certificate-of-title law in all states. They claim that providing each car with a title, a sort of birth certificate, makes it much more difficult to transfer stolen cars. Statistics on car theft appear to substantiate this claim: in the forty-four states that require titles for cars, the recovery rate for stolen cars is much higher than in the remaining six. (Of the six nontitle states, Alabama is the most negligent. In certain counties it is possible for out-of-staters to obtain license plates by mail without proof of ownership.)

The most ambitious anti-car-theft proposal under consideration is the ALPS system (automatic license-plate scanning). This is how it would work if adopted in New York State: An electronic camera mounted at the side of the highway, say at a toll booth, would scan all passing vehicles, recording and recognizing all the numbers and letters on most New York State license plates. The data would be sent by leased phone lines to a computer containing a list of all wanted license plates. If the number were on the wanted list, this fact and all related information on the crime involved would be sent back to the scanning station within two seconds. The local operator would then radio a patrol car parked farther down along the highway to intercept the vehicle bearing the wanted plates. Besides car thieves, the ALPS system would also detect cigarette smugglers, scofflaws and known criminals. Unfortunately, it would only recognize New York State plates, which means that the pros could circumvent it by immediately slapping stolen out-of-state plates over the plates of cars they steal.

To operate ten ALPS scanners on New York City avenues, highways and bridges favored by thieves moving stolen cars would cost an estimated $10,500,000 for five years. Under the worst conditions, this ALPS system is expected to cut the toll of all damages resulting from car theft by a whopping $100 million per year. Not a bad investment for New York State, particularly since the federal government, under the Safe Streets Act of 1965, would pick up a big share of the cost.

The ALPS system has been the subject of studies beginning back in May 1967. A very sophisticated system, it couldn't be operational before 1974 even if funded soon.

Some day, hopefully, the good guys will be given the tools and the powerful legislation to really get the bad guys. In particular, a nationwide link-up of computers maintaining up-to-the-second lists of stolen cars, perhaps tied to license-plate scanners on major routes, should force the interstate, international stolen-car racket into a sharp recession. But one is made uneasy by the chilling thought that then these clever, resourceful criminals would counter by infiltrating the computer rooms and unobtrusively and selectively erasing from the lists of purloined cars and license plates those held in inventory by the stolen-car industry.

Protecting Motorcycles

Sales of motorcycles are rising faster than car sales; thefts of cycles are rising even faster. For example, in California during 1970 one out of ten vehicles stolen was a motorcycle, even though cars and trucks in the Golden State are twenty-four times more numerous in total than cycles. To compound the problem, the recovery rate for cycles is much lower. While 84 percent of stolen cars are recovered in California, mostly in good shape, only 36 percent of stolen cycles are recovered, and most of these are worthless, mere carcasses.

Bikes come in two major varieties: the heavy, high-powered sports models that cost up to $3,000, and the lower-powered, less-costly machines mostly used for transportation and not to show off. The professional thieves concentrate on the former, while the latter are stolen by amateurs who need "wheels."

One professional, known as the "White Phantom," stole only one model of bike, the expensive Harley-Davidson Electroglide. Operating in the Baltimore area with a white panel truck, this well-organized criminal stole up to three machines a night (that was the capacity of his panel truck). At the end of each month, he placed all the stolen bikes in a trailer truck and shipped them off to his "distributor" in California, a state where motorbikes are especially popular.

The White Phantom usually found his targets in the street, but on occasion sneaked into a backyard to grab a machine that the owner no doubt considered safe because it was not observable from the street. The White Phantom and his confederates rolled the machines up a portable ramp or shoved them, if the wheel was chained, into their panel truck. Some bike thieves use trucks with power lift gates to raise the heaviest bikes, which weigh as much as eight hundred pounds, into their trucks.

The point I am making is that it is not sufficient to chain the wheels of a motorbike to the frame to protect the machine—the entire machine must be chained to some immovable object such as a lamppost or sewer grating. If you own one of the really expensive bikes, the best protection is to garage it at night or during the day while at work. If you work in New York, park it in one of the special parking areas for motorbikes.

Even if you garage your bike, you still need a heavy chain and padlock that resist conventional steel hacksaw blades. Heavy-duty chains that can only be cut by an acetylene torch are sold by those who sell the bikes. They cost up to $20 for a six-foot length. The padlocks are sold in any locksmith's shop and cost up to $25.

Despite all precautions, bikes are stolen. Once stolen, motorbikes are rarely recovered because the thieves "scramble" the parts of similar models, making identification very difficult.

In the past several years, attempts have been made to market antitheft systems for motorcycles. Most failed, but one device that appears to be gaining acceptance is the Cycle-Gard, which is made by Alcotronics Corp. This device comes in two versions. The simpler and earlier model is mounted behind the license plate. When armed by a key, it will emit a loud bleeping noise if the bike is moved. The alarm sounds for forty seconds, then stops. If the motion continues, the alarm repeats for another forty seconds, and so on. Powered by two high-grade 9-volt batteries, the device lists for $32.95, including batteries. Cycle-Gard II adds a transmitter and receiver to the basic alarm. If the bike is moved after arming, the alarm sounds and the transmitter sends a signal to the small receiver, which is worn by the owner or set up near his bed. The receiver, which can be as far as three hundred feet from the bike, emits an alarm that sounds like an alarm clock. This more advanced system lists for $89.95. If you have an older Cycle-Gard and want to upgrade it into a Cycle-Gard II, you can buy a kit for $69.95. Obviously, the sensitivity of these systems has to be set so that they don't send out a false alarm every time a heavy truck passes. Alcotronics is located at Church Road and Roland Avenue, Mount Laurel, N.J. 08057.

I can't recommend another antitheft device that is featured in some catalogs of parts for motorbikes. This is a small switch containing a time-delay relay that cuts off the ignition after ten seconds. This action is repeated over and over again if the switch is not turned off. I have three objections to this $8 gadget, which was developed for use on cars. First, it is very difficult to conceal on a motorbike. Secondly, it is no deterrent at all to those thieves who operate by lifting the entire bike into a truck. Thirdly, if it works, the thief may abandon the bike in the middle of a highway.

Protecting Boats

Theft and vandalism of boats is now so common that many boat owners are forced to install expensive locks on all doors and hatches. Or they moor in marinas equipped with brilliant lighting at night plus security guards. The problem of theft of parts of the boat and vandalism is actually more common and perhaps more destructive in terms of total dollar loss to the owners. Sometimes the objective of those who break into boats is not theft or vandalism. At one East Coast marina teenagers were breaking into boats to engage in necking parties—or more serious sex. Although their intent was not criminal, they did some damage, messed up the interiors and also consumed the yacht owners' liquor and food.

Sturdy padlocks and hasps are required to protect boats and whatever is stored on the boat. Of course, the locks should be made of rustproof materials such as stainless steel or brass. That means that they may cost as much as $25 apiece. However, the doors and hatches to which such locks are attached may be made of wood or some material other than steel. Therefore they can be forced or broken open sometimes more easily if the padlock is very massive, giving the thieves greater leverage.

The antidote is some intrusion-detection system. The siren alarms used on cars can also be mounted on boats with motors, which have the battery to power the sirens. If you want to mount an automotive-type alarm system on an unpowered sailboat, then a separate 12-volt battery must be installed—and checked and replaced regularly.

An alarm specifically designed for yachts is available from the Eaton Corp. First introduced about seven years ago, the

Auralarm actually announces which yacht among many at a mooring or marina is being burglarized or vandalized. A pre-recorded message is played over a loud hailer horn in this fashion: "There is an intruder aboard the yacht *Lady Ann* in berth No. 78 South Marina. Please call police to investigate immediately."

Now standard on all large Chris-Craft yachts, the self-powered Auralarm is not inexpensive. The price is $250, plus installation, which runs about $23 per "opening." If your yacht has one door and one hatch, then installation will total about $45—unless you do it yourself. Figure on taking an entire afternoon to install an Auralarm if you do. The hailer horn that comes with the system is still required even if there is a horn on your boat.

There is also a separate charge of $16 for a "custom-pro-grammed" announcement cartridge. The system comes with a cartridge that simply announces "There is an intruder aboard this yacht. Please summon police immediately." This cartridge should be retained for use when away from your home marina. If you switch yacht clubs, then you have to pay an additional $16 for a new cartridge from your dealer. If no dealer in your area carries the Auralarm or equivalent, the address of the nearest dealer can be obtained from the manufacturer: Eaton Corp., Lock and Hardware Division, 401 Theodore Fremd Avenue, Rye, N.Y. 10580.

A lower-cost anti-intrusion system for boats is available from Protective Services Corporation, North Plainfield, N.J. The Electronic Policeman not only protects all doors, hatches and ports, but it also includes a trip switch that indicates if someone is trying to remove the outboard motor. Installed, the Electronic Policeman costs about $140.

Several new alarm systems for boats were announced at the National Boat Show held at the New York Coliseum in January, 1972. One that I found attractive in concept is made by Portstar Industries, Inc., P.O. Box 142, Nyack, N.Y. 10960. Packaged as an install-it-yourself kit, it lists for $90. The system does not draw any current until it is triggered, a most useful feature. When triggered, it actuates a boat's horn and flashes the running or cabin lights. This system also contains an optional device costing $17 that warns if your bilge is filling.

An ultrasonic alarm (see discussion in Chapter V of the limitations of this form of alarm) is also available for mounting in boats—and camping trailers too. Operating off the boat's 12-volt battery, the Bourns Model MA-2 intrusion alarm is supposed to draw a very small current of 1/100th of an ampere, so it won't run down the battery during extended periods in which the boat rides at anchor. The "maximum" range of the unit is from twelve to eighteen feet, depending on the acoustics of the space guarded. The range is adjustable from six feet up to the maximum. The alarm may be connected to the boat's horn. Since camping trailers don't have horns, an accessory bell costing about $10 for a three-inch-diameter bell or a siren for $44, both of weatherproof construction, must be mounted on the outside of the trailer in such a way that the wires to it and the mounting hardware are not accessible from the outside. The alarm will sound for one minute, then stop automatically. If the intruder is still present, the alarm sounds again.

The Model MA-2 lists for $108. The same manufacturer's Models HS-1 or HS-3 heat sensors, which activate at 135°F., can also be connected to the alarm. These sensors cost from $2.25 to $3.25 each, which makes the addition of fire detection a bargain.

Protecting Camping Trailers

At one time it was common for campers to leave whatever valuables they had with them openly inside their tent or unlocked camping trailer. No more. With the phenomenal rise in popularity of camping, a less-honest element has taken it up. Some private camping grounds now offer security guards who patrol at night. The operators of these grounds also suggest that their guests not leave valuables about.

Camping trailers are equipped with door locks, but these are not sturdy and can be easily forced. If you are concerned about the possibility of theft from or vandalism of your trailer, you should supplement the lock with a heavy hasp and padlock.

There's also the possibility that your entire trailer will be stolen, especially if you leave it parked for long periods, either beside your home or stored at some camping ground. To protect your trailer when it is not hitched to your car, use one of the series of sturdy locks that fit over the "female" part of the hitch, the inverted cup which fits over the "ball" part of the hitch on your car. Listing for $13 apiece, they are made by the Master Lock Company, Milwaukee, Wisc. Many campground operators sell them.

An anti-intrusion alarm system specially designed for motor campers is available from Protective Services Corporation. Developed primarily for the Winnebago line of motor campers, the system can be installed in any similar machine at a cost of $285.

Protecting Bicycles

Bicycle sales to adults are up sharply all over the nation. People are buying bikes for exercise and also to get to work. I have at least a half-dozen friends who bike to work during all but the winter months.

But increased sales have also resulted in increased thefts. I know firsthand, because my bike was stolen from in front of my son's school one bright, sunshiny afternoon. I had chained my English racer to a lamppost at a very busy intersection. Some ten minutes later when I went to retrieve it, all I could find of the bike was a few severed links.

Not because I hoped to get my bike back, but to establish a claim on my income-tax form, I took the broken links to the nearby police precinct house and reported the theft. The desk sergeant told me that the chain had been severed by a bolt cutter, a tool that is three feet long and weighs about twenty pounds. It's not a tool that someone carries about easily, or nonchalantly, so the sergeant suggested that the thieves were operating from a truck. I suspect that they pull the truck up to a chained bike, which cuts off the view of anyone across the street. As soon as the coast is clear, one thief hops out of the back of the truck, cuts the chain and hands the bike up to a confederate. It most likely takes less than thirty seconds.

To protect their bikes, my friends who bike downtown to work take one of these two approaches. Some own collapsible bikes, which they take right up into their offices and fold into a closet, and some own true racers, which are light enough to be lifted easily into an elevator and taken upstairs. The others use motorcycle-type welded chains and heavy padlocks with case-hardened shanks. They snake the chain through the wheels and lock the chain about a lamppost. The chain and lock weigh half as much as the bike, which makes pedaling it more work. Some of those with racing bikes remove the front wheel before chaining the bike to a post or rack (many firms in New York now provide bicycle racks for employees). It's very easy to remove and reattach the front wheel of a racer.

Children's bikes are also stolen, especially the popular Stingray models with the wide handlebars and small wheels. Often older children will simply take the bike from another child. The best deterrence is for a child who senses danger to turn around and pedal away as fast as he can—usually the thieves are on foot.

If you live in an area in which children's bikes have been stolen, my recommendation is not to buy the fanciest bike on the market. Stick to the simpler machines with fewer gadgets. They not only cost much less, but weigh less, which makes them easier to pedal. Less likely to attract the eye of thieves, they also represent a smaller loss if stolen.

Another way to make a bike less desirable to thieves is to paint polka dots or stripes on the frame and mudguards. This process of uglification also makes the bike easier to identify in the event of theft.

If you own or can borrow an electric engraving pen (see "Commonsense Measures for Everyone, Everyday" in Chapter II), engrave your driver's license number on the frame, crank and wheels of each family bike.

One of the first antitheft alarms for bicycles is available from Alcotronics. It's an adaptation of their Cycle-Gard for motorcycles, and will cost "under $20." For a description of the Cycle-Gard, see discussion earlier in this chapter.

Chapter IX

HOW TO BUY
SECURITY PRODUCTS
AND SERVICES

"Security" is a tough sell. Many suppliers of security hardware have told me that the only time they make an easy sale is right after a customer has been victimized. It's akin to locking the barn door after the horse has run away.

Because security is so hard to sell, many of the legitimate suppliers of security devices and services tend to overstate the virtues of their product; naturally, they don't reveal any of the deficiencies. Of course, the charlatans and fakers in the field don't hesitate to invent powerful features for their products. For example, Vigilant Protective Systems, Inc., a sleazy supplier of burglar alarms in New York, made the false claim that its very much overpriced alarms were "wired into the police department." (Vigilant's license was ultimately suspended and soon afterwards it went into bankruptcy.)

You must maintain the same attitude of caution and skepticism in the purchase of security products that you assume when making any purchase of expensive equipment for your home or car. More so perhaps, because the purchase of some limited or unreliable security system could generate a false sense of security. And such self-deception could cause one to drop one's guard, neglecting corollary security measures and possibly paving the way to costly victimization.

Here are some rules to follow in the purchase of security systems, devices, services and training courses:

Question "reliability" claims. Many of the newer electronic security systems are touted with claims of "solid-state reliability," "space-age components" and "computer electronics." As a graduate electronic engineer (School of Engineering, Columbia University), I can assure you that the electronics in the grade of product designed for use in the home is of "commercial" quality. This means that it is comparable in quality at best to the electronics in a good color TV set. And you know how color TV sets can go kaput. (It's true that because home-security systems are much less complex than TV sets, they are less likely to fail. But don't be charmed by the claims of the salesman.)

Avoid panaceas. There is no one security product or service that meets all needs. Beware of any salesman or supplier who claims that his product meets all of your needs now and in the future.

Purchase products locally. Despite claims of "solid-state reliability" and similar reassuring statements, all security devices except the simplest of mechanical slide bolts require some service, lubrication or maintenance. Mechanical products wear out in use and electronic products age and deteriorate due to the effects of humidity and self-heating. Solid-state or semiconductor ("transistorized") devices are particularly vulnerable to heat and voltage variations. The voltage spikes induced in power lines during lightning storms or brownouts are especially destructive to electronic devices unless they are equipped with proper overvoltage and undervoltage protection. In case of early failure or improper operation, you want to be able to obtain rapid advice and service from your supplier. That's hard to get from a supplier in another state or locality.

Look for service first. Even if you are wise enough to deal with a local supplier, first make sure that he does indeed offer good service. The only way to find out is by calling up present customers. Start with at least three customers whose names are supplied by the dealer, but try to supplement the list with names of other customers, which you may be able to obtain from the local police precinct house, insurance agent or locksmith.

Check spare-parts inventory. Also check the supplier's local inventory of spare parts for the particular product or system you are considering purchasing. If the supplier has no local inventory but claims that he can obtain spare parts rapidly from the manufacturer, that's one mark against him.

Seek standard parts for electronic devices. In time, your supplier may use up his inventory of spare parts or even go out of business. To protect against this unfortunate eventuality, it's helpful if the electronic devices you purchase are manufactured with easily obtainable components (ones that can be bought at any radio-parts store). One way to check is to ask the supplier to remove the back of the control box and then examine the transistors (the little cans that sit on three legs) and integrated circuits (the long rectangular "bugs" with six, seven or eight legs running down each side) for brand names or trademarks. If there are no names or trademarks on these key components, there is a good chance that they are rejects, substandard or "war surplus" parts not easily purchased locally. (This criterion of "standard parts" does not apply to mechanical or electromechanical devices, which are usually made with custom parts other than nuts and bolts.)

Favor UL approval. Underwriters' Laboratories, Inc. performs vigorous tests on certain classes of security systems, notably those supplied by central-station alarm services. I have visited one of the four branch UL testing stations, and it was well equipped. Because it takes a long time for UL to get around to testing any new gear, it is not likely that any of the newer devices and systems will have UL approval. In addition, some suppliers claim that UL is prejudiced in favor of certain long-time suppliers of equipment. It is very difficult to check such claims. What you can be certain of is that UL approval means that the product is well made with sturdy components: it is not likely to develop a short circuit and burn down your home or place of business. In addition, having a UL-approved security system expedites obtaining insurance against burglary of commercial premises, assuming such coverage is obtainable in the first place. UL approval does not earn discounts on home burglary insurance.

In general, UL approval is a big plus. However, it is subordinate to good local service. If you favor a new device that seems to meet your particular needs and can obtain it from a reliable local supplier, I would advise immediate purchase rather than waiting for UL approval, which can take years.

Most of UL's testing of security products is devoted to burglar alarms for business premises. However, it has performed tests on and approved alarms for vehicles, mostly trucks, but also some alarms suitable for passenger cars. The current approved list for cars includes the following: Models LC-9 and LC-9X, made by Auto-Matic Alarm Systems, Chicago, and the Check-Mate System made by Safetech, Inc., Fairfield, N.J. (see Chapter VIII).

The UL publication listing these alarms contains an important disclaimer. I quote it here to emphasize the importance of proper installation (italics mine): "Listed vehicle alarm units are examined to determine that they are *capable of* being installed and maintained in accordance with the Laboratories' requirements. . . . However, neither the character of installation nor maintenance service furnished by the manufacturer, his authorized agents, or installers is supervised by Underwriters' Laboratories, Inc."

How long in business? The mortality rate among companies in the security business is high. On the reasonable assumption that the longer a company has been in business, the longer it is likely to stay in business, always ask any prospective supplier, "How long has your company been in the business of supplying [whatever it is you are considering buying]?" If the salesman's answer is "Only a few months," then you should proceed with caution. If the salesman claims a long history in the business, then check his claims by asking for the names of local customers. If he is unwilling to provide such names, then he is most likely fudging about how long the company has been in business.

Caution: recent franchisee. Several of the newer home-security systems are sold through franchised dealers. If you know anything about the proliferation of the franchising concept, you must be aware that small businessmen or those with a yen to be their own boss are offered a host of franchise deals in a growing variety of fields: fried chicken, hamburgers and other rapidly prepared foods; car washes; art galleries; clothing boutiques; etc. The franchiser's main criterion in selecting a franchisee is the latter's ability to come up with the required "investment" fee, which can run from a few thousand to tens of thousands of dollars. Next, the franchiser looks for selling ability. Usually, the franchiser does not expect his satellites to have prior experience, so many of the franchiser ads offer "training courses." Now security devices are being offered on a franchise basis, in at least one instance, by a billion-dollar corporation, Westinghouse. Among the many people looking for a franchise offering, there is no reason to believe that those who select security devices as their thing will be the cream of the crop or particularly experienced in advising those who believe they have a security problem. I have met several security-systems franchisees. Although I found them to be very pleasant, appealing chaps and good salesmen, I was not impressed with their insight into security problems. Deterrence of criminals does not yield to the same simplistic solutions as the frying of hamburgers and parts of chickens. In addition, the range of products offered by franchisees will no doubt be limited. Beware in particular of the friend or relative who becomes a franchisee of security products or services. Security is not purchased on the basis of friendship or kinship.

Don't buy from amateurs. There are many outright amateurs who supply security products, usually burglar alarm systems. Often they are no more than TV servicemen. I once met one such amateur, who wasn't even trained as a technician. His "partner" was a bright physicist who turned to designing and constructing home burglar alarm systems when the market for physicists turned soft. They did nearly all the work themselves, even down to making their own printed-circuit boards on which the components were mounted. They charged as much as $1,000 for a system, including installation. The nontechnical partner claimed "absolute reliability," although he didn't even understand how reliability is measured. They had just installed their first system in a brownstone in New York City at the time I met them. I asked how it was working. "Not very well," was the reply.

Avoid door-to-door salesmen. On occasion, security products and services have been sold by door-to-door salesmen. Because of the high commissions associated with door-to-door selling, such products at the very least will be overpriced; at worst they will be frauds. Security products should only be purchased from established suppliers, local if possible, to whom one can turn for service and redress in the event of poor performance.

Beware of buying security by mail. Many low-cost security products, such as self-contained burglar and fire detection systems, but sometimes complete home-security systems, are sold by mail. In general, I am quite skeptical of any products sold in this manner. The claims made in the advertisements are often highly exaggerated. For example, an ad for a wall safe sold by mail carried this claim: "Enjoy bank vault safety in your own home. . . ." If you read Chapter IV, Part A, "Safe-Deposit Boxes, Safes and Security Closets," it should be obvious that even the most elaborate of home safes does not match the security of a bank vault, and certainly not the product in question, which is merely a tin box lined with asbestos. You should examine any security product closely before purchasing it, which is obviously impossible when you buy by mail; the "money-back guarantee" offered with nearly all products sold by mail is not sufficient, particularly if the supplier should refuse to accept the merchandise back. (Fortunately, obtaining redress from mail-order suppliers whose only address is a post-office box has recently been made much simpler. If it is apparent that a post-office box is used for commercial purposes, the local postmaster will supply the name, address and phone number of the box holder.)

Check with local consumer fraud agencies. The various consumer fraud agencies, such as those maintained by some large cities, state agencies, the Federal Trade Commission

(See Appendix to this chapter for a list of FTC offices) and the Better Business Bureau compile lists of businesses known to be of questionable reputation. Check with these agencies before making any purchase of a costly system.

Seeking expert advice. It would be most helpful if you could obtain the advice of some expert in your locality on security products and services and their suppliers. Such experts are few and far between. In some large cities, specialized police groups, such as the Premises Protection Squad or the Auto Squad in New York, do offer sound advice. In general, however, local police departments have little experience with or knowledge of home or auto security devices. Nevertheless, it does make sense to take advantage of whatever advisory services are available in your locality, even if they are completely informal. At the very least, the police can tell you if phone alarms are banned—or, if legal, whether they are effective in that community.

Unfortunately, the security field is full of self-appointed experts, many of whom, if not paranoid themselves, play on the element of paranoia in all of us. If you listen to these orchestrators of paranoia, you will be driven to take extreme measures to insure your safety and the safety of your family and home. (By no coincidence, the preachers of paranoia are often peddlers of overpriced security devices.) The measures may appear to be effective, but I believe that their main effect will be to induce unwarranted anxiety in yourself, your family and in those who visit your home. Few like to live in—or visit—a fortress.

Favor long warranties. Obviously, the longer the warranty, the more desirable the product. Some security devices are warranted for as long as three years; others carry warranties of only ninety days. Ask to read the warranty of any product you are considering. Make sure that the salesman does not make any warranty claims that the manufacturer will not back up in writing.

Seek self-checking features. Some of the electronic alarm systems include self-checking features that enable the user to tell if the system is operating properly, if the switches or contacts are closed, or if the batteries, if such are part of the system, are fully charged. This is an important plus, since self-checking means that you are warned to call a serviceman *before* the system is inoperative.

Demand an instruction or owner's manual. If the product you are considering is electronic or complex in nature, then you should be furnished with a clearly illustrated and simply written instruction or owner's manual that is printed on good paper that will not disintegrate in a few months. Before making any purchase of an expensive, complex system, ask to examine the manual. If no manual exists or if the manual is so poorly illustrated that you can't follow it, forget the system.

Banned products. Certain security products have been proscribed by various governmental bodies. I have discussed the spreading ban against phone alarms and mentioned that siren alarms are still banned (although in common use) in California. I also indicated that certain detection devices that emit radio energy must conform to the regulations of the Federal Communications Commission. Before purchasing any security product, be sure to ask the supplier if there are any local bans on the product or if any are under consideration by local authorities and if FCC requirements have been met. If the product depends on any form of telephone or wireless communication, insist that the supplier include a statement on the bill of sale stipulating that no local or federal regulations are violated.

Long-term service contracts. Be leery of any supplier that tries to obtain your signature on a long-term contract with no escape clauses. In the past, ADT and Holmes, the leading central-station-alarm services, offered only five-year contracts, ostensibly to permit them to recover the high cost of initial installation. As a result of government action in the courts, the central-station services now include an escape clause exercisable at the end of two years and every year thereafter on the anniversary of signing.

High installation charges. Some suppliers make their real profit in charges for installation of what appears to be a reasonably priced system. Even if the supplier does not make a profit on installation, such charges may be surprisingly high, particularly if they call for extensive wiring and mounting of hardware. Before agreeing to the rental or purchase of a security system, make sure you know what you will be charged for installation.

Lease-purchase agreements. A convenient way to try out or test an expensive security system is to rent it for a period of months with an option to apply all or most of the rental charges toward purchase. Explore such agreements with your suppliers. (Of course, if there are heavy installation charges for the system, it would be difficult to arrange to try it out for a few months.)

Tax advantages of purchased systems. If you install an expensive security system that becomes part of your home, then it can rightfully be considered a home improvement. This means that should you sell your home at some subsequent time, the cost of the security system could be deducted from any capital gains achieved in the sale (included under column "h" of Schedule "D" of the federal income tax forms). So there is a tax advantage to purchasing rather than renting a security system. In addition, if you use any part of your home for business purposes, a reasonable part of the cost of installation and maintenance of the system can be charged to business expenses. All of this means that you should carefully collect and keep all records of the cost of the system and subsequent repairs to it.

No sales tax. Another advantage of installing a security system that becomes part of your residence is that you most likely don't have to pay any sales tax on it. A security system that becomes a permanent part of your home (with concealed wiring run behind walls) is considered a capital improvement. To avoid the sales tax, check with your local state tax office. They may ask you to complete a form that is then given to the outfit installing the security system.

Financing your security system. If you decide to finance rather than purchase the system, check with your bank on the availability of cash under the home-improvement loan program. You will most likely find that it costs less to finance the system through your bank than through the dealer, who would most likely arrange a loan at higher interest.

Buying Self-Protection Courses

One sign of the growing crime problem is the sprouting of so many schools that offer courses in self-protection: karate, judo, jujitsu, etc. Unfortunately, some of the operators of these schools, or their salesmen, can best be described as flim-flammers or con men. For example, one gentleman who responded to an ad for a self-protection course naturally wanted to inspect the school's facilities. Before the tour, he was asked to sign a "release" in case he was "hurt." The salesman folded the "release" form so that the prospective student could not read all of it. The form turned out to be a contract for $1,700 worth of lessons. The victim of this deception was smart enough to complain to the Federal Trade Commission, which forced the school to cancel the contract.

If you or your child or some friend wants to take a course

in self-protection, I strongly urge you to first consider this key fact: up to 90 percent of the enrollment of most self-protection classes drop out. In other words, unless the person who wants to take the course is very well motivated and well disciplined, the chances of completing the course are only one out of ten. Self-protection classes—if they are at all worthwhile—are physically demanding. I watched a beginning jujitsu class at New York's big McBurney Y. The first hour consisted of warming-up exercises that at least half the class performed in a lackluster manner because of either lack of interest or inability to perform these simple movements more than once or twice. Later I spoke to the instructor, George Pasiuk, "Judo Commissioner" for all the YMCA's in New York State. Mr. Pasiuk, who is an experienced instructor and one-time judo champion, favors jujitsu over karate for self-protection. His reason is sound: Karate calls for damaging blows, which means that students can never practice on each other. On the other hand, jujitsu involves throws that students can practice on each other without harm—all the classes are held on thick mats. He stresses that judo is a sport and not a form of self-defense. However, knowing judo makes it easier to learn jujitsu.

I asked if anyone can learn self-protection from a book. Pasiuk answered that books are useful but that one first needs a base of knowledge and experience that can only be provided by taking a class. Fortunately, it is very easy to take such a class at a Y, and at a low cost too. And the classes are often co-ed. This means that the YMCAs will accept females and many of the YWCAs will accept males. For example, the Dayton, Ohio, YWCA offers a co-ed judo class for girls and boys ages eleven through seventeen. The ten-week once-a-week course only costs $10. And nonmembers can join that Y for a very low fee. Hundreds of Ys offer similar low-cost classes, which are often smaller in size than classes in commercial schools. If your local Y does not offer classes in self-protection, Y officials suggest that you request that classes be established.

There are no recommended minimum or maximum ages for taking self-protection classes. Children as young as five take judo classes and men and women over sixty have also enrolled. In general, children learn very quickly and women learn faster than men.

In summary, in view of the high drop-out rate for self-protection classes, one should not enroll unless one is very determined to complete the course. To avoid high financial loss, take classes only at a Y, where one is not asked to sign a long-term contract for many hundreds of dollars. Take the course as an exercise in physical training and self-discipline. Pasiuk urges all who take his classes to avoid encounters with criminals. As he put it very well, he teaches his students to "run, but run with confidence."

Where to Complain

Even if you take all the precautions suggested here, some of you will be taken by glib suppliers of security products and services. You will buy a product that does not perform anywhere near the salesman's claims; or the product will not operate at all or fail shortly after purchase; or the dealer will not maintain the product or fail to provide or stock replacement parts; or you will be dunned unconscionably by the supplier or the bank that finances the purchase if you refuse to make further installment payments on an obviously inferior or defective product.

What to do? First, let's assume that you have attempted repeatedly to obtain redress or service from the supplier and can make no headway. If you consider the manufacturer of the product a reputable company, or if the supplier is a branch or franchisee of a large retailer with a good reputation, begin by writing directly to the manufacturer or the head of the retailing organization.

More and more of the giant corporations are setting up customer-service offices or appointing ombudsmen to handle complaints by those who buy their products. Some of these offices are mere generators of form letters that offer soothing phrases. Some, however, are for real. To contact a manufacturer, call the local office or distributor and ask if the company has a functionary who handles complaints from customers. If so, ask for his name and address. If they don't have an ombudsman, ask for the name of the chief executive officer and write to him directly. (To my knowledge, none of the big retailers have appointed ombudsmen, so you have to complain directly to the chief executive officer.) In these letters of complaint, I suggest that you adopt a polite tone, but hint that you will take the matter to governmental agencies if you obtain no satisfaction.

If you obtain no redress from the manufacturer or retailer, or if you can't even locate the manufacturer, which is possible, then you must contact the following organizations, if they exist in your community. Don't contact them one by one in the order given; if you've been taken for a large amount, contact more than one at a time.

The Better Business Bureau. This nonprofit organization set up by responsible businessmen will make representations to the supplier on your behalf. Those suppliers who have true roots in the community and who wish to maintain their reputations may heed the BBB and either redress your complaints or work out some reasonable compromise arrangement with you. The truly unethical supplier, such as the Vigilant Protective Systems, Inc., mentioned earlier in this chapter, will pay no attention at all to the BBB. Unfortunately, the BBB does not take complaints over the phone; they must be in writing.

Postal inspectors. The mail-fraud statutes are very powerful weapons against fraudulent suppliers. They apply even if the supplier's only relation to use of the mail is posting of dunning notices by the bank or finance company that holds your note. If you have been taken by a fraudulent dealer, don't hesitate to call your local postal inspector and ask him to investigate.

Consumer affairs department or agency. In many of the larger cities, the municipal governments have set up departments or agencies to deal with the increasing volume of complaints from consumers about many inadequate products and services. Some of these agencies, through the licensing power of the municipality, have the means to force fraudulent dealers to either stop making unwarranted claims, accept returns of defective merchandise or accept lower payments in line with the true value of the product.

Department of licenses. Many businesses are licensed by the city or state. Pressure can be brought to bear through the local licensing office, which has a powerful weapon at its command: refusal to renew a license at renewal time if the licensee has a history of providing poor products or services. One of the major sources of security products, locksmith's shops, are sometimes licensed, and therefore amenable to pressure from the licensing authority. All guard services are licensed and their employees often registered.

Attorney general's office. The attorney general of your state, an elected official, may take action against unethical suppliers. Call his local office to find out if it will accept complaints—and do something about them.

Governor's consumer affairs advisor. More and more governors are appointing advisors on consumer affairs. Mrs. Virginia Knauer, the President's special assistant on consumer affairs, was previously an advisor to the governor of Pennsylvania.

Federal Trade Commission. Although the FTC is in essence limited to action against products sold in interstate commerce, the courts have interpreted this limitation so broadly that just about all products and services are now subject to action by the FTC. In general, the FTC will take strongest action against a company for which many complaints are received rather than on the basis of an isolated complaint. However, you may not be aware that the company against which you are complaining has come to the attention of the FTC repeatedly. To contact the FTC, check the listings for "U.S. Government" in your local phone book. There are twenty-four field and regional offices of the FTC. If none are listed in your local phone book, see Appendix to this chapter for the address of the nearest regional office.

Credit-card issuer. More and more transactions involving security products will be arranged through use of credit cards. Since the credit-card issuer shares in the proceeds of the sale (up to about 7 percent), he is in effect a partner or co-seller. The law on the responsibility of the credit-card issuer in the instance of a fraudulent sale is still being developed. Ralph Nader, in his group's extensive 1971 study of the giant First National City Bank of New York, attacked the bank for permitting some dealers in allegedly shoddy goods to honor the bank's credit card. The bank responded by withdrawing credit-issuing privileges from some of the dealers, even though it did insist that by law it was not responsible for the goods involved.

In time, the law may hold banks and other issuers of credit cards partly responsible for goods purchased with their cards.

Until the law becomes more definitive on this issue, it is important to recognize that an informal means of redress does exist. If you have purchased some shoddy or misrepresented goods by credit card, and have made a reasonable effort to get the dealer to make good, you should contact the issuer of the credit card. The bank or other issuer will check with the dealer and satisfy itself that you are not a crank or trying to take advantage. If the bank is satisfied, it will credit your account for the amounts involved, even if the merchant refuses to take back the goods in question. Then the merchant is charged for the amount. If the dealer was a fly-by-night and has gone out of business, the bank will "eat the loss." Bankers tell me that this does not happen very often because they don't permit companies in business less than six months to honor their card, and that such companies that do honor their card must have a good credit rating.

Legal Action

If none of the above are able to help you, and you still want to press your claim, then you have to go to court. Fortunately, it is not as time-consuming or expensive to obtain redress in the courts as you might think. First, consider the small-claims court. The upper limit for claims that can be pressed in small-claims courts has now been raised, in line with the general inflation, into the hundreds of dollars in many municipalities. This means that those who have been defrauded in the purchase of substantial products such as furniture, TV sets—or a portable burglar-alarm system—can now obtain redress in the courts without going to the expense of hiring a lawyer. In addition, small-claims courts are often open in the evening, which means that you can press your claims without losing a day's work. The cost is also very low: only several dollars usually to pay for a summons. Unfortunately, it is difficult to collect a judgment against a truly unethical supplier, because they often skip town when the going gets rough.

If the security product that is the subject of a claim is a complete home security system costing over a $1,000, then you can't go to a small-claims court to obtain redress. You must hire a lawyer, which means that you will most likely have to pay him even if you lose your case.

How to Handle Dunning Notices

If you purchased the security device or system on the installment plan, you should refuse to continue to pay for the defective product until it is replaced or repaired, even if your note is held by a bank or finance company. Before taking such a strong action, discuss the matter with your lawyer. Since most lawyers are cautious men, he will most likely advise you to continue to make payments. He knows that banks and finance companies are very tough when it comes to delinquent payments.

But my advice is to stop paying. Go down to the bank or finance company and explain just why you won't pay. The banker or loan officer will undoubtedly tell you that they are not responsible for the product since they purchased the note and are now a "holder-in-due-course." For a long time, the holder-in-due-course provision forced purchasers to pay banks and finance companies even if the product was defective. Now the courts and state legislatures are beginning to question the dubious sanctity of the holder-in-due-course concept, particularly since collusion between fraudulent dealers and the officers of banks that finance purchases has frequently come to the surface (for instance, bankers have anticipated problems with the purchasers and gotten dealers to agree to reimburse them for all legal and collection costs).

Even if the banker or loan officer indicates that he will proceed against you, don't give in; tell him that you will bring the entire matter to the attention of governmental authorities.

If the bank is a national bank, you should contact the local United States Attorney. If the bank is chartered by the state, contact your state banking commission. Tell the authorities that you have reason to believe that there was collusion between the bankers and the fraudulent dealer and that you want the matter investigated.

Incidentally, the actions suggested here against fraudulent dealers in security products apply to all frauds, of which there are far more in other product categories, such as backyard swimming pools, home improvements, food freezer plans and "future-service" deals—computer and truck-driving schools and health clubs.

Obviously, the multifront offensive I suggest against fraudulent dealers is both time-consuming and takes a lot of nerve. The point should be clear: purchase expensive security products with great care and deliberation.

Appendix • Regional and Field Offices
of the Federal Trade Commission

New England: Federal Trade Commission, Regional Office, John F. Kennedy Federal Building, Government Center, Boston, Mass. 02203. (617) 223–6621.

New York and New Jersey: FTC, Regional Office, 26 Federal Plaza, New York, N.Y. 10007. (212) 264–1204.

Pennsylvania, Maryland, Delaware, Virginia and Washington, D.C.: FTC, Regional Office, 2120 L Street, NW (Room 600), Washington, D.C. 20037. (202) 254–7700.

North Carolina, South Carolina, Tennessee, Georgia, Alabama, and Florida: FTC, Regional Office, 730 Peachtree Street, NE (Room 720), Atlanta, Ga. 30308. (404) 526–5836.

Kentucky, Michigan, Ohio and West Virginia: FTC, Regional Office, Federal Office Building (Room 486), 1240 East Ninth Street, Cleveland, Ohio 44199. (216) 831–8874.

Illinois, Indiana, Minnesota and Wisconsin: FTC, Regional Office, Everett M. Dirksen Office Building, 219 South Dearborn Street, Chicago, Ill. 60604. (312) 353–4423.

Colorado, Iowa, Kansas, Nebraska, North Dakota, South Dakota and Wyoming: FTC, Regional Office, 2806 Federal Office Building, Kansas City, Mo. 64106. (816) 374–5258.

Arkansas, Louisiana, Mississippi, Oklahoma and Texas: FTC, Regional Office, 1000 Masonic Temple Building, 333 St. Charles Street, New Orleans, La. 70130. (504) 527–2091.

Southern California, Arizona and New Mexico: FTC, Regional Office, 11000 Wilshire Boulevard (Room 13209), Los Angeles, Calif. 90024. (213) 824–7575.

Northern California, Nevada, Utah and Hawaii: FTC, Regional Office, 450 Golden Gate Avenue, Box 36005, San Francisco, Calif. 94102. (415) 556–1270.

Alaska, Idaho, Montana, Oregon and Washington: FTC, Regional Office, Suite 908, Republic Building, 1511 Third Avenue, Seattle, Wash. 98101. (206) 583–4055.

Chapter X

SECURITY ON

THE JOB

This chapter is addressed to those readers who work—or who employ others. Most of what I have to say deals with measures that businessmen can take to protect their property. However, some of these measures also protect the on-the-job property of employees—so reading the entire chapter isn't a total waste for those of you who are employees. And you will also find out what your boss might be demanding of you in the future to maintain the security of his place of business.

There's another good reason why employees should find out what employers should be doing to protect their businesses from criminals and other intruders, such as vandals: employees should support these measures and not resist any that might be considered restrictive. Why? Because their jobs might very well hinge on these security measures. Criminal depredations are one of the leading causes of business failure in the United States. Even if the company is not put out of business by the action of criminals, a victimized company can become a less pleasant place in which to work. Following a criminal assault, your boss and other executives could understandably turn a bit paranoid and might overreact, instituting highly restrictive and unpleasant security measures.

Some of you may be executives in a position to institute those suggested security measures appropriate to your company. If they work, you should earn some additional standing or responsibility in the organization, perhaps even a raise.

At the very least you should have enough loyalty to your fellow employees to support measures that protect them as well.

Criminal assault on business takes three forms: the threat from organized crime; the threat from employees, particularly embezzlers, who are usually with the company many years; and the threat from intruders such as burglars, petty thieves, pickpockets and vandals.

The second of these causes by far the greatest losses, losses estimated in the billions. No one really knows how many billions because many, perhaps most, crimes by employees are either not detected, or if detected, not revealed to the police (the employer "settles" with the embezzler on some basis or merely fires the embezzler or other dishonest employee).

Organized crime exacts a toll of many hundreds of millions each year from the business world. In many instances, unfortunately, the crooks get their foot in the door through the cooperation or weakness of the head of the firm. The president of the company may decide to deal with a gangster-run union to obtain a "sweetheart" contract, one that forces the union members to work for less pay, fewer benefits or under more onerous or dangerous conditions than other workers in comparable jobs. Or poor business conditions may force the boss to deal with a loan shark, many of whom are associated with organized crime. It's very difficult to convince a businessman in desperate straits not to go to loan sharks. It's better to go into bankruptcy, but he can't believe that.

Many businessmen buy stolen or less-than-fully-taxed merchandise from criminals. They think they are getting a bargain, until the criminals—or the law—move in on them.

As I indicated in the chapter on protecting cars and other vehicles, stolen merchandise is rarely if ever a bargain. Sometimes criminals use offers of terrific bargains in stolen merchandise to con greedy businessmen out of thousands of dollars.

The Color-Television-Set Con

The color-television-set con is one such. A shady character will approach a small retailer of appliances with an offer to sell color-television consoles at some ridiculously low price, say $100 apiece. The con man doesn't come right out and say that the sets are stolen, but he implies the same.

The retailer is told to drive his delivery truck to the loading dock of a well-known department store. There, the con man asks for a payment of as much as he can get away with—half or sometimes all of the agreed-on amount. Then the retailer is told to back his truck up to the dock and the sets will be loaded into the vehicle. Sometimes the retailer is first asked to supply an additional amount, $50 or $100, to go to an indicated shipping clerk, the one who will "load the sets onto the truck."

The retailer backs his truck up to the dock and waits . . . and waits . . . and waits. Impatient, he finally approaches the designated clerk and asks when the sets will be loaded into the truck. The clerk, who is completely innocent, naturally hasn't got the faintest idea what he's talking about. Usually, the retailer is intelligent enough to realize at that moment that he has been taken for several thousand dollars. Sometimes he gives the clerk a hard time, believing the poor clerk is really in on the deal. So the clerk calls a company guard or the cops.

How to avoid such cons and the other criminals acts of the pros should be obvious: don't have anything to do with anyone who offers a shady deal.

Deterring and Detecting Embezzlers

Embezzlers are among the most destructive of criminals. They are also among the least feared. Why? Because they are usually trusted employees, even good friends. And they never have previous criminal records.

Taking advantage of positions of trust, they can rob a company blind. Embezzlers frequently get away with hundreds of thousands of dollars over a period of years.

As I have done elsewhere, I could supply a long check list of danger signals.

Here are a few of the danger signals that really call for scrutiny:

• Be suspicious of any employee who never takes a vacation and who always works overtime or on weekends. He may need the extra time to cover up his depredations.

• Be suspicious of any employee who refuses a promotion out of a position where he handles much cash or approves payments.

• Be suspicious of any employee whose life style suddenly changes. Don't be put off by the stock explanation that he or she "suddenly came into an inheritance."

• If your company is sold and some trusted employee is disgruntled by the sale, or if a long-time employee is not promoted to some position he covets, keep an eye on him. He may take out his chagrin on the company.

Here are some other ways to detect or at least impede embezzlers:

• Suddenly change the standard date on which the books are audited or an inventory of goods taken.

• If one employee has responsibility for preparing accounts payable and invoices and then depositing the resulting checks from customers or preparing checks for suppliers, split up this dual responsibility, or switch the present holder of the job to another position.

• Arrange for all checks from customers to go directly to a post office box emptied by your bank. (This move also offers the added payoff of faster deposit of cash, helpful in times of tight money.)

There are many other approaches and procedures for detecting the unknown, unsuspected embezzler. What is surprising is how many businesses are able to support embezzlers for years and years. Maybe yours is one of them.

Repelling Intruders

In terms of dollar damage, the criminal intruder is the least destructive of all. However, the effects of intrusion are far more traumatic than embezzlement or other white-collar crimes. The disruption and demoralization caused by a small burglary can be immeasurable. If even one employee is terrified, injured—or killed—as a result of a criminal intrusion, the true cost of the loss will be hard to calculate and even harder to forget. (In the event an employee is injured by a criminal, your legal obligation as an employer is covered by the existing workmen's compensation laws.)

Prevention—the Essence of Self-Protection

The basic objective of any security system is to *deter* the would-be criminal from entering your premises in the first place. At the very least, the process of breaking and entering should be as *time-consuming* as possible. Once inside, additional deterrents should protect high-value property, such as calculators or computers, making burglary or spite damage difficult if not impossible.

In most companies, the traditional guards, locks, gates, alarms, etc., are relied upon to provide the framework of protection. Fortunately, ingenious devices and techniques to supplement the familiar ones are coming on the market in great number. Unfortunately, the many promotional claims made for these new products, mostly electronic in nature, could confuse the businessman seeking to raise the level of security of his plant, warehouse, offices or company vehicles.

But the most ingenious mechanical devices may be worthless if your security program fails to screen out strangers during the working day. The most obvious loopholes are often the most likely to be overlooked. The most valuable additions to your present security measures may well be those that do not cost a penny. But they will require the cooperation of all employees.

A well-planned security system must start at the entrances to your premises. Intruders come in two unwholesome varieties: welcomed and unwelcomed. The intruders who are often welcomed into your premises are the delivery boys, messengers, repairmen, salesmen, scrap collectors, drivers or casual visitors who either have a legitimate excuse for entrance, or who fake such an excuse or affect disarming authenticity.

Larceny may not be on their minds when they enter, but an unwatched purse or wallet or an open drawer tempts them to petty crime. Or they see objects of value worth the greater risk of breaking and entering at a more appropriate time, perhaps after first disabling your alarm (the conductive metallic striping on windows and doors can be cut unobtrusively with a razor).

Deterring such intruders is simple yet demanding in terms of employee discipline. An effective system of visitor controls should include these minimum precautions:

• All deliveries and pickups should be made at the reception area or shipping dock. No outside messengers or delivery boys should be permitted to roam your premises.

• All visitors should be registered and escorted to the person they wish to see—and then escorted back to the reception area when their business is complete. If high security is needed, consider badges for visitors (see p. 247 for a discussion of employee identification cards). If your building is large or has areas of varying sensitivity, issue color-coded visitor's badges that limit travel to one area or floor.

• Traffic through your premises by strangers can be cut sharply if an interview room for salesmen, those seeking employment and other visitors is provided off your reception area. This is also a good way to avoid the embarrassment of making all visitors open their briefcases for inspection. (This is standard practice among those companies dealing with the Department of Defense. It works well.)

• Train your executives and employees and guards (if you employ them) to ask any unescorted stranger if he needs directions to where he is going and then escort him there.

• Discourage social callers and other visitors on business other than company business. For instance, don't permit insurance agents during working hours. (This is a security measure that helps pay for itself—passing strangers distract employees from their work.) Retailers are obviously one major branch of business that can't discourage visitors. Some special new techniques for deterring shoplifters are discussed later.

• Finally, a search should be made of your premises each evening before closing to make sure that no intruder has hidden himself to circumvent costly security measures.

• Caution: Introduce a program of visitor control with discretion. Carefully explain its need to your employees, stressing that the aim is to protect them and their property as much as to protect company property. Sudden imposition of visitor controls with no explanation could be resented and contribute to lower morale. No one enjoys a fortresslike atmosphere— at home or at work.

Identification Badges

If you employ guards during working hours, they can do a much better job of deterring intruders if all employees and visitors wear identification badges.

Employee ID badges require photos. Local photographers can provide the photos, but few of them are equipped to make up complete ID badges, which usually calls for laminating the photo inside sheets of clear plastic. Hand-operated laminators are available for as little as $100.

If you have a considerable number of employees and no satisfactory local photography service is available to make up ID badges, consider buying or leasing your own system. The simplest are based on the instant Polaroid camera. Suppliers claim that, in volume, badges can be made up quickly on company premises for as little as fifty cents apiece.

Where required, special codes, such as the Hollerith Code associated with the familiar tab card, can be punched into the ID card. Then the card can be used for other purposes, such as recording attendance, recording completion of jobs, opening doors and opening the gate to a company parking lot. These functions require installation of card readers, and in the instance of the first two, connection of the readers to the computer that keeps tabs on these aspects of the business. Card readers cost about $300 each (see Appendix for sources).

Deterring the Unwelcomed Intruder

Deterring the unwelcomed intruder calls for more than employee discipline; it requires an investment in locks, alarms and a variety of devices and systems. Whatever else you install, you may still want to include a traditional device, such as central-station alarms, for two simple reasons:

• Since many of the newer devices have not been approved by the Underwriters' Laboratories, their use may not earn the user the customary burglary insurance discounts, which can run as high as 70 percent.

• Evidence of forcible entry is still required before a burglary claim can be successfully pressed and payment made. Some of the newer devices cannot by their nature provide such evidence.

But even if you are satisfied with the performance or degree of deterrence provided by your present security setup or program, knowledge of the newer security products can be valuable. Here's why:

• Criminals soon learn to circumvent or disarm security products. Therefore, the mere passage of time may make your present setup less effective.

• Crime insurance premiums may rise so high that you are forced into self-insurance and greater reliance on self-protection, or your underwriter may refuse to issue crime insurance or even cancel your present policy. (See Chapter XI on "Crime Insurance.")

• Demand for central-station alarm service may be so great (stimulated in large part by the Bank Protection Act) that you may not be able to obtain it in your locality—or your present service may decline in performance (due to poor phone service).

How Secure Are Your Doors and Windows?

Locks—on windows and skylights as well as doors—are still the first line of defense against intruders. But a lock is only as secure as the door or window that it guards. (See Chapter III for a discussion of locks.)

Double-cylinder locks are particularly recommended for front doors of business establishments. These are locks that require keys to open from the inside. They are effective against intruders who enter through small windows or skylights, then try to leave through the front door with merchandise or office machines.

If appearance of doors or windows is a consideration, consider the new break-resistant glasses, which crack under but do not give way quickly to the blows of a sledgehammer. (See Chapter III for discussion of high-security glazing.)

Cinderblock wall construction is another concern. Without making too much noise, a burglar with a crowbar can knock out one cinderblock, then pry enough others loose to enter a building. Old-fashioned brick walls are an effective deterrent.

Roofs are another point of entry. If you are in a one- or two-story building, the roof is often quite flimsy. To protect against burglars who enter by cutting holes in roofs, sensing wires may be mounted in the ceiling or a space alarm (see p. 109) installed.

Folding gates over doors and windows are gaining in popularity—and earn insurance discounts in some localities. To protect unobserved access points, these metal gates should slide in strong metal frames. For windows facing a busy street, a simple, unframed accordion gate may be sufficient. If appearance and ease of daily use are a consideration, you should investigate roll-up gates, which retract out of sight. But they are much more costly. (For a discussion of the padlocks required to secure these gates, see p. 73.)

One last access point to check: the airconditioning ducts. If your facilities are centrally airconditioned, make sure that the grill over the outside duct is locked. Provide a heavy-mesh or iron-bar barrier close to the outside grill. If you have an alarm, tie the barrier to it. Burglars have been known to back big trucks up to an airconditioning duct and enter a building undetected through the ductwork.

If you are concerned about the quality of your locks and the access points they protect, hire a master locksmith to check them; he'll charge about $10 an hour.

Central-Station Alarms

Central alarms are still rated the most reliable of all alarms—and earn the highest discounts on insurance. In some high-crime areas, no burglary insurance is available without installation of a central-station alarm.

When a central station receives an alarm, the man on duty calls the police and dispatches guards, who usually bring the sealed keys to the establishment. These guards are armed, but the weapons are to protect themselves. The guards are strongly deterred from using their weapons against intruders. Any arrests based on central-station-alarm reports are nearly always made by the police.

These alarms depend on a direct leased telephone line from your premises to the nearest station of the company providing the service. In some localities, the charges for the leased line are the same to all, but usually the charges increase with distance. Charges for these leased lines average $5 to $10 per month.

Reliability of central-station alarms should be high because the companies providing them claim to test them regularly and because a warning signal is received if the line fails or is cut deliberately. They are supposed to be fail-safe.

Unfortunately, central-station alarms have the reputation for generating a high proportion of false alarms. The Los Angeles Police Department made a study of all alarms received via central stations during a one-week period and found that the false ones totalled 95 percent. An analysis, however, showed that a good third of the false alarms were caused by failure of the employees of the establishment using the service to lock all doors and windows properly and follow other procedures. Loose windowpanes are a frequent cause of false alarms, and the police have come to expect many false alarms whenever there is a windstorm or heavy rain, and also during electrical storms.

The companies that provide central-station alarms are also prepared to guard against other possible dangers such as fire and water leakage and breakdown of deep freezers.

Because installation charges are high, selection of a central-station alarm service calls for care. If you decide to drop the service—or if you move to other quarters—the installation charge is not recoverable (the earliest that many of these services can be canceled is after two years).

An anti-intrusion technique in which the events inside a monitored factory, office building or store are accurately screened by the sounds emitted is coming into competition with the conventional central-station alarm systems. (Larger companies are also buying sound-monitoring gear to be added to in-plant security systems.)

These new services (the first was started in 1967) offer a much lower false-alarm rate than the conventional central-station systems such as ADT and Holmes. The key to their lower rate is the use of human monitors back at the central station. A human can quickly learn to differentiate between the sounds generated by a rainstorm, hail, dogs and cats, children tossing a ball against a window—and a burglar or vandal. While the conventional systems rarely drop below a 90 percent false-alarm rate, the sound systems rarely exceed 15 percent. Some police departments, frustrated by the false alarms, are proposing what has been suggested many times in the past: that a fine ($50) be imposed for each false alarm.

Three other advantages offered by the sound systems are: inherent protection against the "lay-in," burglars who hide on the premises just before closing; rapid detection of teenage vandals whose only objective is to break windows; and much lower installation costs. (To install a sound system, a mike is merely glued high up on a wall. By contrast, conventional systems require a lot of skilled labor.)

Conventional systems can also protect against the lay-in, but this calls for additional expensive interior detectors, some of which are also subject to false alarms.

Because the sound systems are comparatively new (central-station systems have been offering sound-monitoring of bank vaults for fifty years, but these are not listen-in devices; rather an alarm goes off automatically if any sound is heard, which is quite suitable for a vault), they rarely have UL approval, which means few insurers will grant discounts for sound systems. However, UL approval is less meaningful these days because in many cities, burglary insurance is either not available or prohibitively expensive. Therefore many companies opt for self-insurance or add extra protection beyond the insurer's requirements. Some companies have taken both measures. The sound-based central-station services also offer subsidiary protection against holdups, fire and smoke, and boiler overflow. As the sound systems prove themselves, it is not unlikely that the conventional systems will add this technique to their array of services.

To find out if a sound-monitoring service is available in your locality, check the classified phone directory under "Burglar Alarm Systems." Many have been organized under the "Sonitrol" trade name.

Many businesses that cannot afford central-station alarms or which do not require that degree of security install local alarms mounted outside. These alarms are purchased rather than paid for monthly as a service, and unless they are maintained regularly, they cannot be expected to function well.

True to the maxim "you get what you pay for," local alarms are effective in relation to price. Reliability is not high and the very high incidence of false alarms does little to stimulate police action when a local alarm sounds. Nevertheless, a local alarm—when it works—can be expected to scare off intruders, and it does earn limited discounts from some underwriters. If you choose a local alarm, *make sure it can only be deactivated from inside* the premises and that it includes enough delay to allow designated employees to enter the premises and shut it off by key before it goes off to annoy your neighbors. Local alarms require the cooperation of neighbors to be effective.

Why the Guard Services Are Expanding

The old traditional reliable company guard or watchman is gradually becoming extinct. Retired police officers and firemen, two of the major sources of company guards, are more and more reluctant to become bank dicks or company guards. They are retiring at earlier ages and seeking better-paying jobs. Salaries of company guards are rising, as the sources of experienced guards dwindle.

To obtain competent guards, companies are turning more and more to the organized guard services, which are expanding rapidly in number and in size of staff. Already the guard services employ one-third of the more than one million private guards in the United States.

Guard services offer certain advantages. The men come trained—more or less. They are under some supervision at all times, often through unscheduled inspection visits. The number of guards is easily expanded—or cut. The bill includes all charges, such as Social Security, uniforms and vacations. But there is a bill, and it can run over $150 per man per week per shift. That comes to about $25,000 per twenty-four-hour guard station each year.

There are some disadvantages to guard services. They are experiencing difficulty hiring good people. Sometimes they supply men who are no more than warm bodies. Despite claims that all employees are checked out, some guard services hire any halfway presentable man who shows up at what amounts to a morning shape-up. Such guards have been known to engage in pilferage themselves. In addition, these services have been known to supply their best men to a new customer, then slowly downgrade the quality of guard over the months. So you have to check up on the guards from to time. If you are not satisfied, begin by protesting. If your protests are unavailing, find a new guard service—or hire company guards.

Helping Guards to Guard More

To get the greatest return on the high investment in guards, you should consider the various devices that either extend their reach, sustain their alertness or actually keep tabs on their performance. These include: watchman's clocks, watchman's alarm systems, walkie-talkies, closed-circuit TV, employee identification badges, and dogs.

The sturdy watchman's clock is a familiar device that in effect insures that the watchman makes a complete tour of his assigned beat. It records on an inaccessible (to the guard) sheet of paper the exact times at which the bearer visited the various key-equipped stations on his tour. A recent extension of the watchman's clock concept is the tie to an automatic phone alarm. If a watchman fails to visit an assigned station within a certain period, the alarm automatically calls the police or some outside guard service. (See Chapter V for a more complete discussion of phone alarms.)

If your facilities are large enough to require more than one guard on duty at the same time, one of the most effective ways to keep them in communication is by the walkie-talkie radio. These transmitter-receiver combinations are powerful enough to span the largest industrial facilities, and even work well inside steel buildings.

Walkie-talkies are available for as little as $100 a pair. Really not much more than toys, they should not be relied upon for security purposes. The sturdiest walkie-talkies are recommended for one simple reason: guards resent carrying them in addition to other weighty gear such as watchman's clocks, flashlights, nightsticks and guns, and they have been known to show their resentment by "drop-testing" the units out an upper-story window or even dragging them on a line behind trucks. A top-quality walkie-talkie costs about $800 per unit. Reputable suppliers include General Electric, Halli-crafters and Motorola.

Closed-Ciruit TV

If you use guards, their reach can be extended by the use of closed-ciruit television (CCTV). Unlike entertainment TV, CCTV is never broadcast: the signals are confined to coaxial cables between the camera and the receiving monitor.

The CCTV camera can be fixed in place or it can automatically scan an area. In more elaborate setups, a zoom lens can be fitted on the camera for an extra $300 to $400, enabling the viewer to remotely close in if he spots a suspicious situation. Often, a single guard watches more than one monitor, or he can view more than one scene if the monitor is equipped with a split-screen feature. Where one guard must keep an eye on a number of monitors or a succession of views on one monitor, there is the danger that he may miss an intruder on another monitor. To avoid this, the monitors can be equipped with an electronic device that sounds an alarm if motion is detected on the monitor. Such a device costs about $1,500.

In a really high-security situation, or where an intrusion is anticipated, a video recorder can be attached to the monitor or set up with its own camera. The video recorder need not operate 100 percent of the time. It can record at intervals and thereby run longer without needing additional tapes. One such stop-motion machine can record for seventy-two hours before changing tapes.

Incidentally, all the CCTV and video recorders used for security purposes are black-and-white. Color isn't worth the much higher expense, aside from the matter of higher reliability, easier adjustment and quicker and less costly repairs for black-and-white.

Prices of TV cameras have been dropping steadily, particularly now that $200 cameras are coming in from Japan in growing numbers. However, good U.S.-made single-lens cameras still cost about $700 each. The monitors cost about twice as much as home TV sets for the same size screen. However, they are constructed to perform more reliably and last longer than a home TV. Electronics expert Arnold Goldberger suggests that ordinary home TV sets be used as monitors to cut costs, but that a spare set be purchased with part of the money saved. (But the units must be altered so that they can't receive broadcast TV—or the guards might merely entertain themselves.)

Installation costs are not too high unless appearance is a factor. Coaxial cables must be strung between the camera and the monitor, which are often hundreds of feet apart. Before buying a CCTV system, ask for a day-long demonstration. Some cameras and monitors work fine as long as the salesman is unobtrusively adjusting the controls. Make sure that the picture is still sharp after eight hours of unattended operation.

If you buy CCTV to detect shoplifters or pilferers, don't skimp on the quality of the cameras. A poor image won't show some skillful shoplifters and pilferers at work or may confuse your guards into apprehending an innocent person. Settling a false-arrest suit can be very costly.

Many retailers have been achieving some of the "Big Brother" effect of CCTV in foiling shoplifting and pilfering with fake installations. Professional criminals can spot the fakes, but the casual intruder or first-time shoplifter may be deterred by them. To maintain the effect of the fake cameras, a single live camera can be spotted among them. Conversely, the effect of live cameras can be magnified if some fakes are sprinkled among them.

CCTV is another of those security measures that helps pay for itself. Employers have discovered that where CCTV is used to detect shoplifting or pilfering, the honest employees within view of the camera work harder.

Guard Dogs

Guard dogs, perhaps the most ancient of security measures, are again gaining in popularity. Dogs offer one unmatched feature—a sharp sense of smell. They can smell out the lay-in, the intruder who hides on your premises at closing time. This is a favorite means of gaining access to department stores, large warehouses or multistory office buildings. Dogs can also patrol much faster than a guard. However, trained guard dogs, which cost from $600 to $3,000 apiece, should rarely be used without an attendant.

There are certain obvious disadvantages to dogs. Quarters, a continuous supply of water and feeders must be provided for them. In addition, if they are left to roam your premises for long periods, say over long weekends, guess what you will "nose out" on your return.

There is one very handy way to use guard dogs if you can arrange it. Have the dog brought in at closing time to search out any lay-ins, *and that's all.* This is a way to take advantage of the dog's unique characteristic without incurring some of the penalties. Services that offer guard dogs plus handlers for short periods of time are only likely to be available in large cities.

Lighting: a Low-Cost Deterrent

As I indicated earlier, lighting is one of the cheapest deterrents to intruders. The new high-intensity light sources mean that only a few lights are needed to illuminate the entire perimeter of a building, denying an intruder the cover he may need to work his way through a door or window. (If your roof is vulnerable too, consider floodlighting the roof as well.)

Exterior lighting should be matched by all-night lighting of interiors, particularly ground-level spaces that can be viewed from the exterior. The cost of leaving lights on all night is modest. If arranged carefully, moreover, lights can make a building look like a showplace to passersby.

Retailers are urged to leave their cash registers open

(empty, of course) and bathed in light. Safes should also be exposed by light.

Interior Lines of Defense

Despite all of the above measures and precautions, criminals still enter business premises undetected. This means that secondary deterrents are needed to protect exposed valuables. Some very sophisticated secondary deterrents are available. First, familiar, simple and not-too-costly products should be applied.

Secondary Deterrents in Office Buildings

Once burglars or vandals have penetrated a large office building, they are usually free to roam about sacking one office after another. To deny them access from one floor to another, one-way door openers are easily installed on all fire-exit doors, forcing any intruders to go down to the ground level, or up to the roof, if they enter a fire staircase. Better still, equip each door with an alarm that sounds if it is opened. Such alarms cost about $100 per door installed.

These deterrents must be coupled with special measures to control movement of elevators. At the end of the working day, self-service elevators should be set so that they can only return to the ground level and not open at intermediate floors. Or they can be set so that they require an operator, such as the night watchman or guard.

Daytime burglaries and even robberies of one-man or one-girl branch offices are becoming more common in large cities. The obvious deterrent is keeping the door locked at all times, and providing a peephole.

Another useful deterrent for the small office is the low-cost CCTV system. These systems, which are made in Japan, include a camera (to be mounted outside the door), monitor (an adaptation of an eight-inch TV set) and audio link. From her desk, your secretary can view visitors, question them over the audio channel and then open the door by pressing a button that releases a solenoid-operated door lock. At less than $300 per system, they are a buy—but don't expect high reliability at that price. These systems can be purchased at some department stores, such as Sears.

Safes

There is no need for a long exposition on one of the most familiar of the traditional security products, the safe. A well-built safe provides very good deterrence against the amateur burglar and substantial deterrence against the professional. At not too much added cost, safes also protect valuable documents against fire.

However, a safe provides *no* deterrence if it is *not completely locked*. Police who investigate burglaries from safes report that those responsible for locking them all too frequently fail to do the job well. To make it easy to reopen the next working day, the dial is not completely turned, which means that it need only be reset to the last number to spring open. Burglars know this, and usually their first action is to carefully turn the dials of safes in the hope of finding the ones not fully locked. Therefore, you must train your employees—and yourself—to spin the dial of the safe several times before leaving. (For a more complete discussion of safes, see Chapter IV, Part A, "Safe-Deposit Boxes, Safes and Security Closets.")

Retailers and others who collect considerable cash during the working day should know about one of the recent developments in safes. The drop depository safe is in effect a one-way safe that can accept deposits from anyone, but opens only to those with the combination. The least expensive (under $50) drop depository safe has a slot over the door. More sophisticated models have a cylinder in the top into which one places the cash. Spinning the cylinder drops the cash into the compartment. Manufacturers provide window decals that let any robbers know that those present can't open the safe.

If at all possible, place the safe—*well illuminated*—where it can be seen by passersby, the cop on the beat or by a guard on his rounds. If your office is on an upper level, attach the safe to a structural member as near as possible to a window that can be seen from the street. At night, the safe should be illuminated. In this way, if burglars attempt to break into or move the safe, they run the risk of being seen from the street. Or if they drape a black curtain over the window to obscure an attempt to open the safe with an acetylene torch, the obscuring of the normal illumination might attract attention.

Protecting Office Machines

Portable office machines are one of the prime targets of the petty thief, even if they bring but a mere fraction of their value. Readily saleable, office machines are becoming a more attractive target of the thief as they rise in value. While new technology can supplement the means of protecting office machines, the old methods come first. Begin by bolting down all typewriters and machines that are not normally moved about the office. Bolting will discourage the thief, who is usually pressed for time.

To discourage the thief even more, use the various types of locks that secure the machines to the desks or tables on which they are used. These locking devices range from $5 for a type that requires a padlock to $12.50 for a type that includes a built-in lock. If you buy these devices in volume, the price per unit drops by as much as 25 percent. They are available at office-supplies houses.

The elaborate systems developed to prevent thefts of TV sets from motels can also be applied to office machines in very large offices. These systems tell a guard at a remote console that an electric office machine has been unplugged from the power outlet.

A new problem in office security is created by the extremely small size of the latest battery-operated electronic calculators from Japan. They are too small to be bolted to a desk, and securing them would negate their main attraction, which is portability. One obvious means of securing them is to lock them up at the end of the working day in either a safe or lockable file cabinet. Another way to avoid this problem is not to purchase such small machines unless there is a real need for them, such as making calculations in the field.

Of course, you have previously noted down the serial numbers of all portable office machines to aid in their identification in case of theft. If the police department in your locality maintains a computerized identification system (see p. 23), all office machines should also be marked with your license number or the number of some other executive.

New Low-Security Alarm Systems

Even though you may be satisfied with your present alarm system, it's a good idea to be aware of the newer devices that are constantly being developed. Some may be worth considering if the police in your locality begin to downgrade their level of response to present alarm systems.

The lower-security devices range in price from $50 to $1,000 and more, plus installation. At the low end of the cost scale are a variety of self-contained alarms that fit right on the door they protect (see p. 125).

New Proprietary Alarm Systems

If a high degree of security is needed, your best bet is still the central-station alarm or company guards. However, if your plant is far from a central station, the cost of the leased line is not only high, but the distance from the station precludes a rapid response to an alarm. (In many small localities, the police are willing to permit a leased-line alarm to come right into police stations. Check the availability of such extra protection in your area. However, before approving this kind of arrangement, check the degree of response with other businesses that have already installed these direct alarms. Since the police are not paid any premium to monitor alarms, the reliability of response may be poor or haphazard.)

Even guards can't be expected to cover every situation. Therefore, additional electronic security measures may be indicated. The most elaborate electronic security devices connect into a console that is supervised by a guard.

The console provides indications of intrusions, fire, smoke, water leakage or any other emergency condition desired. Leading suppliers of such elaborate systems, which generally go into large facilities, are listed in the Appendix. The many different kinds of sophisticated and conventional detectors discussed in detail in Chapter V, "Electronic Security Systems," can be hooked into these proprietary systems.

If you are turned off by the high cost of high-security devices, remember that these costs can be cut by concentrating high-value documents, materials or merchandise in one space or room that requires only a single alarm or a smaller, less-costly system.

New Weapons Against Shoplifters

Deterring shoplifting is one of the most difficult and sensitive security assignments. If the controls are too strong, then customers are deterred from entering. If too lax, shoplifters will soon take all the slim profits out of a retailing operation.

One of the most popular techniques used against shoplifters is closed-circuit TV. Electronic technology has also created several new antishoplifting systems that may find applications elsewhere, such as in deterring internal thefts of valuable tools or irreplaceable magnetic tapes from computer rooms.

The older of the antishoplifting systems depend on the attachment of a passive reflector of electromagnetic (radio) energy on items selected for protection. Anyone attempting to leave the store—or that part of the store selling high-priced items—with an item that contains a reflector must pass through a narrow archway equipped with electronics that creates an invisible electromagnetic field inside the archway. The reflector reflects enough energy to either disturb the field pattern or trigger the electronic system (the inventors are sensibly secretive about the exact mechanism to keep professional shoplifters from finding an antidote). Naturally, the reflector has to be removed with all merchandise tags at the time of sale.

The latest in electronic antishoplifting systems operates on the principle of magnetics. In the Stoplifter system, an inexpensive magnetic label is attached to each item to be protected. If the label is not demagnetized at the checkout counter, it disturbs a magnetic field at the eight-foot-wide exit gate, setting off an alarm. Because the labels cost as little as three cents apiece in volume, there is no need to reuse them.

Since the Stoplifter system is quite new, I have not yet had an opportunity to observe one of the few installations. However, I did study the older Knogo system. In the latter system, which was first offered in the mid-1960s, the reflector is a sturdy plastic card. It is attached by a special steel rivet, generally in some conspicuous part of the item (nearly always a garment). The reflector is removed by a powerful yet safe electric chopper mounted on the checkout counter. If a shoplifter succeeds in removing the reflector, it usually tears the garment enough to make it unwearable or unsaleable.

The security chief in a major metropolitan department store reported that the system detected 178 "incidents" in a little more than six months, permitting the store to recover $10,416.13 worth of merchandise. But these savings have to be balanced against the following expenses: the archways rent for $50 a month. This department required seven archways, which usually must be erected in pairs to meet municipal requirements for width of exits. Equipment for each of three wrapping desks rents for $50 a month per desk. Installation costs several thousand dollars, and there is also the rental of many thousands of tags (reflectors) at $50 a month per thousand.

Also, making the system work requires much supervision and good discipline: detectives must spot-check garments to make sure that each has a reflector attached and they must remove and lock up the choppers at night to make sure that housekeeping employees don't use them to remove reflectors.

Another antishoplifting system of more recent origin is offered by Sensormatic Electronics. The reflector used by Sensormatic is quite unobtrusive and is attached by an easily cut plastic loop. However, it can also be concealed on a garment so that a shoplifter can't find it. More powerful or more sensitive electronics are apparently used on the Sensormatic gate because the gate is between two to three times the width of the Knogo archway. This means only one gate is needed to meet many municipal regulations on widths of exits.

The Sensormatic system appears to offer much the same advantages and disadvantages of the Knogo system. That includes one important disadvantage for any chain-store operation: corresponding departments in all stores in the chain must be equipped with the system or commonplace transfers of merchandise are impeded by the need to either take off or add on the tags.

Still another new antishoplifting system requires no electronics at all. It is specific against the shoplifter who attempts to conceal stolen goods in shopping bags containing merchandise for which he has paid. The antidote is simple: make the bags transparent. Since ordinary plastic bags are usually not strong enough, Continental Extrusion Corporation offers extra-strength bags with reinforced handles called Security-Totes. These bags can be sealed by stapling, by pressure-sensitive adhesives or by heat sealing. They cost from one and one-half to three times as much as paper bags, depending on size and quantity, but only a few cents apiece.

Protecting Company Vehicles

Thefts of and attacks on vehicles are up sharply: the number of cars stolen will pass one million in 1972. In New York City, some underwriters are refusing to insure Cadillacs, while others insist that alarms be installed to obtain insurance on expensive cars.

Hijacking is skyrocketing, causing insurance rates on truck cargoes to spiral. The major deterrent to hijacking or thefts from company trucks is careful checking of the backgrounds of drivers and dispatchers. Hiring standards must be carefully maintained prior to Christmas and at other times when temporary drivers are often added. The experts claim that most of the crime associated with truck cargoes is based on collusion with or information supplied by employees.

One simple deterrent to thefts from trucks is *not* providing drivers with keys to the cargo compartments. Another is the

well-known Babaco alarm (Babaco supplies about 85 percent
of the truck alarms installed on over twenty thousand trucks
and two thousand salesmen's cars). To obtain an insurance
discount for a truck alarm, it should generally be leased
rather than bought. The leased alarms (cost: $100 per year)
are supposed to be tested by the supplier about every two
months.

Some truck alarms help pay for themselves because the
same key is required for the ignition and cargo compartment,
forcing the driver to shut off the engine to make a delivery.

Truck alarms are not very effective against hijackers, although they can be rigged so that they sound off if a hijacker
attempts to open the door to the driver compartment.

Another company has developed a cargo-locking system
based on special plastic cards. The driver's card alone can
start the engine. Both the driver's card and another card in
possession only of the dispatcher and recipient open the
cargo compartment.

Attacks on vehicles used to make collections from customers are also on the rise. One obvious deterrent is not
using drivers or salesmen to collect money: induce your customers to pay by mail. If you can't change their payment
habits, consider mounting of drop depository safes (see p.
37) on collection vehicles. Naturally, the driver is not given
the combination. The safe has to be securely bolted or welded
to the chassis.

If your salesmen carry valuable samples in their cars (supplied by the company or themselves), install an alarm. The
most effective—the Babaco alarm—is also the most costly.
The installation fee is about $100. (See Chapter VIII, which
discusses auto alarms.)

If company—or employee—cars are subject to stripping or
vandalism in the company parking lot, deterrence costs jump.

If the lot is small, consider fencing it in and then giving each employee a key to the padlock on the gate. If the company employs guards, perhaps the guard post can be relocated to guard the parking lot as well as the entrance to the building. Elaborate automatic systems are also available that permit only those who hold special plastic cards (see p. 247) to open the gate to the lot.

Development of new protection devices is at its highest level and new products are entering the marketplace at an unprecedented rate. The result should be wider choices, better products and hopefully better values too. New devices are essential, because skilled criminals soon learn how to thwart those on the market.

But the rush of new products can also create problems for businessmen seeking security. Therefore, my recommendations in Chapter IX, "How to Buy Security Products and Services," apply with equal force to business as well as residential premises.

Appendix · *Sources of Equipment*

In general, the best product to buy is the product that is sold locally. This is your only assurance that the service and maintenance that are essential to the proper functioning of a security system are quickly and easily available. Your local classified telephone directory will provide a good starting point for your investigation of products and equipment. In addition, I have listed below some of the major manufacturers and suppliers of security devices. If you are interested, I suggest that you write them directly and ask whether they have branch offices or distributors in your area.

Proprietary Alarm Systems (for Large Installations)

American District Telegraph Company (ADT), 155 Avenue of the Americas, New York, N.Y. 10013.

Honeywell, Inc., Commercial Division, 2701 Fourth Avenue South, Minneapolis, Minn. 55408.

Johnson Service Company, Milwaukee, Wisc. 53201.

Notifier Company, 3700 North 56th Street, Lincoln, Neb. 68504.

Mosler, Inc., 1561 Grand Avenue, Hamilton, Ohio 45012.

Sound-Monitoring Equipment

To purchase sound-monitoring equipment for inclusion in an in-plant system, contact your local central-station sound system or the following:

Executone, Inc., 29-10 Thomson Avenue, Long Island City, N.Y. 11101.

Honeywell, Inc., Commercial Division, 2701 Fourth Avenue South, Minneapolis, Minn. 55408.

International Alarm Research, 4494 Elizabeth Lake Road, Pontiac, Mich. 48054.

Mardix, 900 Stierlin Road, Mountain View, Calif. 94040.

Multra-Guard, Inc., 12750 Twinbrook Parkway, Rockville, Md. 20852.

Sonitrol Corp., Daleville, Ind. 47334.

Specialized Telephone Alarms

There are a large number of suppliers of telephone alarms, and more are entering the business all the time. The three manufacturers listed below offer unique variations. Banks, gas stations or other establishments handling large sums of money may be especially interested in investigating either Eaton or Mayday. Both offer small pocket transmitters that actuate nearby phone alarms by radio signals.

Mayday Protective Systems, a division of Electro-Nite Company, Comley and Decatur Roads, Philadelphia, Pa. 19154.

Eaton Corp., 401 Theodore Fremd Avenue, Rye, N.Y. 10580.

Steffens Security Systems, Inc., 233 Broad Street, Elizabeth, N.J. 07208, offers a watchman's station tied into a phone alarm.

Truck Alarms

Babaco Alarm Systems (see your local telephone directory).

Ever-Guard Alarm Systems, 512 West 20th Street, New York, N.Y. 10011.

Pushbutton Electronic Locks

Permaloc Security Devices, Inc., 8226 Fenton Street, Silver Spring, Md. 20910.

Systems for Opening Doors Based on Plastic Cards

Detex Corp., 53 Park Place, New York, N.Y. 10007.

Digital Identification Systems, 9200 Glenoaks Boulevard, Sun Valley, Calif. 91352.

Holobeam Security Systems, 560 Winters Avenue, Paramus, N.J. 07652.

Industrial Instrumentations, Inc., 14 Prospect Street, Marblehead, Mass. 01945.

Employee Identification-Card Systems

Avant, Inc., P.O. Box 88, Concord, Mass. 01742.

General Binding Corp., 1101 Skokie Boulevard, Northbrook, Ill. 60062.

Security on the Job

Polaroid Corp., Cambridge, Mass. 02139.

Sipco, Inc., 20727 Dearborn Street, Chatsworth, Calif. 91311.

Card Readers

For coded plastic ID cards—to record attendance or jobs completed.

Programming Devices Division, Sealectro Corp., 225 Hoyt Street, Mamaroneck, N.Y. 10543.

Antishoplifting Systems

Check-Mate Systems, Inc., Pickering Creek Industrial Park, Lionville, Pa. 19353.

Continental Extrusion Corporation, 2 Endo Boulevard, Garden City, N.Y. 11530.

Knogo Corp., 112 State Street, Westbury, N.Y. 11590.

Sensormatic Electronics Corp., 2040 Sherman Street, Hollywood, Fla. 33020.

Stoplifter International, Inc., 6116 North Central Expressway, Dallas, Tex. 75206.

Chapter XI

CRIME INSURANCE

"Crime insurance isn't your first line of defense; it's your last!" This advice given to me recently by a prominent insurance consultant sums up the proper attitude to maintain toward crime insurance. No amount of insurance can make up for the aggravation and disruption of a burglary or auto theft or the trauma of a robbery in which you are *not* injured. Of course, if you are injured, there's certainly no way to make up for bodily harm or persisting pain. And we are not even considering the horror of murder or rape.

However, crime insurance does have an important role to play in making up for the economic burden of crime. The loss of a substantial part or all of your assets is a great shock. In this chapter, I review the obvious forms of crime insurance, such as coverage for burglary, auto theft and floaters for jewelry; less obvious coverage, such as for theft of luggage and credit cards; and finally, the need for liability coverage. As a result of recent federal legislation, burglary insurance is now once more available in some states where it was practically impossible to obtain because of extremely heavy losses.

Most crime insurance is obtained as part of a package in which it is the lesser aspect of coverage. For example, coverage against theft of your car is included in the "Comprehensive" portion of the auto policy, which deals with fire and theft. However, in most localities, comprehensive coverage is a small portion of the cost for good reason. The economic loss from car accidents exceeded $16.2 billion in 1970, compared to the FBI's estimate of only $140 million * for car theft losses nationally. However, some substantial fraction of those billions lost through accidents must be ascribed to one very common form of criminal behavior—drunken driving.

There are certain communities in which comprehensive costs are very high, comparable to accident coverage. I mean cities such as New York, Newark and Los Angeles. The cost of comprehensive for a car can literally run ten times higher in New York City than if the same were registered in a suburban community in New Jersey a few miles across the Hudson River.

To what extent are you liable if your car is stolen and the thief hits another car or injures or kills someone, especially if you contributed to the crime by leaving your key in the ignition? This is an interesting question that is specifically addressed in the new no-fault auto liability legislation passed to date in the states of Florida and Massachusetts. In these states, the owner of the car is specifically held not liable for any damage or injury if his car is stolen. Since the no-fault

---

* Other experts consider the FBI's estimate quite low. They would assign a higher average value to stolen cars at the time of theft than the FBI's estimate for 1970 of $948, and also indicate that the FBI's total figure does not include damage sustained by recovered cars, which are often a total loss. However, even if the FBI's figures are doubled, the total would still be very small compared to the total losses due to accidents.

concept is spreading (because it does cut the costs of car insurance by eliminating costly litigation), it's a reasonable assumption that in time no car owner will be held liable if his car causes damage or injury while being driven by a thief.

But what if you're the victim of a car driven by a thief? If your own car was damaged, then you are protected by your own policy—if you carry collision protection. If you or a member of your family was injured or killed, then you are probably covered by the provisions for uninsured drivers that are now common in most of the states. This means that your own insurer pays.

However, you may not be satisfied with the payment obtained through the uninsured-motorist provision. If so, you have two courses of action. If you can prove that the owner of the car contributed to the theft by leaving the ignition keys in place in the car, then you may have a case against the owner. At least two courts (one in New York State and one in Pennsylvania) have recognized the contributory negligence of the car owner in such cases and come out with high judgments against him. In both instances, a death was involved. Conceivably, this concept of contributory negligence could spread throughout the nation, unless it is blocked by legislative action, as in the no-fault laws of Florida and Massachusetts.

Another course of action is to sue the thief in civil court— assuming that he has some assets, or his parents have some if he is a minor. However, this is a very rare action because so few thieves have visible assets.

Compensation for Innocent Victims of Crime

In several states, the innocent victims of any violent crime, including those struck down by thieves driving stolen cars, may now be compensated for medical expenses and loss of income as a result of progressive legislation. New York and California were the first states to acknowledge by such legislation that society must help bear the burden when it fails to protect innocent victims of violent crime. The pioneer laws were passed in 1965. Since then, similar legislation has been approved in Hawaii, Maryland, Massachusetts, Nevada and New Jersey.

Payments approved by crime victim compensation boards take into account the victim's financial resources and the extent to which the claimant's medical bills have been covered by Blue Cross, Blue Shield, Medicare and other private or public forms of insurance or compensation. Claims must usually be filed within ninety days, but may be filed as much as a year after the injury occurs under certain circumstances in some of the states. Once a claim is filed, it is investigated by employees of the boards. The maximum amount that may be paid under such legislation ranges from a low of $5,000 in California to $10,000 in Hawaii, Massachusetts and New Jersey, to $15,000 in New York and $45,000 in Maryland. However, some of these figures may be raised through legislative action. New York is one of the few states that pay for income lost as a result of the crime; most pay only medical expenses.

A number of other states are considering similar legislation and the National Commission on the Causes and Prevention of Violence has proposed a federal program with the same objectives.*

---

* As this is written, legislation is before the Senate to provide federal payments of up to $50,000 for the victims of violent crimes. The bill, which has powerful sponsorship, also provides for federal grants of up to 75 percent to states with similar programs, which, if this legislation becomes law, should stimulate many more states to pass legislation to compensate the innocent victims of violent crime.

Federal Crime Insurance

The federal government has already gotten into one form of crime insurance. Because burglary insurance for both commercial and residential premises was not available or prohibitively expensive in certain areas due to the high crime rate, the federal government has stepped in with a program to stimulate insurance companies to provide coverage. In many instances, this coverage is essential if small shops are to remain in business in high-crime areas.

Federal crime insurance is not available directly from the government but through designated insurance companies in the normal manner. This is how it works. If losses due to criminals result in claims against the insurer that exceed the premiums received, the federal government makes up the difference.

To keep the federal government out of the insurance business, some of the state governments have stepped in with their own crime insurance programs.

As of this writing, the states in which federal crime insurance is available for small businesses and homes are: Connecticut, District of Columbia, Illinois, Maryland, Massachusetts, Missouri, New York, Ohio, Pennsylvania and Rhode Island. California and Michigan have state-administered crime insurance programs.

To obtain coverage under the federal crime insurance program is not simple. Small businessmen must meet certain standards for security that originally could have cost hundreds of dollars. Now these security standards have been relaxed somewhat. For a home that comes under the plan, the standards call for proper locking devices on doors and windows. After applying for coverage, an inspector is sent around by the insurance agent to check the applicant's premises.

Coverage under the federal crime insurance program is not high. Residential crime insurance is sold in amounts from $1,000 to $5,000, subject to a $75 or 5 percent deductible, whichever is higher. For businesses, crime insurance covers robbery outside the premises to a limit of $5,000, unless an armed guard accompanies the insured's messenger. Coverage for business premises ranges from $1,000 to a high of $15,000. Deductibles run from $50 to $200 or 5 percent of the gross loss, whichever is higher. Premiums vary too, naturally declining * as coverage increases, and are grouped into three categories: low risk, average risk and high risk. Theft of autos and embezzlement are specifically exempted from coverage under the federal program. However, policies cannot be cancelled for repeated losses.

Few businesses and homes were covered under the federal crime insurance program as originally set up. Part of the poor response has been ascribed to lack of publicity for the program. Federal Insurance Administrator George K. Bernstein criticized the insurance industry for not pushing the program, which representatives of the industry denied. To encourage those in high-crime areas to take out policies under the program, the original requirements have been modified. Now a small businessman is no longer required to take combined burglary-theft coverage. He can take either one at lower rates. For example, $1,000 worth of burglary insurance now costs $90 per year, while $1,000 coverage for robbery costs $108 per year, both with a $50 deductible.

Jewelry Floaters

In many large cities, it is very difficult to obtain coverage for jewelry. Many who live in those crime-ridden cities have experienced sudden cancellation of or refusals to renew their

---

* In rate per $100 of coverage; total premiums go up with total coverage, of course.

jewelry floaters, despite the fact that they never made a single claim against the insurer over years, even decades, of paying premiums. Where coverage for jewelry is available, the cost in some areas will be up sharply and deductibles are up to 20 percent (the insured absorbs the first 20 percent of the loss). Also, the insurer may demand that you install a wall safe, keep your jewelry in it when not being worn, and install a burglar-alarm system as well.

Rates filed with the insurance department of your state may not be very significant when a jewelry floater is sought. Coverage at the filed or "regulated" rates will simply not be available, and your broker will be forced to turn to an insurer not licensed in your state, such as Lloyds of London. These unlicensed but legitimate insurers will accept the policy at rates as much as twice those filed. In New York State your broker will ask you to sign an affidavit that indicates you are aware that you are paying more than the filed rate and that the insurer is not licensed in the state.

The actual charges will be based on the neighborhood in which you live, the nature of your residence, your prior loss experience, if you spend much time traveling and staying at hotels, and how well you're known. When it comes to jewelry floaters, there's no business like show business: well-known entertainers are charged particularly high rates because they are so often the targets of criminals.

If you now have a jewelry floater, you can take some consolation in the fact that in certain states, such as New York, the insurer can't cancel your policy after a theft—until the policy expires. At that time, the insurer may raise his rates, or cancel.

Your home owner's or tenant's policy does provide limited protection, usually $500, if your jewelry is stolen, and coverage applies to both on- and off-premises thefts. However, in

New York City and its suburbs, theft coverage on furs and jewelry is limited to a maximum of $250 on premises, with off-premises protection available for an added premium.

"Insurance" for Credit Cards

Credit cards are now a prime target of certain criminals. Many credit cards were stolen in the mail, before persons to whom they were issued ever got them. Now that the federal government forbids the unsolicited mailing of credit cards, this form of theft should decline. But credit cards stolen by pickpockets, purse-snatchers and burglars are practically an article of commerce in the criminal community. Out of some 150 million credit cards now in force, as many as 300,000 may be stolen each year. To protect themselves, the issuers of credit cards have developed elaborate systems to detect lost or stolen cards (about 1.2 million cards are lost each year). Highly sophisticated systems are under development that will allow retailers to instantly detect lost, stolen or overdrawn credit cards presented to them.

Up until early 1971, the holder of a lost or stolen credit card could be held liable for all or a large part of any unauthorized purchases made with his errant card. The way to avoid such liability was to quickly notify the card issuer of the loss or theft of the card. Unfortunately, some card holders were not aware of the loss of their cards, particularly if the cards were duplicates taken from his home by a burglar or if the thief cleverly removed only the most easily passed cards from the card holder's wallet or purse and returned the rest.

As a result of new federal legislation, the liability of card holders for unauthorized use of their cards is limited to the first $50 of improper use per card. And the card holder may not even be liable for that amount if the issuer failed to provide him with a self-addressed prestamped notice to be returned when the card is stolen or lost.

Nevertheless, no one should have to bear even a loss of $50 per card if they report the loss of the card quickly. Many of the issuing organizations maintain twenty-four-hour phone service so that lost cards can be reported. If you are one of those rare people who carry an extraordinary number of credit cards, the mere process of reporting the loss of many cards could be a nuisance. To protect yourself, you should consider subscribing to a credit-card protection service. These services, which are listed in the classified phone book under that heading, take over the burden of notifying all the organizations that have issued cards to you in the event of their loss. (Naturally, you have to provide them with a list of all your cards and their serial numbers.) In the event of loss, you only have to make one phone call. The service does all the rest. It first phones all the issuing organizations, then sends telegrams or follow-up letters as required. Typical charges for this service are $5 per year for the first ten cards, plus twenty-five cents extra for each additional card.

You can add coverage against any liability for loss of all credit cards issued to your family to your home owner's or tenant's policy. The added cost is only $3 per year for the minimum coverage of $1,000 and $6 per year for the maximum coverage of $10,000. This coverage also includes the cost of your legal defense in case the company issuing the card sues you.

Luggage Insurance

If you are a steady traveler, luggage insurance makes a lot of sense. It's cheap and covers you for all of your loss beyond the very limited amounts that the air, bus or rail lines will pay in the event of loss or theft. Of course, insurance for luggage does not cover all the contents of the luggage. Don't expect furs and jewelry worth many thousands of dollars to be covered without separate floaters.

Home Owner's or Tenant's Policy

Every home owner and apartment dweller should take out an all-inclusive policy known either as a home owner's or a tenant's policy. The prime element in a home owner's policy is coverage against fire. A tenant's policy does not require coverage of the structure, for which the landlord obtains coverage. However, a tenant's policy does provide coverage against loss of the *contents* of the apartment due to fire or water damage as a result of efforts to put out a fire.

Home owner's policies come in four increasingly comprehensive forms: basic, broad, special and comprehensive. Basic coverage protects against fire or lightning, windstorm or hail, vehicles, aircraft, vandalism, theft and breakage of glass plus a few others. Broad coverage adds protection against weight of ice, snow or sleet, freezing of plumbing, etc., sudden and accidental injury from electrical shock plus more. The comprehensive form covers all perils except for such unusual ones as earthquake (see discussion of danger from earthquakes in Chapter VII, Part A), flood or tidal waves. Special coverage combines elements of both broad and comprehensive coverage. Some policies also provide for added living expenses while awaiting rebuilding of a home damaged or destroyed by fire. For an excellent guide to liability insurance, I suggest that you write to the Insurance Information Institute, 110 William Street, New York, N.Y. 10038.

An important point with regard to home owner's and tenant's policies: Many neglect to arrange for coverage to commence the moment they take title to the home or become responsible for their new apartments. Instead, they wait until they move in, which could be weeks or even months after they become responsible for the residence. In the meanwhile, their houses or apartments could suffer great damage from fire or vandals and thieves.

Chapter XII

WHAT TO DO IF VICTIMIZED—AND AFTERWARD

If you follow all the suggestions and rules that I offer in the previous chapters, your chances of being victimized are much lower than average. However, I doubt that anyone can maintain the level of self-discipline that I urge, especially for extended periods. I must be candid and admit that I have trouble myself adhering to the entire regimen, even though I pride myself on possessing that degree of self-discipline essential to the professional writer. Even if you do follow every suggestion, a proportion of you will be robbed, burglarized, lose a car to thieves or become the victim of a confidence man. I do not and cannot offer absolute security, just a quite high level of deterrence based on reasonable measures that demand as little of you as possible in terms of time, energy and money. And frankly, I can't offer much in the way of deterrence against murder, assault or rape because a substantial majority of these crimes are perpetrated by relatives, friends or acquaintances of the victims, not by criminals.

When Confronted by a Robber

The violent crime you are most likely to experience is robbery. There are three types of robbers you may encounter: the mugger, the purse-snatcher and the holdup man. Muggers and holdup men are usually men (though their ranks have been swelled lately by women who are or play the role of prostitute) who choose their victims and situations well. There is a high probability that they are armed. Even if no weapon is displayed, they may claim a concealed weapon. In any event, strength of force is on their side because of the weapon or because their victim is a woman or an elderly man. Don't fight with them. Give them what they ask for. Whatever money, jewelry or other valuables you are carrying with you are not worth risking a severe injury, maiming—or death. You can always make more money, and your valuables should be covered by insurance (unless it is not available in your community).

Give your valuables to the robber or robbers readily. Don't delay, because the delay may incite them to harm you: remember, they are twice as nervous as you are. Speak to them calmly. Don't make any quick movements. If you have to reach inside your jacket or coat, tell them in a calm manner just what you are doing: "I'm only reaching in to take out my wallet."

If the robber or robbers want to pull you into a dark alley or other spot where you can't be seen by passersby, immediately offer to give them your valuables. Tell them: "Here's my wallet [purse], watch and rings. You don't have to march me into that dark alley to get what you want."

If the robbers begin to beat you, you have no choice but to fight back as best you can. But start screaming as loud as you can. If you can break away and run, do so. But keep on screaming.

In contrast to the mugger, the purse-snatcher is more commonly an immature robber. Mostly teenagers, they sometimes choose as victims younger women who fight back. If you are an older man or woman, you are well advised not to hold on to your purse or briefcase. Teenage purse-snatchers don't hesitate to shove or pull their weaker victims to the ground or to stun them by striking them in the face. Under such attack, the victims may suffer serious injury, or death.

If you are walking down the street and you hear the sound of someone running behind you, move back against a wall as quickly as possible. That makes it more difficult for the purse-snatcher to knock you down. If you are indeed the victim of a purse-snatcher, again, start screaming as loudly as possible. If you carry some kind of noisemaker—and are self-possessed enough to remember that you have it— use it.

What to Do after a Robbery

Assuming that you have not been harmed and are physically able to do so, try to alert the police as quickly as possible. If the robbery takes place in the street, ring the doorbell of the closest home and ask whoever comes to the door to call the police. If there is a police emergency call box nearby, use it (hopefully, you know the location of those call boxes in your neighborhood). If you were mugged in the lobby or corridor of an apartment building, ring the nearest door bell and ask the occupant to call the police. If you were attacked in the elevator, push the emergency button as soon as the robber or robbers leave. The noise of the emergency bells (one is usually mounted under the cab and another at ground level) should panic the robbers into running, which would make them conspicuous to any police who respond to the noise of the bell.

Next, try to write down as detailed a description of the

robber or robbers as possible. The longer you wait, the more details you'll forget. Follow this list of descriptive items:

• Sex (with the increasing incidence of robberies by males posing as females this is not as obvious an item as might appear).

• Height and build.

• Age.

• Race.

• Eyes: Color? Wear eyeglasses? Condition of eyes: normal or glazed; dilated pupils or droopy eyelids?

• Weapons claimed or displayed (in left or right hand?).

• Hair style (real hair or fake—toupee or wig?).

• Mustache, sideburns or beard?

• Dress: hat (style, color, ornaments?); jacket (belted?); pants; unusual belt; shoes or boots (style and color); gloves; general condition of dress (neat or wrinkled, stained and torn; new or worn).

• Jewelry: rings, watches, earrings or bracelets?

• Scars, tattoos, discolorations, acne, pimples, teeth or fingers missing, birthmarks, or other disfigurements?

• Speech: any accent or dialect; any slang used?

• If more than one robber, did they call each other by any nicknames?

Next, write down as detailed a description as possible of everything that was taken from you: money, jewelry, keys, credit cards, watch, purse, wallet, etc.

If your house and/or office keys were taken by the robber(s), and they also took any document(s) that carry your address and/or the address of your place of employment, immediately arrange for a locksmith to change the cylinders or the pins in cylinders in all locks for which keys were lost. If there is someone at home, call them and alert them to the fact that a criminal has a set of keys. If your office keys were taken, alert any guards and your superior to the fact that your office keys are in the hands of a criminal. If there is no one on guard at the building in which your office is located, ask the police to send a man to guard it or ask a fellow employee to guard it. If the premises are protected by a central-station alarm service, alert them to the possibility of an illegal intrusion.

When the police arrive, if you are physically able to do so, join them in searching nearby shrubbery and waste cans if your purse or wallet were taken. Often, robbers will simply remove all cash, credit cards and other valuables and discard the looted purse or wallet in a convenient garbage can or behind some bushes. Call your local post office to find out if any wallets were found in a nearby post box.

If any of the items taken were covered by an insurance floater or home owner's policy, call your insurance agent as soon as possible.

Ask for a copy of the report that the police prepare and include this document with those you retain to help in preparing your next income-tax return. You are permitted to deduct the value of stolen items from your gross income for tax purposes but only if these items and their values were noted in an official police report. Retain photocopies of any appraisals or sales slips for those items with this document. If you live in one of the several states that reimburse those who suffer injury at the hands of criminals and subsequent loss of income, contact the local agency that handles this form of crime insurance and check your eligibility. If eligible, request one of the forms required. (See discussion of reimbursement of innocent victims of crime in the previous chapter.)

Finally, go home and try to relax. You've been through a trying experience that takes much more out of a victim than imagined. Even if you were not harmed physically, your body has most likely undergone a shock. However, the full impact of the experience may not hit you for a day or two. After my mother received a superficial stab wound in an attempted street robbery, she went to work the next day, then suffered a severe physical letdown the second day after the attack. If you can do so, don't go to work for a day or two after a robbery until you are certain that you have regained your composure. If you have any question about physical shock, go to your physician and ask for a checkup. Follow his advice on when to return to work.

Robberies Involving Vehicles

A rare form of robbery is practiced against victims in or on vehicles. To an increasing extent, robbers approach parked cars or cars at stoplights and attempt to enter them, or hold up victims in deserted subway cars or attempt to knock bicycle riders off their bikes and rob them—as well as steal the bike. If you follow the advice I offer in Chapter II, "Commonsense Measures," it is easy to avoid this form of attack.

However, let's assume that you are the victim of this kind of attack. If you are in your car and a stranger attempts to enter it while the motor is running, step on the gas (since most cars have automatic shifts, this is a matter of split seconds). Even if he has a gun, step on the gas. If there is a car stopped ahead of you, bump into it. That will cause the occupants of the car ahead to get out, which would be enough to send the robber(s) scurrying away.

It is now a risky matter to ride in a subway car alone. At first, robberies in moving subway trains took place mainly at night, but when the transit police in New York increased their night patrols, the robbers shifted to daytime attacks. If you become aware of the strong probability of victimization before the attack begins, move quickly to the emergency cord and grab ahold of it. There is less chance of attack if you are scared enough to pull the cord and halt the train, because this breed of robbers always time their attacks to take place just before the train enters a station, so they can exit quickly. They don't want to be stuck on the train. (However, they may be experienced enough to know that it will take the motorman several minutes to appear after the cord is pulled. In this case, you will be robbed anyway.) Of course, if they catch you unawares, you must give them all your valuables. After they exit, pull the emergency cord to stop the train. Then get out at the station and call for help or go to the change booth, all of which are equipped with phones. Hopefully, a policeman might be near enough to hear your call and pursue your attackers.

Theft of bicycles is increasing rapidly throughout the urban parts of the country. Sometimes the criminals are bold enough to take a bike away from its rider. (A young cousin of mine was attacked by two other bike riders while bicycling down Manhattan's fashionable Park Avenue in daylight. He was able to hold them off until passersby came to his rescue. When I asked how they could have hoped to make off with his bike, he explained that they are skillful enough to mount their own bikes and pedal away holding the stolen bike upright.)

If you are attacked while on a bike, you should attempt to ride away as fast as possible. If you are cut off and unable to flee, hold the bike up as a shield between you and your attackers, just in case they are carrying knives (bicycle thieves rarely carry guns). If they do take your bike, report it as quickly as possible to the nearest police precinct. (To cut down on widespread theft of bikes, officials in several cities have proposed registering bikes and providing them with plates.)

Women on subway platforms are targets for a sophisticated kind of purse-snatcher. These young robbers will either grab a woman's purse by reaching out from between the cars or from the window of a moving train as it starts to leave the station, or, working in pairs, one will grab a purse while the other holds the doors open. As soon as the actual purse-snatcher jumps on board, the second boy lets the doors close and the train starts moving. The former approach is the more common one, and the best way to avoid it is not to stand close to the edge of the platform. If you are the victim of this form of underground purse-snatching, run to the change booth as quickly as possible and ask the attendant to phone ahead to request the transit police to stop and search the departed train. If the train moves with the usual delays, there's a chance that it can be stopped before reaching the next station.

A friend who recently returned from Italy told me of a new form of purse-snatching practiced in some Italian cities. Robbers in cars reach out through an open window and snatch the purses of women walking near the curb, then speed away. The remedy is not to walk near the curb and not to hold your purse in the hand nearest the street.

What to Do after a Burglary

Statistically, the crime that you are most likely to suffer is burglary. In 1970, there were over six times as many burglaries reported as robberies of all kinds.

If you arrive home or at your place of employment and sense that a burglary is in progress, don't rush in. Although few burglars are violent, some might harm you in their rush to escape. Instead, go to the nearest phone and call the police. Make sure you give them the exact address and floor number. (As I explained in Chapter III, the first action of burglars after entering an apartment is to chain the door shut—if there is a chain on the door. So if you find your door chained from the inside inexplicably, a burglary is in progress.) In case you do enter during a burglary, retreat.

If you arrive after the burglary, you must call the police immediately. Then call your insurance agent. If the burglar(s) emptied all your bureau drawers on the floor and dumped all your books too, don't start to clean up. Let the police see the exact condition of your home, which may give them some clues as to the identity of the burglars. Instead, use the time before the police arrive to find out what has been taken. Check where your luggage is stored—burglars often fill luggage with loot. Try to prepare a list of all that was stolen, using that list of valuables you already have prepared if you followed my suggestion in Chapter II, "Commonsense Measures." If any credit cards were taken, report their loss as quickly as possible.

If there is no evidence of forced entry, call a locksmith immediately to change the cylinders. Ask the police to check the condition of the locks for evidence of picking. (However, few policemen are trained to detect picking.) If there is strong evidence of picking, make sure that you retain the discarded cylinder(s) as evidence in case any questions are raised by insurance adjusters or the Internal Revenue Service on claims for losses. If there is no evidence or slight evidence of picking, there is a strong presumption that your apartment was entered by means of a key provided by an insider. Immediately check with those to whom you've given duplicate keys. If you've followed the procedure recommended in Chapter III, then the envelope in which you sealed your keys before giving them to the super or agent may provide evidence of unauthorized use.

If you have prepared the list of valuables as recommended

under "Commonsense Measures," you should be able to determine quickly all that is missing. However, there is still a good chance you may not discover that a valuable item is lost for weeks or even a month after the burglary. If this happens, call the police and your insurance agent and ask them to add the item to the list of lost property. Sometimes the police recover stolen property months or even a year after its loss.

After Your Car Is Stolen

Even if you take all the precautions discussed in Chapter VIII, there's still a good chance that your car will be stolen. Particularly if you live in the thieves' favorite hunting grounds, such as Cleveland, Los Angeles or New York. What should you do if your car is missing? First, make sure that it is really stolen. Maybe you can't remember where you parked it? Or you forgot that you promised to lend it to your wife's kid brother? False alarms, which run about eight thousand per year in New York City alone, are a big nuisance to the police, and embarrassing at the very least to the owners. If you are so embarrassed by a false alarm that you fail to report that you've found your car, you are merely postponing the moment of truth. When you try to reregister your car at the end of the current registration period, computers used by some state motor vehicle bureaus will embarrass you far more by flagging you as a receiver of stolen property.

If your car is truly missing, you should report the theft quickly to the police: call the local police emergency number, not the auto squad, if there is one in your city. Then call your insurance agent. A policeman will come around soon to take down the details. From his report, the license number, VIN (vehicle identification number) and other details will be entered into the police department's computer, the computer at state police headquarters and finally into the FBI's computers at the National Crime Information Center in Washington.

You may get your car back in a few days if it was stolen by joyriding juveniles. If the car was taken by pros, there is very little chance that it will reappear at all or in working order. At best, it may be recovered as a "basket case," stripped down to the frame.

If the car is abandoned by joyriders and subsequently towed away by the police, you have acquired a headache. Claiming a stolen towaway can be an all-day project fraught with frustration. After collecting the necessary proof that exonerates you of the towaway and illegal parking charges, you may have much trouble locating your car: sometimes the police move the towaways from one pound to another depending on how long they have been held. And if your registration was lost with the car, you will simultaneously suffer Excedrin headaches 1 through 99.

Two fairly common circumstances could greatly delay return of your recovered car. First, if the district attorney needs to hold the car as evidence because it was used in the commission of some crime. To get your car back, then, may take a court suit. And the insurance agency won't settle because the car is no longer missing. Secondly, if the VIN was either noted incorrectly or entered incorrectly into the computers, forcing the police to write to the state motor vehicle bureau to find out who owns a recovered car. The state agency may take weeks to reply. By that time, you've most likely settled with the insurer.

Beginning two days after you report your car missing, your insurer will pay for a replacement rental car at the maximum rate of $10 per day for no more than thirty days. There are many agencies that will rent at that rate, which includes one hundred free miles per day. Beyond the hundred-mile-per-day average, you pay a mileage charge. Of course, you have to pay for the sales tax and may pay the usual $2 per day for complete coverage. This brings up still another ugly aspect of car theft. If you report your car as missing, you may soon receive phone calls and letters from rental agencies offering replacements. In certain cities, someone is being paid off by the agencies to report all "alarms."

In case your car is recovered but requires repair, you can keep the rental car until yours is returned—but reimbursement still ends after thirty days. Sometimes it takes a lot longer to get your car back, especially if the manufacturer can't supply needed parts. This is one reason why procurers of "nose clips" thrive: they deliver quickly.

What about theft of rental cars? If a part of the rental car or the car itself is stolen, you're not liable. The $2 per day extra charge for complete coverage only applies to the first $100 of damage due to collision—and nothing else. All other damages are covered by the basic rental charge. Thefts of spare tires by customers are a problem for car renters. To avoid all aggravation, always check to make sure that any car you rent has a spare. However, if you forget to check and the agent later accuses you of taking the spare, tell him he's got no case.

Property stolen from cars is covered by your home owner's or tenant's policy, as indicated earlier in Chapter VIII. The coverage is limited to $1,000 or 4 percent of the face value of the policy, whichever is higher.

What to Do after Being Conned

I assume that none of those who buy this book are gullible enough to be taken by the various kinds of flimflammers. However, there is a fair chance that your parents or other elderly or sick relatives, friends or retired employees will be taken by a "bank examiner," "Reverend," "Sister," "Brother," "Bishop," "reader and advisor," "Naturopath" or other unlicensed medical practitioner. If any such friend or relative mentions that he or she has given or has been asked to give large sums of money to a person who promises quick recovery, enormous profits or other good fortune, take the victim to the police. Ask the victim to preserve for police scrutiny any correspondence, cards, documents or amulets received from his "benefactor."

Sex Crimes

The category of crime for which the victims are least likely to press charges is sexual crimes. In Chapter VI, "Apartment House Security," I detail the incident of a man who molested over a dozen women, yet was not reported. This is most unfortunate because of all criminals, the sexual criminal is the most certain to repeat. He's an unbalanced if not psychopathic individual who can't control his urges.

One reason that women often fail to report or press charges for sexual crimes is that there is an unspoken implication that the woman in some way "led the man on." Proving rape charges is, of course, a very unpleasant experience for women.

If you or a member of your family is a victim of a sexual crime, it is particularly important that you report the crime and also press charges. Otherwise, you may in a sense be responsible for the other victims of that sex criminal.

A woman who is threatened by a rapist is, of course, under extreme stress. Nevertheless, it is surprising how many times women have talked their attacker out of following through. If you can remain calm when confronted by a rapist who is carrying a weapon or depending on superior physical strength, you may be able to talk your attacker out of proceeding, or at least delay him until help arrives. For whatever consolation it offers, it is helpful to know that a drug is now available that prevents pregnancy after sexual intercourse, and by as much as three days. It is widely prescribed for victims of rapists. The drug, diethylstilbestrol—DES for short—produces some side effects, but they are minor compared to the added trauma of bearing the child of a rapist.

What to Do If Your Child Is Kidnapped

Kidnapping is a rare crime, so rare that it is not even included among the crimes compiled in the FBI's *Uniform Crime Reports*. However, contrived demands for ransom of children who are merely absent from home are not so rare, although I can find no statistics on this vicious form of confidence game. Several years ago, many of the parents of students at one of the leading colleges for women in the East received demands for "ransom" of their allegedly kidnapped daughters. Of course, none of the girls were kidnapped, but many of the frantic parents were unable to quickly check the whereabouts of their children. Apparently, those making what could have been prank calls were using a directory of students published by the college. The directory included the home phone number and address of each student. This directory is no longer published.

If you ever receive a call from anyone claiming to hold your child, immediately ask to speak to the child. If they can't bring the child to the phone, you can assume that the call is either a prank or the work of a con man. If your child is indeed kidnapped, you should contact the police, preferably through your lawyer, who, presumably, would be able to follow the instructions of the police more calmly than parents on the verge of hysteria.

One way to avoid being made the victim of pranksters

who claim to be kidnappers is to always know the where-abouts of your immature children and to train them never to go off with strangers. Obviously, it is very difficult these days to expect teenagers to keep their parents informed of their whereabouts.

Guarding Against the Thief in Uniform

After victimization by criminals, too many Americans are exposed to victimization by an even more distasteful crim-inal, the thief in uniform. The sensational revelations in late 1971 of the Knapp Commission in New York and earlier scan-dals in Chicago show that too many policemen are corrupt. Once corrupted by payoffs from pimps, gamblers, madams and drug distributors, they take advantage of their uniforms to victimize those they are sworn to protect. After a burglary of a commercial establishment, some of New York's "Finest," assured that the owner was not likely to appear soon, pil-fered articles of value, blaming all losses on the burglars, according to testimony before the Knapp Commission. (As a result, one of the most valuable services that the uniformed guards sent by central-station services can perform is to guard against pilferage by the police who respond to their emergency call.) Such pilferage is not limited to New York City.

And if the police will steal from burglarized businesses, why should private residences be exempt? Now, in most in-stances, it is the occupant of the home or apartment who calls the police. Since the occupant remains on the premises, corrupt policemen do not have an opportunity to steal. But if the police are called by neighbors or an automatic phone dialer or alerted by a local alarm, they are likely to enter a home when the occupants are not present. What's the remedy? If your home is equipped with an automatic phone dialer (despite the severe limitations of these devices), it should be programmed to also call a neighbor or some friend or relative who lives close by. Ask any such to proceed as quickly as possible to your home when an emergency message is received. Of course, they should first call the police or fire department to make sure that the emergency message has been received. However, caution your neighbors or friends not to arrive *before* the police and blunder in on the burglars. Tell them to delay entering until the police arrive. Once the police arrive, they should ask to enter the premises as soon as the police are certain that the burglars have departed, or after arrests have been made. Under most circumstances, the police should welcome the presence of someone who can tell them where to locate the occupant of the residence.

In the event of a robbery or assault in which someone has been severely injured or killed, it makes sense for all valuables on the person of the victim to be removed by a friend or relative—or at least be inventoried by them. If you are not up to going through the pockets or purse of a dead or severely injured person, ask the policeman or ambulance attendant present to do so for you. Make up a list of the valuables and sign it. The same applies to someone who dies of natural causes or an accident, or loses consciousness due to illness or an accident.

Valuables must also be removed from the persons of those who are severely injured or who die as a result of a fire. One of the most shocking aspects of the infamous Coconut Grove fire in Boston more than thirty years ago was the disappearance of valuables from the bodies of many of the more than four hundred victims.

There is still another way in which the police may take advantage of the victim of a crime. Naturally, any victim is upset. When a young, attractive woman who lives alone is the victim of a burglary, mugging or purse-snatching, one of the policemen who respond may suggest that he return later when he goes off duty to protect the victim. He expects to remain all night. Sometimes young locksmiths called in late at night by a young woman to repair a door or lock damaged by a burglar will make the same gallant offer. If you are in need of company or of moral support after victimization, call a friend to come over and comfort you.

What to Do after Victimization

After you've been the victim of a crime, the police may make certain demands of you, assuming that you are physically capable. You might be asked to identify your attacker in the case of robbery or assault, or come down to identify your property in case it has been stolen. Do so. One of the factors contributing to lower police morale and effectiveness is the refusal of victims of crime to aid in the prosecution of criminals after good, hard police work results in their arrest. A policeman is justified in asking what's the point of spending many hours or even days catching a criminal, if he is then released because the victim refuses to press charges.

Sometimes the victim does not press charges for fear of retaliation by the criminal or his cohorts. Such threats are generally baseless because the first person suspected if a victim of a crime is harmed or his property vandalized is the criminal under prosecution. If you are pressing charges and you receive a demand to drop them or suffer in some way, immediately bring the threat to the attention of the police and the district attorney. They should provide a guard. If the police offer protection, take it. Don't be a hero.

If you cooperate with the police in the prosecution of a criminal, you can expect to experience much frustration and aggravation before the case is resolved. The lawyers who represent criminals are skilled in obtaining postponements and delays of trials. They know that if the trial can be delayed long enough, the victims and witnesses will lose their will to aid the prosecution. No matter how discouraged you become with a criminal prosecution, persevere. Nothing encourages criminals to pursue their careers in crime so much as the knowledge that they are not likely to serve time even if caught red-handed.

If you employ someone who is aiding in a criminal prosecution, be tolerant of his absence due to court appearances. If he is willing to contribute his time and energy to do his civic duty, you as an employer should be willing to continue his salary, just as you would if an employee were called down for jury duty.

What to Do If You Witness a Crime

In your lifetime, there is a strong likelihood that you will witness a crime. If the crime is robbery or assault, there is a good chance that you will become a victim too if you interfere. The intelligent action is to call the police as quickly as possible. Of course, if you carry a noisemaker, use it—or blow your car horn. If the criminals flee on your approach, try to follow them if you are in a car. If they enter a building, there is little likelihood they will exit from the same entrance. This is a good opportunity to get out of your car and call the police.

On occasion you may observe a policeman who needs help in subduing a criminal—or in holding off a hostile mob. Time and time again I urge in this book that citizens not play policeman. If you see a policeman in need of aid, call the police. If you tell them a policeman is in danger, they will respond in an amazingly short time. If you do go to the aid of a policeman or someone under criminal attack and are hurt yourself, you are entitled to compensation in those states that provide for the innocent victims of crime.

If you are a witness to a crime, use the guide printed earlier in this chapter to help you to prepare a detailed description of the criminals. And cooperate with the police and the district attorney in helping to prosecute the criminal.

INDEX

Index

305

Index

Index

Mortise locks, 56
Motorcycles, 211–214; chaining, 212; padlocks, 212
Motors Insurance Corporation, 209
Muggers, 31–32; automatic cash-dispensing machines, 33; being followed by, 33
Muggings, 12; apartment houses, 136–139, 157–158, 192–193; drugs and, 158; elevators, 192–193; impact of, 136; minority groups, 137; New York City, 136–139, 157–159; police, 138; self-service elevators, 157–158; women, 12, 31–32, 137–138, 154–155
Murder by con men, 21
Murphy, Patrick V. 139

Nader, Ralph, 235
National Alliance for Safer Cities, 12
National Auto Theft Bureau (NATB), 198, 205
National Commission on the Causes and Prevention of Violence, 275
National Crime Information Center, 198, 293
National Earthquake Information Center, 176
National Locksmiths Association, 84
National Rifle Association, 14, 15
National Rifleman, The, 14
National Safety Council, 13
National Transportation Safety Board, 180
Neighborhood factors, 178–181
New England Home Security Company, 130
New York Association of Locksmiths, 73
New York City, 16; advice on security, 227; automatic license-plate scanning (ALPS), 210–211; building codes, 144–146; car strippers, 200; cost of holding persons, 17; defensible space, 162–170; electric engravers, 24; electronic security systems, 148–153; housing projects, 163–170; muggings, 136–139, 157–159; professional evaluators, 139–142; tenant patrols, 141, 146–148
New York University Project for

the Improvement of Security in Urban Residential Areas, 162–170
Newman, Oscar, 137–138, 154, 162–170
Noisemakers, 114–115
Nonviolence, 12–14
Northern Electric Company, 128
Novar Electronics, 125

Office machines, 37, 261–262
Optical Controls, Inc., 110
Overcoats, checking, 32
Owens, Charles J., 146–148

Padlocks, 72–74; Abloy, 73; bicycles, 218; boats, 214; camping trailers, 217; motorcycles, 212; shrouded, 73–74
Pan American Airways, 49
Panic buttons, 113–114, 161
Pape, Mrs. Gerald, 168, 172
Park East, 157
Pasiuk, George, 231
Passports, 42
Peace officers, telephone calls from, 28–29
Peepholes for doors, 68
Penthouses, 192
Pepper, Claude, 24
Perimeter systems, 107–109
Pets, 24–25, 94–100; cost of, 95–96; identification tags, 24–25; registering, 25; reward for lost, 28; tattooing, 25; *See also* Dogs
Photoelectric beams, 110
Photographs of valuables, 23
Physicians, when traveling, 42
Pick-resistant cylinders, 50, 61–64
Pivot locks, 75
Plastic glazing, 81–82
Police: automobile theft and, 198; control by, 7; crime by, 297–299; emergency call boxes, 34; entrapment by, 10; minor duties of, 10; muggings, 138; as professional evaluators, 139–143; returning to the beat, 9–10; supporting higher salaries for, 9; telephone calls from, 28–29
Police ban automatic dialers, 105–107
Police locks, 59
Poll-taking, 28

INDEX

Index